The Democracy Own

★ ★ ★ *The* ★ ★ ★
DEMOCRACY
OWNERS'
MANUAL

*A Practical Guide
to Changing the World*

J IM   S HULTZ

R UTGERS   U NIVERSITY   P RESS
New Brunswick, New Jersey, and London

Third paperback printing, 2003

Library of Congress Cataloging-in-Publication Data
Shultz, Jim.
The democracy owners' manual : a practical guide to changing the world / Jim Shultz.
p.   cm.
Includes bibliographical references and index.
ISBN 0-8135-3037-7 (cloth : alk. paper) — ISBN 0-8135-3038-5 (pbk. : alk. paper)
1. Democracy.   2. Political participation.   I. Title.
JC423 .S53 2002
323'.042–dc21   2001031788

British Cataloging-in-Publication data for this book is available from the British Library

Manufactured in the United States of America

Design by John Romer

In Memory of Christopher G. McKenzie
Teacher, Patriot, and my Best Friend

✳ ✳ ✳ *Contents* ✳ ✳ ✳

* * * *Acknowledgments* * * *

My son, Miguel, was looking recently at the acknowledgments I wrote in my last book and pronounced, "Hey, don't you think you should thank your family first instead of last?" I think he is right. So, first, let me thank my wife, Lynn Nesselbush. Lynn supported my writing the book from the first and throughout. She also read every word of the manuscript and pummeled me with edits, most of which I screamed at and then incorporated, to the book's great benefit. I thank her, Miguel, and my daughter, Elizabeth, for all their support, especially when I was grouchy.

This book would not have been possible without the foundations and funders who lent it their support. Thank you each—Tom David and Lucia Corral Peña of the California Wellness Foundation, Yvonne Carrasco of the David and Lucile Packard Foundation, Bruce Sievers of the Walter and Elise Haas Fund, and Nelson Holl of the California Consumer Protection Foundation.

A special note of recognition is owed to my four friends and colleagues at the Advocacy Institute, Michael Pertschuk, David Cohen, Kathleen Sheekey, and Maureen Burke. It has been a pleasure working with them over many years developing trainings and materials for those brave souls who venture into public advocacy. Many of the ideas presented here come from our work together. Another special thank you goes to Mariko Takayasu and Rick Paddock, my trustworthy editors and comma assassins, and to Marlie Wasserman at Rutgers University Press for believing in the book and not flinching when she found out her author was living in Bolivia.

Many wonderful friends and colleagues gave their time to read over drafts of the book's chapters, sharing their experience and insight. Each deserves to be recognized by name: Angie Wei, Anna Aliaga, Carol Cohen, Cynthia Williams, Dane Waters, David Cohen, Debbie Laveen, Emily Goldfarb, Emily Hobson, Ingrid MacDonald, Iris Lav, Jean Ross, Jorge Hurtado, Judith Bell, Kim Alexander, Lee Cridland, Lenny Goldberg, Leo McElroy, Margaret Marr, Marion Standish, Maryann O'Sullivan, Michael Pertschuk, Ruth Holton, Santosh Seeram, Steve Phillips, Susan Sandler, Tomiko Conner, and William Muir. Other friends contributed with stories, ideas, and in the quest to find a suitable publisher. I want to thank each of them as well: Amy Dominguez-Arms, Beth Keifer, Betsy Imholtz, Francisco Herrera, Jim Boyd, Lois Kazakoff, Lois Salisbury, Mark Paul, Michael McCauley, Neil Chethik, Paul Getsos, Peter Schrag, Rosa de la Vega, and Virginia Ellis. Thanks as well to my Democracy Center coworker, Martha Nissen Stabler, who dealt ably and cheerfully with all my requests for help.

There are others too numerous to thank here by name, the wonderful activists it has been my pleasure and honor to train, counsel, and work with over many years and on three continents. I know that many of you will see here some of the many lessons that you taught me. Finally, thank you to Simone the wonder dog, who regularly trotted into the office where I was working to bite my arm and demand attention (which in dog language means "stop writing and get a life"). Okay girl, the book is done, let's go see if there is water in the river.

Jim Shultz
Cochabamba, Bolivia
February 2001

The Democracy Owners' Manual

✳ ✳ ✳ *Introduction* ✳ ✳ ✳

What is democracy and why an "Owners' Manual"?

For many, the word "democracy" conjures up one idea solely, the right of the people to elect their leaders. By this measure, 118 of the world's 193 countries are democracies, encompassing a bare majority of the world's people.[1] But elections alone are not democracy's true measure. In many nations, the United States among them, the fairness of those elections is in serious doubt. More importantly, the mere fact that a government is elected is no guarantee that it will dedicate itself to protecting the public interest. All manner of rights, civil and economic, are trampled on or neglected daily by governments that are allegedly "democratic."

Democracy, therefore, requires a broader definition. To have what Lincoln called "government of, by, and for the people," we must have a democracy that is participatory, one in which the people understand the key public issues of the day and are equipped and willing to actively influence the action taken on them. By this measure, U.S. democracy is in steady decline. As Robert Putnam observed in his landmark essay, "Bowling Alone: America's Declining Social Capital":

> It is not just the voting booth that has been increasingly deserted by Americans. Since 1973 the number of Americans who report that 'in the past year' they have 'attended a public meeting on town or school affairs' has fallen by more than a third. By almost every measure, Americans' direct engagement in politics and government has fallen steadily and sharply over the last generation. Every year over the last decade or two, millions more have withdrawn from the affairs of their communities.[2]

Some will counter, "Yes, fewer and fewer people may be taking an active role in political life, but many are choosing instead to invest their energies, more productively, into individual acts of service and charity, through their churches, or food programs for the poor, or outreach to people who are ill." I have great admiration and affinity for people who engage in direct service and charity. It is something I have always made time for in my own life as well. However, charity and personal acts of service are not enough to solve the problems in our midst. The real aim of charity must be justice, and justice requires bold acts of democratic participation. If the poor do not have enough food, then the rules of our economy must be challenged. If the sick are unable to get health care, then we must demand that our government take responsibility to guarantee that care.

I come to this challenge of democratic participation with three basic premises, ones that also form the basis of the book in your hands. First, I believe that we have both the right and the responsibility to be involved in the decisions our democracy makes. These are decisions not just about who we elect, but about how our public officials exercise power once we give it to them. Second, I believe that when we do become involved in public issues we have a responsibility to understand them. Our aim should be a democracy that is not only participatory, but also informed. Third, I believe that public participation can have an enormous and positive impact, but that to be effective we need to understand the basic tools of democratic activism and how to use them wisely.

I used to own an old Volkswagen, which broke down reliably every time I tried to drive it up or down the length of California. On many occasions, I was saved by a greasy, dog-eared owner's manual that I kept in the glove compartment; it taught me such things as how to fix a leaky fuel filter with Scotch tape. There are two ways to own a car and two ways to live in a democracy. One is to know nothing and put your fate in the hands of others, most usually at great and unneeded expense. The other is to know enough to take back some of that power, at least enough to keep a careful watch over the so-called experts (be they car mechanics or presidents). Helping people arm themselves with such knowledge about democracy is what this book is really about.

The Democracy Owners' Manual has been in my mind to write for a long time. My own involvement in political work started when I was very young, a teenager growing up in Richard Nixon's hometown during his presidency and the Vietnam War. A teacher of mine changed my life forever when he asked me one day, "Do you want to make a difference?" I spent most of the next few months walking door to door for George McGovern—getting attacked by dogs twice, participating in one of the most lopsided election losses in U.S. history, and starting out on a path of political activism that has continued for three decades.

In the years since, my focus turned from election campaigning to the task of organizing and empowering regular people. It has been my great fortune to work side by side with hundreds of incredible people infected with the spirit of public action. These leaders have included the founders of Mothers Against Drunk Driving (MADD), PTA parents trying to improve their schools, welfare recipients seeking to speak out on welfare reform, South African health workers seeking to build a health care system for all, and the brave people of Cochabamba, Bolivia (where I now live), who scored the new century's first victory for global economic justice, taking back their local water system from the powerful Bechtel Corporation. Throughout this wild diversity of activism, I have always found that the people involved have shared one characteristic in common—commitment to social change and a willingness to work for it.

The Democracy Owners' Manual is drawn from all these experiences in public activism as well as from my academic education in public policy, my teaching of policy to university students, and from nearly a decade of advocacy trainings carried out by the Democracy Center. It is a book about how to participate, smartly and effectively, in the work of public change. Part 1, "Five Key Debates That Democracies Decide," is dedicated to a set of issues that I believe are fundamental in a democracy: what is government's job; the rules of politics; taxes and budgets; public rules for business and the marketplace; and society's rules for individuals. Herein lie almost all of the debates that democratic activists are likely to encounter. The goal of the chapters in part 1 is to help readers develop their own thinking about these issues and about the arguments they will use when engaged in these debates. Part 2, "Tools for Democracy's Activists," covers the main elements involved in taking public action: developing a strategy; research and analysis; organizing; building and maintaining coalitions; messages and media; lobbying; ballot initiatives; and use of the Internet. The goal of these chapters is to give readers a better sense about how to use each of these elements, peppered with dozens of real-world examples of public advocacy in action.

Some of you who pick up this book may be newcomers to public activism. For you, the book is an important preview of what to expect and a treasure chest of ideas and stories to help you think about your own way forward. Others of you will be old hands at advocacy and activism. For you, I hope the book will be a source of some new ideas and also an important resource as you explain and teach what you know to others. *The Democracy Owners' Manual* is not intended as a prescription or formula designed to fit every issue or situation. Anyone who tries to tell you "This is how you do it, it always works" is either arrogant or foolish, and is also wrong. There is no one answer, and this book doesn't pretend otherwise. Ultimately, the wisdom that comes from this book will derive not from what I have written on its pages but from what is drawn forth from you as you read it, from your experiences and your insight sparked to life by what you read.

I also want to add a few words about a few words used in the book. Several friends with whom I have worked in the struggle for immigrant rights urged me not to use the term "citizen" so often in the book, arguing that it excluded immigrants, people who also have a right to speak out and be involved. I didn't take that advice and do use the term "citizen" frequently here, but with the following sentiment. If you wander through the dictionary definition of the word, past the part about "a person entitled by birth or naturalization to . . . ," you come to the idea of a "resident," and it is in this sense that I use the term. If you live in a place, work there, raise your kids there, and make your life there, in my view you have a right to care about and influence what happens there. Wherever we live, we are citizens in our right to help shape the world that shapes our lives. In the book, I also use the terms "advocate" and "activist" interchangeably, depending on which suited me from sentence to sentence. For me, they mean the same, someone who takes nonviolent action to bring pressure on the powers that be in pursuit of a public goal. As for "American," another term I use frequently in the book, I agree with those who point out that the United States can't exactly claim exclusive rights to a term that, geographically to be sure, applies to everyone living from the northern outposts of southern tip of Argentina. However, it is what we in the United States call ourselves and will continue to for many years to come, so I do here as well.

Finally, before the book begins, let us be clear about one other point. Democracy, most of all, is about power. Even if, on paper, we all have just one vote and are supposedly equal in the eyes of the law, the truth is that we are far from equal. How much actual political power we have depends on how much money we have, what social connections we can call on, our race, our sex, and many other factors that tip democracy's scales steeply toward some people and away from others. The public activism that this book seeks to inspire and strengthen is activism that aims to right those scales back toward equality, to help those with less power get more.

Confronting and influencing those with power, many of whom exercise it with unimaginable arrogance, is no easy task. Those who walk down that road should be prepared to lose more often than they win and to devote far more time and energy to it than they had ever planned. As the abolitionist Frederick Douglass observed, "People might not get all that they work for in this world, but they must certainly work for all they get." Nevertheless, history is filled with noble efforts of public action in which, through persistence, struggle, courage, and clarity, the world has been made a better place. My hope for this book is that it makes the work of those who read it more effective and more powerful, always with the aim of more justice, more freedom, more equality, and more democracy, the tool that delivers all the others.

PART ONE

Five
Key
Debates
That
Democracies
Decide

CHAPTER ONE

What Is Government's Job?

We the people of the United States, in order to form a more perfect union, establish justice, insure domestic tranquility, provide for the common defense, promote the general welfare, and secure the blessings of liberty.

—FROM THE PREAMBLE TO THE U. S. CONSTITUTION

At the heart of democracy are public choices, the decisions that we must make together as a people. Most of these have to do with what we expect from our government. Where do we want government in our lives, and where do we want it to stay out? How will we use the power of government—from the public purse to government force—to protect and advance the values and objectives we hold most dear?

Some people have a strong philosophy about these questions. For them, understanding the philosophy on the other side is important, both to challenge their own ideas and to understand the opinions they are up against. Others don't have a ready-made set of opinions about government's role and form their attitudes issue by issue, circumstance by circumstance. For these people, understanding this philosophical debate is an opportunity to shed broader light on the specific public issues that interest them.

Some people look upon government as a protector, keeping us safe from the abuses and excesses of a hostile world. Others look at government as an intruder, getting in the way of our liberty and freedom and making it harder for us to blaze our own trail. Most of us probably fall somewhere in the middle, welcoming government involvement in some instances and opposing it in others.

This essential debate, what is government's appropriate role, is at the center of six fundamental and familiar public questions: What are our interests abroad and how should we protect them? What measures should we take to protect ourselves against crime? What steps should we take to assure liberty and equality for all? What public services do we want government to provide and how shall we pay for them? What public rules should be imposed on businesses and the marketplace? How do we assure that government itself is a genuine democracy? The chapters that follow in this section address most of these questions in great detail. First, however, let us look at the philosophical debates that underlie them all.

PROTECTING OUR INTERESTS ABROAD

Five centuries ago Machiavelli wrote, "A prince must have no other objective, no other thought, nor take up any profession but that of war, its methods and its discipline, for that is the only art expected of a ruler."[1] Today many would still argue that government has no responsibility more important than to safeguard the security and the foreign interests of the nation. In Machiavelli's day, the power to determine what those interests were and how to protect them resided squarely in the hands of whoever sat on the throne. Today, issues of foreign policy, and especially of making war, are public questions subject to democratic debate.

What are a nation's foreign interests? When should it act to defend them and by what means? Few would disagree that when a nation is directly threatened it has a right to defend itself, including the right to take up arms. The United States has only on rare occasions faced foreign attacks on national soil—the Revolutionary War, the War of 1812, and in more modern times, Pearl Harbor. Today, the direct threats we face come from missile attacks or terrorism, such as the assaults on New York's World Trade Center—first, the 1993 bombing, and then its complete destruction in September 2001.

A different case is when close allies are threatened. In the earliest days of World War II, U.S. isolationists declared that Europe's war was not ours and quoted George Washington's farewell guidance against "foreign entanglements." Those who wanted the United States in the war argued that with global power in the balance and a despot on the loose the nation could not stand idly by. Today the United States is treaty-bound to come to the aid of allies under attack.

In the aftermath of World War II, for nearly half a century, the United States defined its primary foreign interest as the battle against communism. Following a policy aimed at "containing" communism's advance, the United States sent troops to battle in Korea and Vietnam and sponsored and funded wars in El Salvador and Nicaragua. We also built up an enormous nuclear arsenal to deter that of our adversaries. Backers of this cold war credit it with the breakup of the Soviet Union, the liberation of eastern Europe, and preventing communism from taking hold in Latin America. Critics charge that the United States became zealous and blind, needlessly killing thousands in Vietnam and plunging Central America into a decade of civil war that had far more to do with poverty than with communism. Cold war critics also argue that, in the end, eastern-block communism collapsed more from internal rot and resistance than from U.S. war making.

In the aftermath of the cold war, with the United States the undisputed remaining superpower, our legitimate foreign interests have become even harder to define. In its "war on drugs" the United States is now employing many of the same techniques it once used against communist insurgencies—military advisors, military equipment, and military aid. Supporters of the drug war argue that only military action can stop the flow of illegal drugs from countries such as Colombia and Bolivia. Critics question the right of the United States to delve so deeply into the internal affairs of poor nations and charge that military buildups do little to stop the net flow of drugs into the United States and end up deepening violence and repression in those nations. In addition, critics point out that, dollar for dollar, nonmilitary options such as improving drug treatment and education at home are far more effective.

The other current debate over U.S. intervention deals with how we should handle the world's despots and gross violations of human rights, a debate that has created sharp disagreements among both hawks and doves. In the spring of 1999 when the United States began bombing Serbia to pressure Slobodan Milosevic to cease his "ethnic cleansing" campaign against the people of Kosovo, supporters from both the right and left justified it as a human rights action. The United States could not stand idly, they argued, in the face of mass slaughter, as the world did in 1994 when 800,000 were killed in ethnic warfare in Rwanda. Many conservative opponents of the bombing countered that U.S. interests were not directly at stake. Many progressive opponents warned that the bombing was itself a slaughter of innocents.

Sending in troops, providing military aid, and dropping bombs are not the only forms of intervention the United States has at its disposal when it wants to pressure or support a foreign government. It also wields powerful economic weapons, imposing sanctions against those we oppose, providing aid to those we support, or using that aid as a bargaining chip with those we wish to influence. In the 1980s when opponents of apartheid pressed for U.S. sanctions against the white regime in South Africa, the Reagan administration opposed them, warning that it would be only the innocent and poor who would suffer. At the same time those same officials pushed hard to maintain economic sanctions against Nicaragua and Cuba, arguing that in those cases sanctions were essential to force both countries to respect human rights. More recently, the same debate is raised by a decade of economic sanctions against Iraq, an embargo intended to force Saddam Hussein to allow international weapons inspections. According to one United Nations report, an estimated five thousand Iraqi children die every month because of inadequate medical care and insufficient food supplies, a situation linked directly to the sanctions.[2]

The ongoing debate over where and whether to intervene in the name of human rights or democracy (Bosnia, Rwanda, Haiti, Kosovo) is not an easy one to resolve. We may not have a direct self-interest in such interventions; in fact, our narrowest self-interest may well be to steer clear of harm's way. Despite our increasing global interconnectedness, it is still possible for great numbers to suffer unimaginably on the other side of the world while life in the United States remains unaffected. The debate turns instead to hard moral questions. If we have the strength to intervene and stop suffering, do we have the moral responsibility to do so? Do we have the right to do so? If the only intervention we can make to stop the killing of one group of innocents will cause the death of another group, is it justified? How much risk, how many dead and injured of our own are we willing to accept in order to intervene in violence against another people? In the end, will the intervention we make actually accomplish what we say are our objectives?

It is also a sad fact that our political leaders, regardless of party and regardless of political stripe, have lied to us long and consistently in matters of foreign policy. It was only history that told us that the Gulf of Tonkin was a ruse, that the CIA helped install the brutal dictatorship of Augusto Pinochet in Chile, that the military units we funded in El Salvador massacred hundreds of innocents in the village of El Mazote, and that Gulf War Syndrome was not just some figment of a hypochondriac's imagination. It is for this very reason that our interests and actions abroad must be publicly debated. With stakes so high and governments so ready to distort the truth, it is on these issues more than any other that we must remain vigilant, informed and active.

PROTECTING PUBLIC SAFETY AT HOME

When Americans are asked in opinion surveys what public issues concern them most, public safety and crime nearly always comes in close to the top of the list. As with protecting our safety against threats from abroad, protecting our safety at home is also one of government's most important responsibilities.

The philosophical debate about crime, its causes, and how we ought to deal with it is marked by deep differences of opinion. Political conservatives believe crime occurs because there are people who are determined to steal and commit violence and are often encouraged to do so because the punishments they face are not certain, swift, or severe enough to create a meaningful deterrent. A politician with this point of view might proclaim, "The reason we have people running wild on the streets, robbing our homes and injuring the innocent is because of weak laws and weak-kneed judges that let these people get away with it, and the criminals know it!" Political progressives more often look at crime in terms of economic and social causes, arguing that its main roots can be found in poverty and the lack of appropriate services and opportunities for those at risk, especially youth. A politician of this perspective might declare, "You can't deal with crime until you give poor communities some other viable economic option for survival and until we start intervening early in the lives of young people who might be tempted to walk the criminal path."

That difference of perspective carries over into the debate about how we ought to punish crimes once they are committed. Conservatives argue for strictness—tough sentencing, long prison terms, prison construction, and, in murder cases, the death penalty. Progressives propose a different approach—treatment for those whose crimes are related to drugs, non-jail alternatives for those whose crimes are nonviolent, investment in education rather than prisons, life terms without parole in lieu of execution.

There are also differences between conservatives and progressives about what ought to be a crime. Drug use is the leading example these days. Conservatives want government to treat virtually all drug use as a criminal offense, punishable by incarceration. Others advocate reforming drug laws with a focus on "harm reduction"—policies that include decriminalizing the medicinal or personal use of marijuana, providing clean needles to heroin addicts as a way of preventing the spread of AIDS, and dealing with heavy drug use through treatment rather than jail time.

Conservatives argue that the death penalty is justified in serious cases as a deterrent ("dead people don't murder again") and as an instrument through which government provides "an eye for an eye" justice for victims and their families. Death penalty opponents argue that statistics do not show that it has any provable deterrent effect on would-be killers and that by coldly inflicting death government only perpetuates the idea that killing can be a legitimate act. Death penalty opponents also argue that its victims are disproportionately people of color.

On the issue of guns and gun control, conservatives see such weapons as an instrument of self-protection in a hostile world and object vigorously to gun control as government interference with their "right to bear arms." Proponents of gun control see guns as instruments of violence, aimed more at the innocent, and therefore want government to protect people by restricting access to guns and reducing their number.

Between these two perspectives, on most all crime-related issues, there is an expansive middle ground where the two views mix into compromise. Prevention and intervention can be an important part of government's approach to crime concerns, yet people can still be held accountable for the crimes they commit. Government can deal with drug use that is damaging to people and society without making a criminal offense out of use that is a personal choice by adults. Guns can be removed from the hands of those who would use them do harm without sweeping away the rights of those who choose to keep a protective or recreational weapon in their home.

ASSURING LIBERTY AND EQUALITY

At its founding, the United States declared itself bound to a set of publicly declared principles. First among them was the protection of civil liberties and the commitment to human equality. Enshrined in both the Declaration of Independence and the U.S. Constitution, these two principles have been at the heart of some of the nation's most heated debates about what role government should have in our lives.

It was liberty from government that was first translated into a set of specific rights. Enshrined in the Bill of Rights, among others, were freedom of speech and assembly, trial by jury, protections against self-incrimination, and unlawful intrusion of soldiers or police into our homes. These rights are reflective of their time. They focus on limiting government intrusion into private spheres, a reaction to the trampling of such rights by the British monarch. However, the declaration that "all men are created equal" was not so quickly translated into specific laws. It was a bold promise at direct odds with the personal practices of those who made it, many of whom owned slaves. As Representative Jesse Jackson Jr. explains, "The Constitution and our whole political system evolved to maintain the power of white slaveholders."[3] The centuries since have seen a long and difficult struggle to convert those noble words into actual legal rights.

The most prominent of these struggles have dealt with race—ending slavery, establishing the right to vote regardless of color, abolishing segregation in schools and public services, and banning discrimination in housing and employment. Similar battles have been waged to extend basic civil rights to women, gays, the disabled, and others. The debate over the extension of this basic package of rights has had a similar echo to it for two centuries. Those in favor have argued that the nation must stand true to its promise of equality for all. Those opposed have argued that government has no right to force people to socialize or do business with people they choose not to deal with. Today we hear those same arguments in the debate over extending similar rights to gays.

The first step in protecting basic civil rights has been for government to tear down the formal mechanisms of discrimination, to eliminate segregation laws and bans on direct prejudice in housing and employment. The most heated debates in civil rights are whether the government should go further, extending preferences and special outreach, such as affirmative action, to make up for past discrimination and to push toward actual equality with greater speed. Proponents argue that as long as race and gender remain magnets for discrimination, government has a responsibility to tip the scales back toward equality. Opponents argue that although government must work hard to prevent direct bias and assure equality of opportunity, it cannot seek to implement equality of outcome (through racially weighted admissions to universities, for example) without creating yet another form of bias.

PROVIDING PUBLIC SERVICES AND ASSISTANCE

Another essential part of government's job is to provide public services and assistance. We expect government to provide many different kinds of services. These include huge projects such as highways, which we can only buy if government takes charge of organizing, financing and operating them; economists call these types of projects "public goods." We decide to provide other services, public schools being the clearest example, on a public basis to ensure that everyone has access to them. While many families do send their children to private school, not all can afford to or want to. Long ago in the nation's history we decided that public education should be made broadly available to every child, with government being the means for doing so.

Other public services and assistance are more controversial. In health care, for example, the United States has a mixed system. The majority of people receive their health care through private coverage, most often through their employer. Government may set some rules for how these private systems operate but they are still private systems. Other people, especially the poor and the elderly, receive their health care through public systems such as Medicare and Medicaid. Virtually all other wealthy countries have chosen differently, creating national health systems that cover everyone, paid for out of tax dollars instead of private premiums. Advocates of a public heath care system for the United States point out that our dependence on private care leaves millions without any health coverage at all, wastes enormous amounts on marketing and overhead, and subjects private health care patients to abuses as health insurers pursue maximize profit at the expense of patient care. Opponents of a public system contend that it will reduce innovation, end up rationing health care services to everyone in order to stay within budgets, and convert health care into a public bureaucracy akin to the state department of motor vehicles.

Public assistance for the poor is also a controversial topic in the United States. Since the Great Depression, federal, state, and local governments have provided the nation's poor with a safety net, including subsidized medical care, housing assistance, food stamps, and direct cash payments known as welfare. Supporters of public assistance warn that without government support many families will be forced into homelessness, unable to afford adequate food, and cutoff from the health care they need. Critics of welfare charge that it fosters dependence on "government handouts," is unfair to poor families who work hard to succeed on their own, and is a drain of public resources that could be better spent elsewhere. In 1996 the United States Congress approved a national welfare reform package that put strict limits on welfare benefits and required families to work in order to receive them.

In the aftermath of welfare reform, however, many studies have documented the serious gap between what poor families can earn when they do work and what it actually costs to live. One such study in Sonoma County, California, found that while a local family of two adults and two children would need an income of $17.74 per hour to meet all their basic needs, one-fifth of the families in the county earned an average of less than half that.[4] Low-income working families face similar wage/need gaps all over the country. In terms of government policy, that leaves us with a choice. We can either force private employers to boost minimum wages and benefits until the gap is closed, or government can fill the gap with publicly subsidized services such as housing, day care, and health coverage. If we choose to do neither than we are accepting that millions of families will not be able to make ends meet, even if they work full-time.

Once we decide what services we expect government to provide, the next question is how we expect government to pay the costs—the perennial debate over taxation. Debates over taxes are a matter of tradeoffs. If we want our taxes to be less, then our levels of services will be less (or at the federal level our deficits will be higher). If we want to give a tax cut to one group of taxpayers, without reducing services or increasing debt, another group will need to make up the difference. During the 2000 presidential election, for example, critics of George W. Bush's proposed federal tax cut pointed out that its high cost would cut deeply into the funds that might otherwise be used to hire new teachers, fix public health care systems such as Medicare, or be used to pay down the national debt.

Taxation debates are driven by two other questions as well—fairness and the larger effects of taxes on the economy as a whole. In tax policy, "fairness" usually refers to the principle that people with higher incomes should pay a higher portion of their income in taxes because they can afford to, and people with lower incomes should pay a lower portion. Some taxes, such as income taxes, are generally more "progressive," meaning they follow this principle that the well-off pay more, the poor less. Other taxes, such as the sales tax, are generally considered to be "regressive," with the poor paying a larger share of their income. Finally, economists, politicians, and taxpayers alike argue over the effects that taxes have on jobs and the economy. Businesses traditionally employ the argument, when faced with a tax increase or pushing for a tax cut, that higher taxes mean less production, less employment, and higher costs passed on to consumers. Whether this is true and to what extent varies depending on the specifics. In many cases businesses overstate these side effects in order to bolster the case for lower taxes.

MAKING RULES FOR THE MARKETPLACE

The other area where government plays a major role in economic life is in its power to set rules for the marketplace. Few would argue that government has no role to play in the economy. Without contracts enforceable by law, courts to resolve disputes, and the basic protection of private property, most of the private economy could not function. The debate over how far government should go beyond these basics centers on two questions: When is government intervention in the marketplace warranted? When government does intervene, in what manner should it do so?

The most compelling argument for government intervention in the marketplace is when public rules are needed to protect us from harm and abuse. In some cases this happens to us as consumers, when businesses conspire to raise prices, sell dangerous products (such as Firestone tires that fall apart at high speed), or deny access to essential services (as when heath insurers deny care to people who are ill). In other cases businesses take unfair advantage of workers, forcing them to work long overtime for no extra pay, exposing them to dangerous chemicals, or firing them without just cause. Without public rules businesses can also do serious damage to the environment, dumping pollutants into the air, land, and water because it is cheaper and easier to do so than to pay for cleaner methods of production. In cases like these, most people expect government to act on our behalf, establishing public rules to prohibit this type of market behavior.

Many people, especially the leaders and owners of the affected industries, argue against intervention by government. They insist that the marketplace has its own, more efficient mechanisms of self-correction. Consumers will find out which products are overpriced or unhealthy and switch to ones that aren't. Businesses will act responsibly in order to preserve their good name. There are certainly instances where this is true. It has taken, for example, no rule making by government to get computer manufacturers to lower their prices and improve their products over the past decade. That was the result of innovation and competition. However, there are many instances where competition and goodwill alone are not enough to get the market to act in the public interest, and then government must enter the picture.

Not all methods of government intervention are alike. The most traditional is "regulation," whereby a government agency establishes a specific rule for companies to follow. This, for example, is how the United States Environmental Protection Agency (EPA) regularly imposes specific antipollution requirements on companies. A variation on regulation is for government to set standards, such as how much pollution a factory can produce each year, but then leave it to the company to determine what technology and methods it will use to most efficiently meet that standard.

In other cases government provides financial incentives (such as tax breaks) or disincentives (such as fines) to encourage companies to act in a more publicly responsible way. Still another approach is to subject companies to civil lawsuits by those they have harmed or criminal prosecution of their managers for the most serious offenses (such as consumer deaths). Again, opponents of government intervention argue that such rules only end up boosting prices for all of us and stifle innovation by making businesses subject to the whims of faraway bureaucrats and trial lawyers. To be sure, there is no shortage of examples where government bureaucracy has made running a business unnecessarily difficult. As with most all public policy, the challenge is to analyze the situation wisely and balance the interests involved—public protection and business efficiency—in a thoughtful way.

It is also important to note that the increased globalization of the world's economy has made effective rule making in the marketplace even more difficult. With the world's biggest enterprises operating in dozens of countries at once and with capital and investment able to leap hemispheres with the touch of a keyboard, individual nations have become less and less able to implement effective consumer, labor and environmental protections. Companies subject to these rules make the threat, "If you do try to impose minimum wage laws/antipollution measures/etc. on us we will go somewhere else." Many can and do. Part of the answer is to develop international agreements that afford such protections worldwide and to establish public institutions to monitor and implement such agreements.

MAKING SURE OUR GOVERNMENT IS A DEMOCRACY

Finally, the work of government is the integrity of government itself, assuring that public policy is deliberated and crafted through a process that is genuinely open and democratic. If government is to be, in Lincoln's words, "of, by, and for the people," than the people must have open and equal access to their government.

The most serious challenge to this principle today is the increasing and alarming role that money plays in our political system. At the local level, in state legislatures, in elections for Congress and for the presidency, campaigns are becoming dominated by the flow of contributions made by wealthy special interest groups to politicians. These same groups later come calling on those same politicians seeking public favors. The conflict is a clear one. If the money given were in the form of a bribe, stuck in a politician's pocket, the act would be illegal and we would be aghast. Because those funds instead go into the candidates' campaign coffers, the transaction is legal and accepted, but the effect is little different.

Campaign reform advocates propose a series of reforms to change the role that money plays in election politics—limits on campaign spending, caps on campaign contributions, and the replacement of special interest funding with public financing to qualified candidates. Opponents of reform argue that the flow of money in politics is a form of free speech, protected by the First Amendment. The United States Supreme Court has largely affirmed that view, blocking the way to limits on political spending. Nevertheless, the concern among voters is evident, and around the nation voters are approving political reform through ballot measures and applying pressure for reform on their local officials.

In addition to the regulation of money in politics, other rules are important to making government more open and democratic. These include open meeting laws, guarantees of access to government information, and rules against financial conflicts of interest by public officials. In the end, however, there are certain ingredients of an effective democracy that no government rule can provide. These ingredients are civic participation, a commitment to learn and understand the issues that government debates and to play an active role in influencing the action government takes on those issues.

CHAPTER TWO

The Rules of Politics

There are two things that are important in politics. The first is money and I can't remember what the second one is.

—OHIO POLITICAL BOSS AND U.S. SENATOR MARK HANNA, 1895[1]

In a representative democracy we place the authority and power of government in the hands of those we elect. The rules that govern those elections and the exercise of power afterward determine the course of every other public issue we care about—civil rights, foreign affairs, public education, and many others.

The presidential election of 2000, with its high-stakes drama over uncounted ballots, raised new doubts among many Americans about whether the rules of politics are really quite as fair and democratic as many might have believed. In fact, the fight over ballots in Florida touched on deeper doubts about political fairness that have been growing in the United States for many years. For four decades, participation in U.S. presidential elections has been in steady decline.[2] Election campaigns have become multimillion-dollar marketing campaigns that seem farther and farther beyond our ability to influence as average citizens. It is no surprise that in a 1997 poll published by the *Los Angeles Times,* 69 percent of those surveyed agreed with the statement "People like me have almost no say in the political system."

Making our political process more democratic includes understanding the rules by which the political game is played and being involved in making those rules. Our goal should be to have a political system that is fair, ethical, open, and accountable. How well we address these issues will determine the integrity of our democracy for many generations to come.

CAMPAIGN FINANCING: DEMOCRACY FOR SALE

Suppose you were going to list the job qualifications needed to run for president, Congress, the state legislature, or the city council in any big city. Somewhere very near the top would be this: "Applicant must know a lot of people with money and have a strong ability to get it from them." There is no real question that fundraising has become the number-one activity in election campaigns and the ability to raise funds the number-one qualification.

With each new election, the number of dollars spent by candidates at the national, state, and local level leaps higher at extraordinary rates. For example, during the 1998 election, congressional candidates and the national Democratic and Republican parties spent a total of more than $1.3 billion, a 17 percent increase in just four years.[3] That year the average winner of a House seat spent $775,000, the average winner in the Senate more than $5 million (and in the more hotly contested races for both, much, much more). In 2000, with a presidential campaign added in, the total spending on all national races combined came close to $3 billion.[4] In states both large and small, the money trend is the same. In California, a competitive race for the state senate can cost nearly $2 million.[5] In much smaller Connecticut the average cost of winning a state senate seat has doubled in just ten years.[6] Running for public office has become a big-money enterprise, shutting out those who aren't prepared to play by money's rules.

RETURN ON INVESTMENT

There should be little debate about the intentions of all this campaign giving. Wealthy special interests, from Microsoft to the alcohol industry, pour millions into candidate and party coffers. They do so not to support democracy, and often not even with the direct aim of helping specific candidates, but to buy access and friendship from whoever wins. The biggest givers cover their bets with huge donations to both sides. A 1999 Common Cause study identified more than three dozen major corporations that had given $50,000 or more to both the Democratic and the Republican national parties; among them were AT&T ($832,400), American Airlines ($348,056), Microsoft ($252,100, and Anheuser-Busch ($231,450).[7] There should also be little debate about the effect of such giving—public policy made under the influence of those who can afford to pay for it.

All this big campaign giving is based on a simple business principle—"return on investment"—and few investments deliver as powerful a return as changing government policy in your direction. Federal tax changes in 1997, for example, slashed taxes for companies investing in new machinery and equipment, a windfall worth as much as $18.3 billion over ten years. The main organizations that lobbied for the change, the Chemical Manufacturers Association, the American Petroleum Institute, and the American Iron and Steel Institute, poured more than $22 million into Republican and Democratic coffers during the six years preceding the vote. That may seem like a huge sum to most people, but in relation to what it helped win it was only a tiny fraction.[8]

Political contributions in the initiative arena can also provide a hefty return. In 1990 California alcohol makers spent $27 million to defeat a state alcohol tax initiative that would have boosted wine, beer, and spirits taxes by $750 million per year. That political investment delivered a twenty-eight to one return in the first year alone, far better than they would have made opening a new brewery or distillery.

Another effect of dollar politics has been the near elimination of serious challenges to incumbent office holders. During the 1998 congressional elections,

347 of the 401 House incumbents running for reelection either faced no opponents or spent at least twice as much as their challengers. All 347 won reelection.[9] In the Senate that same year, where incumbents also outspent their challengers an average of 2 to 1, more than 90 percent won reelection.[10] Incumbent lawmakers have maintained similar advantages in fund-raising and reelection at the state level.[11]

The pivotal role of cash in politics also affects the underrepresentation of ethnic minorities and women in the process.[12] San Francisco school board member Steve Phillips, a leader in California's African American community, says, "As much as people would like to not admit it, the economic status of one's ethnic community makes a big difference, and that is why a lot of black candidates can't win outside majority black districts."[13] Similarly, a recent study by the Center for Responsive Politics concluded that although women may vote in larger numbers than men, they are still responsible for only about one-quarter of large individual contributions to candidates, parties, and political action committees.[14]

It is not only good people that get filtered out of politics by big money but also important ideas. As *Nation* editor William Greider writes, "The most pernicious influence of big money is not the repeated scandals in which contributors buy politicians quid pro quo. The far greater damage from relying on major corporations or wealth holders to finance candidates in both parties is how this automatically keeps provocative, new ideas off the table—effectively vetoed before the public can hear about them. Money doesn't just talk in politics, it silences."[15]

HOW DID WE GET HERE?

Somewhere in our national history, more by accident than by intention, we decided that political campaigns should be financed with private contributions, a choice that has slowly converted our democracy into one more commodity for sale. How did that happen? In the nation's earliest days campaigns were inexpensive, waged with personal appearances, cheaply printed pamphlets, and perhaps a newspaper ad or two. Fund-raising scandals were no more serious than the charge made against a young George Washington that he had distributed a little rum, wine, and hard cider to some of the 391 voters in his Virginia legislative district.[16]

As the nation grew, however, so did the relationship between money and politics. A national economy of small businesses evolved into one of enormous corporations. Banks, railroads, oil conglomerates, mining companies, and power utilities all began to amass economic clout and look for ways to turn their financial resources into influence and outright control of the political process. At the same time, campaigning also grew more expensive, with more voters and higher costs to get out the message. By the start of the 1900s, the relationship between big money and politics was well entrenched. As Frank Norris wrote of the railroads in his 1901 epic, *The Octopus*, "They own the ballot box . . . they own us."

The twentieth century saw the relationship between money and politics sky-rocket to new heights. As the New Deal and political reforms in the 1960s started poking government's nose more actively into the affairs of business, with labor, environmental, consumer protection, and other types of regulation, corporate interests began turning their attention to politics, with campaign contributions and expensive lobbying being their main tools. Labor unions grew as well, dominating, in a smaller way the campaigns of many Democrats. The nature of political campaigning also changed dramatically, relying more and more on the expensive mediums of radio and television. Between 1956 and 1968, overall spending for all U.S. campaigns doubled, pushed by a sixfold increase in spending for broadcast advertising.[17] The transition from a few barrels of rum to corporate contributions totaling hundreds of millions of dollars happened so slowly and steadily that Americans barely stopped to ask the question "Does it still make sense to fund our political campaigns with private contributions?" As one of the architects of the American Revolution, Thomas Paine, wrote, "A long habit of not thinking a thing wrong gives it a superficial appearance of being right."[18]

AGENDAS FOR REFORM

The challenge to big money's influence over politics is not new. At the beginning of the 1900s, President Theodore Roosevelt called for a ban on all political contributions by corporations and advocated public financing of federal candidates.[19] For a century, political reformers have tried to build a wall between money's influence and the nation's democracy. However, efforts at reform involve a tough juggling act. Many of the obvious changes—a cap on campaign spending, for example—run directly into a series of rulings by the U.S. Supreme Court that equate political spending with free speech. As reformers attempt to create campaign rules that can survive legal challenge, most have relied on some mix of several reforms.

Public Disclosure

One of the chief reforms in the wake of the Nixon Watergate scandal was to mandate tough disclosure of the political contributions made to candidates for Congress and the presidency, a reform also adopted by most states and cities. Those who care to peruse the mammoth files buried in the Federal Elections Commission (FEC) in Washington and in state and local election offices around the country can find a treasure trove of information about the path of cash from contributors to candidates. Advocacy groups, journalists, even political opponents use this information to help sketch a public picture of where political cash comes from and what it might be buying. Such filings are the original source of many of the figures used in this chapter.

Technology promises to make this information even more accessible, moving it out of government offices and onto the computer screens of millions of

Americans. The FEC already makes much of its reporting available via the Internet, as do many states. Reforms are underway across the country to require campaigns to file their campaign reports electronically, giving the public easy Internet access to the smallest details of that information.

Many reformers argue that, to be effective, disclosure must go one step further, by requiring that campaigns clearly disclose their top contributors in their paid ads. Large corporate givers, who fear that their true identity might rally voters against them, often try to hide behind unrevealing or even misleading pseudonyms such as "Californians Against Unfair Taxes" or something similar. In this case it was only through tough disclosure laws that voters were able to learn that the real money behind "Californians Against Unfair Taxes" was actually tobacco giant Philip Morris. Nevertheless, disclosure alone without changing where political money comes from is of limited value, roughly akin to getting a better look at a street mugging without making any effort to stop it.

Contribution Limits

The other mainstay of the post-Watergate reforms was new federal limits on campaign contributions to candidates: $1,000 for individuals, $5,000 for political action committees. Most states and localities have also set limits on political contributions. Supporters of strict contribution limits argue that they block the big money that gives donors disproportionate influence and shifts the emphasis to small donors. As Derek Cressman of the U.S. Public Interest Research Group testified to congress, "Candidates would then raise their funds from ordinary citizens and the candidates who raised the most money truly would be the candidates who had the most public support."[20]

Conservative opponents of contribution limits denounce them as an attack on free speech. Senator Mitch McConnell of Kentucky, Congress's leading campaign reform opponent (and one of Congress's top fund-raisers), has called contribution limits "the most dangerous assault on core constitutional freedom in American history."[21] The argument that unrestricted contributing is free speech has been denied over and over again, however, even by conservative U.S. Supreme Court Justice John Paul Stevens, who wrote in 2000, "Money is property, it is not speech."[22]

Other critics, from both the left and right, warn that contribution limits by themselves really just force candidates to spend more time scrambling for smaller donations and less time thinking and talking about the issues. In fact, many argue that in the absence of an alternative source of funds, such a public financing, candidates are able to stay truer to their principles if they are allowed to receive and rely on large, even unlimited, contributions from their core supporters. As some point out, if antiwar presidential candidate Eugene McCarthy had had to follow the current federal contribution limits in 1968, he wouldn't have had access to the huge contributions from wealthy Vietnam War opponents that made his challenge to President Lyndon Johnson possible.

The other criticism of contribution limits on candidates is that big cash just finds its way into campaigns through other paths. For example, contributions made directly to political parties (known as "soft money") are not restricted, and donations of $1 million and more are common. The same is true for "independent expenditures," the money spent directly by groups (from the National Rifle Association to the League of Conservation Voters) to either promote or attack candidates.

Without restrictions on all forms of campaign giving and without public financing as a substitute for private fund-raising, the benefits of contribution limits are severely limited. They create a system that one candidate called "more loophole than law." The Center for Responsive Politics warns that the disclosure and contribution limits reform formula adopted after Watergate "only served to sanitize, rationalize, and legitimize the same old system of privately-financed federal elections dominated by wealthy individual and corporate contributors."[23]

Limits on Campaign Spending

The fund-raising efforts of dueling candidates are often compared to the cold war nuclear arms race between the United States and the former Soviet Union. What each side wants is based on what it thinks the other has or is going to have. As a result, campaign spending nationally, in the states, and locally, has exploded. In addition to the increased costs of television, radio, and direct mail advertising, each new increase fuels the belief among candidates and their supporters that they have to keep up. As campaign spending increases, so in turn does the dependence of candidates on wealthy special interests.

Placing some reasonable limits on what candidates can spend is a key step toward rolling back that dependence. However, spending limits run up against a long-standing brick wall erected by the U.S. Supreme Court's 1976 *Buckley v. Valeo* decision. Although the Court let stand the limits on campaign contributions, it declared that mandatory limits on campaign expenditures were a violation of the First Amendment's guarantee of "free speech." Some reformers are hopeful that the Court can be challenged to change that opinion, but many others have begun searching for an alternative that can pass Court muster.

The most common alternative is "voluntary" spending limits, which reward candidates who comply by giving them some mix of public funds or advertising. Since candidates agree to these limits voluntarily, there is no forced restriction on free speech. Voluntary spending limits tied to public financing have been in effect for presidential candidates since 1976. More recently, Maine, Massachusetts, Florida, and cities across the nation have adopted voluntary limits. Critics of voluntary spending limits argue that candidates who abide by them risk being clobbered by two forms of spending that the Supreme Court says cannot be restricted: independent expenditures and the unrestricted ability of wealthy candidates such as Ross Perot or Steve Forbes to pour unlimited amounts of their own cash into their own campaigns.

Public Financing of Campaigns

Supporters of publicly financed campaigns make the case that if we really want to eliminate the corrupting influence of big money in campaigns then we need to go back to the original question: Is the public best served by having candidates dependent on private contributions? If we are not served by such a system, then we have to provide an alternative way for candidates to finance their campaigns and that alternative is public dollars.

The idea of public campaign financing inspires deep objections among its opponents, with warnings that politicians will use taxpayer dollars to pay for the same slick, substanceless campaigns that voters already despise even when they're paid for by someone else. Critics charge that taxpayer dollars that could otherwise go for schools or other public services would instead "flow to those on the fringes of American politics." Law professor Bradley Smith writes, "Perennial presidential candidate and convicted felon Lyndon LaRouche took in a cool $825,000 in taxpayer-provided matching funds in 1988 alone." He goes on to quote Thomas Jefferson, "To compel a man to furnish contributions of money for the propagation of opinions which he disbelieves, is sinful and tyrannical."[24]

When Jefferson wrote that he probably wasn't anticipating a nation in which candidates would need a million dollars to run for Congress or corporations could pour tens of millions into the campaigns of public officials, swaying their votes on public questions worth tens of billions. There is no question that some portion of our tax dollars would end up supporting candidates whose views we despise, just as now some portion of our tax dollars are used to support government programs we disagree with. Public financing could, however, make it possible to draw into politics people whose main skill is not fund-raising.

Far from being a radical concept, public financing has been available in presidential contests for nearly three decades, and across the nation many states and cities have also adopted some form of public funding. In 1996 Maine voters approved a "Clean Money Campaign Reform" initiative offering full public financing to candidates who reject special-interest contributions and agree to campaign-spending limits. Similar reforms have been adopted in Vermont, Arizona, Massachusetts, and in New York City, Los Angeles, Long Beach, Seattle, Tucson, and Sacramento.[25] A 1996 national Gallup Poll reported that 64 percent of voters support a system in which the "federal government provides a fixed amount of money for the election campaigns of candidates for congress and all private contributions [are] prohibited."[26] Despite conservative objections, it appears that citizens are warming fast to the idea of using tax dollars as a way to retake control of their government.

Free Broadcast Time

For more than thirty years, radio and television broadcasters were required, as a condition of receiving their federal broadcast license, to provide free airtime to political causes that couldn't afford to purchase it. The Fairness Doctrine" adopted by the Federal Communications Commission (FCC) in 1949 provided at least some measure of balance in access to the nation's powerful airwaves. Under pressure from broadcasters and other business interests, the FCC gutted the rule in 1992. Many political reformers advocate that such a fairness requirement be reimposed and expanded, offering free time both to candidates and to initiative campaigns that can't afford to buy that media access.

VOTING SYSTEMS: RIGGED, FAIR, AND OTHERWISE

The rules that govern how we vote and how our votes are counted can also seriously tip the advantage toward one group or another. Here too there are public issues that citizens need to understand and seek to influence.

Voter Registration

One of the first things that we learn as new voters is that the law requires us to register prior to the election in order to be eligible to vote. Originally, the practice of requiring voters to register was a reform aimed at preventing voter fraud, a response to fears that people would vote more than once or use false names.[27] However, voter registration also puts one more obstacle in the way of voting, at a time in which voter participation is already in marked decline. Although it may seem reasonable to require voters to register at least a month in advance, many people don't pay much attention to elections until the very end of a campaign. It may only be in the last week that they find some candidate or issue compelling enough to get them to the polls, and by then it is too late. Less restrictive voter registration rules would make it more possible and more likely that a larger and more representative electorate would go to the polls.

Some voter participation advocates favor eliminating registration altogether, claiming that concerns about voter fraud are exaggerated since it can be controlled with the help of identification checks and modern computer technology. Two states, Minnesota and South Dakota, allow citizens to register to vote up to the day of the election. Minnesota's same-day registration law is widely credited for the surprise 1998 election victory of Reform party gubernatorial candidate Jesse Ventura, who benefited from a groundswell of excitement at the very end of the campaign.

Short of same-day registration, there has been an effort in recent years to make voter registration more accessible. One main strategy has been to build voter registration into the work of government agencies. The "motor voter" program gives citizens the opportunity to register when they renew their driver's licenses. In many states voter registration is offered to people receiving assistance in welfare offices. The National Voter Registration Act of 1993, which mandates that certain government agencies aid citizens with voter registration, resulted in 4.5 million new registered voters nationwide in just its first six months.[28] Many nonprofit groups—

clinics, churches, child care centers and the like—have started to register voters as well.

Reapportionment

Another issue that has a huge effect on who wins and who loses elections is the manner in which we draw the boundary lines for legislative districts—otherwise known as reapportionment. Federal and state laws require that the boundaries of congressional and legislative districts be drawn so that each has an equal population, thereby giving equal electoral weight to each potential voter. However, the country's population is constantly growing and moving. Every ten years, following the U.S. census, each state is required to redraw the boundaries of these districts to equalize once again the number of residents in each one. It is a process loaded with politics, and it has produced some of the nation's most notorious partisan manipulation.

In brief, reapportionment works like this. Two congressional or state legislative districts that are adjacent to one another may have grown over the decade by very different rates. For example, one district may have experienced a ten-year surge in population while the population in a neighboring district may have remained quite stable. To make the two districts equal again in population, the boundaries must be redrawn. Some of the neighborhoods and voters in the populous district will be shifted into the less populous one—but which neighborhoods and which voters? The answer may determine who wins elections in both districts for a decade to come.

Let's say the populous district is made up of 50 percent Democrats and 50 percent Republicans, a "swing seat" considered winnable by either party and that the sparsely populated district is already securely Republican. If the lines are redrawn in a way so that nearly all the voters shifted out of the district are Republican, the GOP district remains safely GOP but in the other district the registration split might suddenly become 60 percent Democrats and 40 percent Republicans, a big advantage to Democratic candidates. Similarly, if the district gaining voters has a large Latino population, say 55 percent, it would generally be a strong seat for Latino candidates. However, if all the new voters added to the district are white, the Latino population might drop to 40 percent and the seat would no longer be so easy a win for Latino candidates. The potential for manipulation in the hands of those who control reapportionment is endless.

In most states, these lines (both state and congressional) are redrawn by the state legislature, a highly political process in which the party in power seeks to move the boundaries to its maximum political advantage. During California's 1982 reapportionment, as a young legislative assistant, I was called into the office of Assembly Speaker Willie Brown, shown the new district maps, and asked if there were any changes the assemblywoman I worked for might want. District lines are redrawn in all kinds of odd shapes to move blocks of desired or undesired voters from one district to another, a process known as "gerrymandering," named for the salamander-shaped district lines drawn in 1812 by Massachusetts Governor Elbridge Gerry to benefit his party.[29]

Political reformers have tried, with little success, to squeeze the politics out of the reapportionment process. Some have proposed specific standards for district lines, such as avoiding the division of cities, towns, and neighborhoods, or keeping together blocks of ethnic groups and educational districts. Reform groups have also tried to turn over redistricting to "independent" commissions, usually made up of judges. Common Cause argues, "The farther the reapportionment process can be removed from the direct participation of legislators, the less likely incumbent or partisan interests will negatively affect the process and its outcome."[30] Partisan resistance to these reforms runs high, and with the spoils so great, squeezing politics completely out of the reapportionment is probably impossible.

Vote Counting

Before the surreal drama over uncounted votes in Florida in the 2000 presidential campaign, few Americans probably thought seriously about how their votes are actually counted. However, when the election of the President came down to a few hundred votes out the entire nation, the issue of how votes are counted suddenly took center stage. In most of the United States voting is done by punch machine, a technology that goes back to the 1960s. During the Florida controversy, the manufacturers of the punch machines admitted that, at best, they could guarantee an accuracy rate of 99 percent. In Florida that margin of error translated into a number of votes far larger than the vote gap separating candidates Al Gore and George W. Bush.

With so much at stake, there is enormous potential for conflicts of interest in the decisions that are made about how votes should be. The fact that these decisions were made in Florida by appointees of one candidate's brother heightened suspicions of partisanship. Reform groups argue that there must be clear rules assuring that every vote is counted, regardless of what delay that might entail. Some have suggested that such disputes should be handled by a special nonpartisan commission with broad public credibility. Another solution lies in upgrading the technology used for voting in the United States. As many pointed out during the Florida drama, in a country that uses computer technology to conduct millions of transactions per day, there are clearly ways to use that technology to design a system of voting in which voter confusion is minimized and every vote is counted.

Moving Beyond Two Parties

The two-party system is deeply imbedded in U.S. political life, though not everyone is happy with the choices. Not all democracies are designed so narrowly, and many political reformers in the United States think a system that gives us more options would serve us better. Recently, voters in the United States have shown more interest in third parties, with both the Reform party and the Green party winning some high-profile local and state races. These parties and others claim, however (with reason), that they suffer serious electoral handicaps, struggling to be listed on the ballot in some areas, excluded from public debates, and often ignored by the media in favor of the candidates from the two major parties.

Much of that handicap has less to do with legal barriers than with the United State's long two-party tradition. Many voters ask themselves, "Why should I throw away my vote on a third party, even one more in tune with my views, and forfeit the chance to influence the outcome between the two real contenders?" Green party candidate Ralph Nader's candidacy for President in 2000 raised this question in earnest, given that his vote total more than surpassed the vote margin that gave George W. Bush his victory over Al Gore in key states.

Other democracies, including Germany, Spain, Denmark, Sweden and many others, offer voters a system that does not force them to choose between principle and pragmatism. Under the voting method known as "proportional representation," legislative seats are apportioned based on the percentage won by each party. A Green party victory of 10 percent of the vote means taking 10 percent of the total legislative seats and having a substantial say in the government (as was exactly the case not long ago in Germany). Proportional representation is used in a limited way in the United States, to divide up delegates among candidates in some states' presidential primaries and at the city-council level in communities such as Cambridge, Massachusetts, and Peoria, Illinois.

Advocates of proportional representation argue that it makes third parties a viable choice for voters, giving a voice to political minorities and broadening the scope of public debate. The reality is that the United States is a long way from adopting such a major reform as this one, but interest in third parties is growing, and making more political space for them is becoming a more important issue.

ETHICS IN GOVERNMENT

After the elections are over and the winners take power, the struggle for honest government is still just beginning. The work of government must be open and visible and the influence of money in that work must still be limited. Conflicts of interest must be watched for and brought out into the open. Here as well, public vigilance over the rules of politics is crucial.

Open Meetings and Access to Information

John W. Gardner, the founder of Common Cause, once wrote, "The two chief obstacles to responsive government are money and secrecy."[31] The best way to keep our government honest and accountable is for the process of government to be transparent. Government deliberations and decisions should take place in the public spotlight, where members of the public can watch and participate. Common Cause suggests a set of rules for all government bodies—legislative and administrative—to protect public access and accountability. These include: advance public notice of at least seventy-two hours for all public meetings and a requirement that all meetings be open to the public; the tape recording of all meetings and the keeping of detailed minutes available to the public; and that violations of such public meeting laws be treated as a serious offense.[32]

Equally important is public access to the records of government, including copies of proposed bills and regulations, government reports, correspondence—all the material that makes up the paper trail of government action. If the public does not have access to this information, key decisions can be made without the public ever knowing or being able to exercise its right to influence the outcome. At the national level the Freedom of Information Act spells out the public's right to information and the process for getting it (For more information about the U.S. Freedom of Information Act see chapter 7 of this book.) Many states have similar laws. Here as well, the rules are important. The definition of what "records" are available to the public should be as broad as possible, and exemptions (such as personnel records and medical records) should be kept narrow. Government records and documents should be available at a low cost and accessed easily, something made even more possible by the World Wide Web.

Making government more open and accessible is important, but at the same time we need to recognize the inequities in how such access gets used. Too often the culture of public participation in government—attending hearings, preparing testimony, meeting with officials—is primarily a middle- and upper-class, usually white, activity. It is a culture many people don't feel comfortable participating in; as a practical matter, many people don't have the luxury of taking time off from work to be present. Open government means not only opening the doors to those who are already knocking, but also reaching out actively to communities that don't participate as readily. This may mean holding public meetings at different times (in the evening after work, for example) or out in the community instead of in city halls or state capitols. It also means working directly with groups that have strong roots in underrepresented communities to help overcome the barriers that still keep those communities outside the political process.

Conflicts of Interest

There is always a need to watch carefully for how money tries to buy its way into the democratic process, creating "conflicts of interest" in which officials charged with watching out for the public interest end up watching out instead for themselves or someone who has done them some favor. Simple disclosure is the baseline against this kind of conflict. As with disclosure of campaign contributions, elected and appointed government officials should be required (as is the case nationally and in many states) to disclose their main financial interests such as outside income and property holdings. It was through such state disclosure filings that consumer groups in California discovered that the state agriculture secretary was in the business of growing peaches while simultaneously using his state authority to affect peach prices; revelation of the conflict eventually forced the secretary's resignation.

Another important good-government reform prohibits "revolving door" employment, the practice of public officials moving back and forth between private employers and government positions that set the rules for those private employers. For example, in 1993 the U.S. Food and Drug Administration (FDA) ruled that milk produced using the controversial hormone rBGH did not need to bear warning labels advising consumers that the hormone was used. The decision was made by an FDA official who had previously been an attorney for the hormone's manufacturer, Monsanto. After his favorable ruling for Monsanto the official then went back to work for the corporation.[33] Many states have adopted rules to prohibit this kind of back-and-forth employment between regulators and those they regulate.

Finally, there is a need for rules to limit what is permissible activity between government officials and lobbying groups. Lobbyists provide an important function in the democratic process, furnishing lawmakers and other officials with essential information about public problems and the possible effects of different policies. Lobbyists represent groups ranging from animal rights activists to oil companies, although lobbyists representing corporate interests far outnumber all the others and have far more resources to do their job. In most cases the information they share is important. The problem begins when lobbyists start to provide officials with something more than information.

The most serious conflict is the millions of dollars of campaign contributions that many of these same lobbying groups funnel to candidates. One night a lobbyist is attending a lawmaker's fund-raiser, and the next morning that same lobbyist is meeting with the lawmaker about a bill. Campaign contributions aren't the only way lobby groups use cash to woo policy makers. A practice long targeted by reformers is the honorarium game, in which officials are invited to an association's meeting to give a short talk and then rewarded with a speaker's fee of $500, $1,000, $5,000, or more. This is a conflict perhaps even more serious than a campaign contribution, because it goes right into the official's own pocket. Lobby groups also offer lawmakers perks ranging from free sports tickets to free travel. During his 1996 presidential campaign, Senate Republican leader Bob Dole used the private jet belonging to the Chiquita Banana Corporation, while at the same time pushing Chiquita's request for government trade assistance.[34] Bans on honoraria, gifts, and perks to public officials are essential.

While we may not all be equal when we go into the marketplace to buy a car, a shirt, or a house, when it comes to our democracy, equal is exactly what we are supposed to be—one person, one vote. The fight to preserve that principle has run through more than two centuries of U.S. history, from the granting of the vote to blacks and to women to the fight against poll taxes. In our time, the principle of political equality is neither less urgent nor any less under attack, especially from the power that money wields in our political process. Working to assure that our political system remains open, fair, and equal to all is one of the most important challenges our democracy faces in the century ahead.

Taxes and Budgets

Following the Money

Our Constitution is in actual operation; everything appears to promise that it will last; but in this world nothing is certain but death and taxes."

— BENJAMIN FRANKLIN

When I was growing up in southern California in the 1960s and 1970s, my family's life was touched everyday by the things that government paid for. My parents purchased our home with the help of a federal loan program for veterans. I started my education at the local public elementary school and learned to love books at the small county library a block from my house. During the summers I spent my days playing games and doing crafts at the local county park. A new state freeway cut my father's work commute and brought him home to us earlier each night. Later I was able to go to college at the University of California at Berkeley, paid for mostly with government scholarships and financial aid.

As with many families, these were things we could not have afforded on our own. They were all made possible because people in that era made a commitment to dedicate a portion of their incomes to make certain public investments. Taxes and public budgets were them mechanism by which they did so.

It is through taxes and budgets that we make many of our most important and enduring public decisions. Yet, for most people, there are few issues that seem as complicated, shrouded in the jargon of economists and lawyers. At their essence, tax and budget matters boil down to two basic questions, each one having more to do with values than with economics or arithmetic: What public services and projects do we want to buy? How do we want to pay for them? In a democracy, it is critical that these questions be understood broadly and decided in a public way.

TAXES: HOW MUCH AND WHO PAYS?

No one likes paying taxes. Most people really hate it. We are caught in the paradox described by conservative economist Milton Friedman: "Many of us welcome the additional government spending; few of us welcome additional taxes."[1] Yet taxes are, as Benjamin Franklin says, "certain," and for that reason, deepening our public understanding of tax issues is crucial.

As we think about and debate tax policy it is important to keep in mind that we use taxation to accomplish three very different things all at the same time. First and most important, taxes are how we raise the funds to pay for public services and programs. Second, we use the tax system to close, at least slightly, the enormous gap between the wealthy and the poor, taxing those who can afford it to help finance services for those who can't. Finally, we use taxes to influence the private economic decisions of both businesses and individuals, through a multitude of special tax breaks and incentives. Often these different objectives are in competition with one another. As we debate how to balance them we return again to certain fundamental questions: How high or low should taxes be? What is fair? What are the costs of our attempts to influence private economic behavior and are they worth it?

How High or Low Should Taxes Be?

"Our taxes are too darn high!" It is a rallying cry that has echoed loudly throughout the United States for several decades, beginning with the great antitax revolts of the late 1970s and continuing through President Reagan's tax-cutting crusades in the 1980s. Cutting taxes has continued to be one of the major issues in every national election since. As we look behind the rhetoric on this issue, two important questions make our choices clearer.

If we cut taxes, what programs will gets cut? Who wouldn't like to see his or her tax bill cut and have a little more cash in hand? However, every dollar that gets cut from taxes also gets cut from a program somewhere in the budget. Too often, tax cut advocates pretend that the money to pay for cuts will come out of thin air, ignoring the program cuts that will inevitably follow. President Reagan's antitax revolution went even further, arguing that every dollar cut from taxes would, through economic growth, actually generate an even larger number of dollars for the public treasury (the infamous "Laffer Curve"). The result of that economic experiment was a whopping $1.5 trillion increase in the U.S. national debt.[2]

Citizens involved in tax debates need to focus public attention on the specific tradeoffs involved when tax cuts are proposed. Who will receive the tax cut and how will the public benefit from it? Where will the money come from and at what public cost? In 1996, for example, then-California Governor Pete Wilson pushed hard for a 15 percent cut in the state's personal income tax and bank and corporation taxes. His proposal would have reduced state revenue by $4.7 billion a year. Opponents countered that although most of the benefits of the tax cut would go to the wealthiest 10 percent of the state's taxpayers, the costs would fall hardest on the state's schoolchildren, a cut of about $480 per pupil.[3] Californians did not look kindly on a tax cut for the wealthy at the expense of their children's education, and the Wilson plan was stopped in its tracks. It is precisely this kind of clear tradeoff—tax cuts versus programs—that the public needs to understand during tax debates.

The second question is, What are the economic side effects of raising or cutting taxes? When taxes are raised, that money doesn't come out of thin air, either.

It eventually comes out of someone's pocket. Those who advocate tax increases must take into account the potential economic side effects. The most heated debates about the effects of tax hikes usually deal with the potential impact on businesses and jobs. Business groups are quick to warn that if they are required to pay higher taxes (or they don't get a tax cut they are asking for) they will cut back or relocate their operations. These threats are often enough very effective at wooing policy-makers and the public to their side.

How true is this "business flight" warning? In some cases, tax increases can indeed motivate businesses to cut back or move, and tax advocates need to take note. In other cases, however, businesses are just enacting the political version of "crying wolf." Taxes are just one part of what goes into a business's decisions about where to set up shop. Higher on its list of considerations, and a much larger factor in the cost of doing business, are the costs of real estate, labor, employee housing, transportation, and the general quality of life in a given area.[4]

In 1993, executives at Taco Bell threatened to move their corporate head-quarters from Irvine, California, to Plano, Texas, if they didn't receive a hefty tax break from the state. Lawmakers responded quickly with an expensive new tax break proposal dubbed by critics, "run for the border," after Taco Bell's well-known advertising slogan. As lawmakers prepared to give in to Taco Bell's demands, the move unraveled on its own, thanks to the marketplace. The landlord of Taco Bell's headquarters, fearful of losing a major tenant, lowered the corporation's rent by even more than the proposed tax break. In the end, lawmakers ended up abandon-ing the expensive tax cut.[5]

While warnings about business flight should be taken seriously, citizens also need to assess these claims with a critical eye. Such warnings, for example, are much more credible in relation to local taxes, because some businesses are able to move easily across city or county lines where taxes might be lower. These warnings are less credible when a business's key resources are immobile (such as an oil re-finery) or if it must stay close to a labor force or customer base tied to its location. The same guidelines apply when evaluating warnings that high-income individual taxpayers will move because of dissatisfaction with local or state taxes.

What Is Fair?

When it comes to taxes in the United States, for nearly a century we have defined "fairness" according to one basic principle: people who have less should pay a smaller portion of their income in taxes and people who have more should pay a larger portion.[6] This principle of paying taxes based on what you can afford is called "progressive taxation," and the idea behind it is to make things at least slightly more equal between those who have little and those who have much.

To be sure, not everyone believes that this style of paying taxes is a fair deal. As one wealthy California lawyer wrote in the *Los Angeles Times*, "McDonalds doesn't charge me $23 for a cheeseburger just because I earn 10 or 20 times the me-dian income and could pay the price."[7] He is right. The private marketplace does not

PROGRESSIVE, FLAT, AND REGRESSIVE TAXES			
Income Level	**Progressive** *Tax / % of Income*	**Flat** *Tax / % of Income*	**Regressive** *Tax / % of Income*
$200,000	$50,000 /25	$40,000 /20	$5,000 /2.5
$80,000	$16,000 /20	$16,000 /20	$5,000 /6.25
$20,000	$2,000 /10	$4,000 /20	$5,000 /25

give people a price break based on their income, which is why it becomes so important that the tax system make an effort to do just that. Unfortunately, most state and local taxes in the United States today are not progressive. In fact they are just the opposite. When people with lower incomes pay a larger portion of what they earn in taxes than people with higher incomes, this is called "regressive taxation."

The leading challenge to progressive taxation today comes from proponents of so-called flat taxes. With a flat tax everyone would pay the same percentage income tax rate regardless of how they much they earn. The most direct effect of a flat income tax would be lower taxes for the wealthiest. But, cleverly, flat-tax advocates have made their proposals more popular by linking them to the idea of making taxes simpler. Sparing taxpayers painful hours with a calculator by closing complicated tax loopholes is an idea with merit. However, making taxes simple and lowering taxes for the wealthiest are two very different things. A leading flat-tax champion, millionaire publisher Steve Forbes, makes his case based on fairness:, "With the flat tax, we're all on a level playing field, just as it should be in the United States of America."[8] But the fact is that the wealthy and the poor are on anything but a level playing field, and a flat tax just sets that inequality in concrete.

Tax Loopholes—The Drain at the Bottom of the Revenue Pool

It has often been said that tax codes most resemble a Swiss cheese, full of holes that let people with smart lawyers escape from paying their fair share. Popularly known as tax loopholes, national and state tax laws are filled with special tax credits, deductions, exclusions, exemptions, and other exceptions from the general rules. In policy jargon these special loopholes are called "tax expenditures," because they spend tax revenue that governments would otherwise collect. The federal government has more than 130 tax expenditures, which result in the loss of billions of dollars of federal revenue each year.[9] In some states, such as California, the cost of these tax expenditures rivals the total spent in the regular state budget.[10] Some tax expenditures, such as the deduction for interest paid on home mortgages, are well known and widely used. Others are obscure and questionable. California, for example, has a sales tax exemption for the purchase of poultry litter and another for the hot meals sold to airlines.

The practice of granting tax breaks for special purposes is not inherently bad. If, for example, a state decides it is an environmental priority to subsidize the installation of solar energy equipment, then giving homeowners a $500 break on their taxes might be more efficient than setting up a bureaucracy to dole out $500 checks. However, while the effect is the same as spending money through the regular budget, the scrutiny given to how these billions of dollars are spent is not.

Tax expenditures are like a hole draining water from the bottom of a swimming pool. Every time an exception is created that lets more tax revenue out from the bottom, there is that much less money coming into the budget to spend on public programs such as education, health care, parks, and libraries. Yet, compared to regular spending, there is remarkably little attention paid to how much is draining out through tax breaks. When a lawmaker proposes spending $1 million in the regular budget on a new health clinic, that proposal is weighed against other ways to use the same money. If the project is an ongoing one it must be brought up and defended each year, and its budget is limited to the amount appropriated, nothing more.

In contrast, tax expenditures escape these careful rules. In most cases they can be approved without any consideration of the effects of lost revenue and whether the public benefits of these breaks are actually worth the millions of dollars in taxes they give away. In addition, most tax breaks continue indefinitely without any automatic review and with no limit on what they can cost. While debates over spending through the budget force consideration of the tradeoffs involved, debates over giving away new tax breaks virtually ignore them.

In some cases huge amounts are given to businesses or others to entice them to do what they would have done anyway. A California "enterprise zone" program delivered millions of dollars in tax breaks to businesses as an incentive to hire new employees in targeted low-income communities. An analysis of the program found, however, that only one-fifth of the businesses who received the tax breaks actually hired people they wouldn't have hired otherwise. As the California Budget Project noted, "The majority of the businesses received benefits for doing exactly what they would have done in the absence of the program."[11] Who could defend, with a straight face, a regular spending program that wasted four-fifths of its funds? Through tax expenditures, special interests are able to lobby their way to millions of dollars at public expense, and most of these breaks are also notoriously regressive, handing out the biggest benefits to the wealthiest taxpayers. The federal home mortgage interest deduction, for example, costs more than $50 billion each year, more than half of which goes to the wealthiest 10 percent of all taxpayers.[12]

Changing the way governments create and scrutinize tax breaks is key to creating a tax system based on fairness and to protecting the funds needed to finance public services. Tax expenditures should be built into the budget process and treated the same as any other budget item, with their public value weighed against other uses for the same money. The costs of tax breaks should be limited to a specific amount, just like other budget items, and they should receive the same level of public scrutiny as other spending, making them subject to review and renewal every year. These are the budget rules that our schools, parks, and public clinics must live by. Spending through tax breaks should be no different.

Tax Deductions versus Tax Credits

When political leaders do decide to offer taxpayers some form of tax break, it makes a world of difference which type they choose. The difference between "tax deductions" and "tax credits" is a good example. Let's say that lawmakers decide to offer state taxpayers a break to help with child care costs. One method would be to offer a $1,000 tax deduction, which allows people to "deduct" that amount from their taxable income before calculating how much they owe in taxes. Consider how such a policy benefits wealthy families far more than it does poorer ones.

A family with an income of $150,000 annually might pay an income tax rate of 40 percent. A deduction of $1,000 would save them $400 in taxes. A family earning $25,000 a year might pay a tax rate of 10 percent. For them the deduction would be worth only $100 in tax savings. These two families might have nearly identical child care costs, but the more affluent family gets a tax break worth four times as much. Alternatively, lawmakers could design the benefit as a tax credit. This means that qualifying families would each receive the same set cash amount, $250 for example, subtracted directly from the family's total taxes owed. Under this approach the two families would receive the same benefit. These are the nuances of tax policy that many citizens ignore but that are important in terms of tax fairness.

THE BASIC TYPES OF TAXES AND HOW THEY STACK UP

Citizens who become involved in tax issues, whether nationally, at the state level, or locally, will find that most governments use a similar mix of taxes to raise their public funding. For each kind of tax, there are important issues to be aware of and to address.

Personal Income Tax

The personal income tax is the great equalizer among taxes used in the United States. It was introduced in 1913, at a time when almost all federal funds came from taxes on basic necessities such as food and clothes. As a result, the poor paid taxes on nearly all they earned, while the well-to-do paid taxes on just a small part of their earnings. The personal income tax was designed to make things fairer by taxing the income that people earned, beyond what they needed for basic survival.[13] The personal income tax is now the leading source of revenue for federal government, and for many states as well. It is also the one tax we pay that is truly progressive, falling most heavily on those who can afford it and most lightly on those who can't. Its progressive nature is all the more important because it offsets the regressive character of other taxes.

To maintain the income tax as progressive it is important to defend income tax rates that are "graduated," which means that the percentage tax rate each person pays increases and decreases along with that person's income. For example, a person earning $100,000 a year might pay a tax rate of 30 percent, while a taxpayer earning $25,000 a year would pay 15 percent. It is this principle that the wealthy should pay a larger share of their income in taxes that is most under assault by proposals for a flat tax. Next, income taxes should include deductions or credits that reduce the taxable income of those who earn the least, lowering their overall tax bills. Such tax breaks include the standard exemptions and deductions familiar to most taxpayers (for children, for example) and special credits targeted to low-income families. Finally, we need to scrutinize very carefully that deductions and loopholes that primarily benefit those with the highest incomes and have the effect of excluding their earnings from taxes.

Capital Gains

While most people make their income from working and wages, the wealthiest make a large share of their income from capital and investments. Taxes on profit from the sale of stock or other investments are known as capital gains taxes. Some argue that this income should be given special treatment, either taxed at a lower rate or not at all, as a way of encouraging investment. Others counter that lower taxes on investment income would have little or no effect on business decisions; they support treating investment income the same as any other. "In all my business lifetime," notes one corporate CEO, "I have never heard an entrepreneur say, 'I am not going to start and expand my business because when I cash out, I'm going to have to pay twenty eight percent on my gains instead of twenty percent.'"[14] Nevertheless, in 1997 Congress cut the capital gains 50 percent for the wealthiest investors.

Sales Tax

Sales taxes on the products we buy are notorious for being regressive, falling most heavily on those least able to pay. The lower a person's income, the more of it she or he needs to spend on the basic goods subject to the tax. People with higher incomes spend just a portion of what they earn on these basics. A study by Citizens for Tax Justice found that the wealthiest fifth of the population paid less than 2 percent of their income in sales taxes, while the poorest fifth paid almost 6 percent.[15] Yet the sales tax remains one of the taxes most widely used by state and local governments across the nation. When politicians decide to raise taxes, the sales tax is usually the one they pick, in part because of its relative "invisibility" compared to other taxes. You can see your income taxes draining out of your paycheck, but sales taxes just quietly leak out of your wallet every time you make a purchase. This makes the sales tax less painful to taxpayers than other taxes, and makes raising it more attractive to politicians.

In addition to its heavier burden on the poor, the sales tax is also an erratic source of revenue for public services. With every economic downturn, sales taxes take a nosedive as people purchase less. Over the long term, the sales tax is also an unstable source of revenue for a different reason. Sales taxes are collected mainly on hard goods, such as lawnmowers, furniture, and clothes, but not on services (especially high-cost services used by corporations, such as financial services, lawyers, and computer programming), which is where our economy is growing most. Each year a larger portion of economic activity falls outside the sales tax, and the revenues from it lag further behind economic growth, to the tune of tens of billions of dollars a year nationwide.[16]

One way to make the sales tax fairer is to exempt more basic goods, such as food, clothing, and medicine, from the tax, lessening its weight on people with low incomes. Sales tax rates could also be lowered, shifting our reliance more to progressive taxes such as the income tax. Finally, to help the sales tax keep pace with the new economy, we could follow the lead of several states and expand the tax to include services such as legal fees and financial services.

Property Tax

The property tax is the number-one revenue source for cities, counties, and school districts around the country. It has also been a lightening rod for some of the hottest antitax revolts in the nation. Sales and income taxes are collected when we're moving money around anyway (be it in a paycheck or in a store), but in many localities property tax bills are mailed to homeowners once a year, to be paid in one lump sum, raising taxpayer temperatures higher each time. The property tax is also wildly unequal. Wealthy communities with expensive properties raise a bundle. Low-income communities with low-value property raise far less than what they need to sustain their communities, with local schools usually being the first casualty.

Property taxes are based on a simple formula. Local officials calculate a property's assessed value, which is then multiplied by a percentage tax rate set by each community. For example, a home with an assessed value $150,000 taxed at a rate of one percent would pay a tax of $1,500. All property tax reforms manipulate that formula in one way or another. An example of shortsighted reform is the infamous Proposition 13, approved by California voters in 1978. Among its provisions, the initiative rolled back the assessed values on every property in the state (including corporate-owned property) to what they had been in 1975. It then prohibited those lowered assessments to rise to a property's current value until the property was sold. While most houses are eventually sold and reassessed, corporate property often stays in the same hands for decades and ends up being taxed based on what it was worth a quarter-century ago (at a cost to public services of up to $5 billion per year).[17]

There are other ways to provide more equitable property tax relief to homeowners. Some states use a policy called a "circuit breaker" which, like its namesake in a home electrical system, shuts off homeowners' property tax bills by limiting each family's property tax bill to a percentage of its income. Other communities assess or tax business property separately, which allows tax relief to be targeted to private homes. California gives a special tax credit to renters, taking into account that a large chunk of the property taxes collected on rental housing gets passed on to tenants.

Corporate Taxes

Corporations benefit from many expensive public services that tax dollars provide: fire and police protection, public transportation, access to the courts, an educated workforce, and many others. Corporations also pay taxes to support these services, including many of the same ones families pay: income tax, property tax, and sales tax. Some corporations and industries also pay special taxes to offset costs they create (such as contributions to the superfund for cleaning up toxic waste). However, corporations also spend hundreds of millions of dollars each year on lobbying efforts to keep corporate taxes as low as possible, often with great success. The result has been a methodic shift of the tax burden off corporations and onto families.

Excise Taxes

Excise taxes are levied on specific products, usually in connection with their public costs. Gasoline taxes are used as a way to raise money for roads and transportation projects. Taxes on alcohol and cigarettes (so-called sin taxes) have two purposes. One is to raise revenue for programs that deal with prevention and health costs related to smoking and drinking; the other is to raise the price of the product to discourage its consumption. In California a twenty-five-cents per pack cigarette tax approved by voter initiative funds an aggressive antitobacco education campaign that has led directly to a 40 percent decline in per capita smoking.[18] Such excise taxes are also extraordinarily regressive, however, falling much more heavily on low-income taxpayers than on those with high incomes.

Tariffs

Until the early 1900s, taxes on imported goods were the major source of federal revenue and were used to protect U.S. industries from foreign competition by raising the price of foreign products. Trade tariffs were also among the most heated political issues of the time. As Mark Twain observed, "I don't know of a single foreign product that enters this country untaxed, except the answer to prayer." Today, however, tariffs are not a major source of revenue in the United States and are used mainly as a tool (still controversial) to give domestic products a competitive edge.

Payroll Taxes

In every paycheck, U.S. workers see some of their wages deducted for Social Security and Medicare, the public retirement and health care programs on which millions of citizens depend in their old age. However, the way these taxes are structured puts a far heavier burden on low-income workers than it does on people with high incomes. For Social Security, for example, all workers pay a tax at one flat rate

(6.2 percent), but only on the first $72,600 of their annual salary. The result is that a worker earning $35,000 a year ends up paying tax on all he or she earns, at a tax rate of 6.2 percent. A worker who earns $135,000 a year ends up paying taxes on just a portion of his or her wages, at a total tax rate closer to 3 percent. Extending the tax to higher incomes would make the tax more equitable and could either cut the rate for lower-income workers or raise extra cash to help keep Social Security financially solvent for the next generation.

Fees

Governments also raise revenue by charging fees for using certain public services. Advocates of such fees argue that it passes the cost of these services onto the people who use them, especially when fees are assessed on developers and other businesses for services from which they benefit, such as sewer construction. However, when fees are charged for services used by low-income families they can end up being one more regressive source of revenue. Especially when fees are charged for services such as entrance to public zoos and parks, use of public clinics, or participation in school sports programs, it makes it difficult, if not impossible, for poorer families to use those services.

BUDGETS: SEEING THE STORY BEHIND THE NUMBERS

If tax matters are often difficult to understand, budgets can be downright impossible. Public budgets are generally incomprehensible collections of numbers left to a few anointed wizards to assemble and interpret. However, as citizens we have a right to understand the story behind the numbers. Doing that means understanding the right questions to ask and also seeing through the numbers games that politicians and others often use to keep the real story under wraps.

What to Look For—Making Comparisons

Making sense of public budgets means keeping your eye on the numbers and trends for the budget as a whole and for the slice of the budget pie that concerns you most, such as schools or health care. For either one, there are four key comparisons that will help you understand the story behind the numbers.

How much are we spending compared to how much is needed? Is there enough money allocated to do the job? If it costs an average of $7,500 a year to educate an elementary school student and there are one million students in your state, have policymakers allocated $7.5 billion? If there are 1,000 pregnant women each year in your city who can't afford prenatal care and it costs an average of $1,000 to provide such care, how close does the budget come to the $1 million needed? If there is a gap between what is needed and what's been budgeted, then people who care about the issue need to focus on whether that gap should be filled by cuts in other programs or by increasing taxes.

How much are we spending now compared to what we spent before? Is our commitment to public services or to one specific service increasing or decreasing? For example, a 1994 study by the Center on Budget and Policy Priorities found that for fifteen years California was steadily spending less and less each year on infrastructure projects such as roads and bridges (no surprise to many of the state's traffic-clogged commuters).[19] Citizens need to ask, Are the trends in our budgets taking us in the direction we want to go?

How much are we spending compared to others? Sometimes the most telling facts about public spending come from comparing ourselves to other countries, states, or communities. What do we spend on welfare, schools, or public health care compared to our neighbors? A 1999 report by analysts in Massachusetts, for example, found that the state ranked last in the nation in the percentage of personal income dedicated to building and improving school buildings.[20] Comparisons such as these are another way to get a clearer sense of the real story behind government spending numbers.

Who's getting a bigger slice of the budget pie and who's getting a smaller one? Ultimately, each item in a public budget is in competition with every other item. A dollar spent on health care is a dollar not available to spend on something else. Another key is how much public money we allocate to different priorities. For example, during the 1990s, California's spending on prisons and jails has increased by an average of nearly 10 percent a year, while the budget as a whole increased by only 6 percent and spending on higher education grew by just 4.5 percent.[21] Once state lawmakers debated where to build new campuses for the prestigious University of California, but now they debate where to build new prisons. Citizens need to ask if these are the priorities reflect what they want from their government.

Watching Out for Numbers Games

Comparisons like the ones just described can help get to the truth behind budget numbers, but sometimes that truth can be covered up by some budgetary number games that citizens should watch for.

When a dollar isn't a dollar. Every year, presidents, governors, and mayors roll out budgets and proclaim the millions of new dollars they have added to this year's spending over last year's. Getting at the truth, however, requires a little more analysis. While the "actual" dollars for a particular program may have increased, that increase may still lag behind what it takes just to keep up with increases in the number of people being served and added costs due to inflation.

For example, your governor might proudly announce a 3 percent increase in state spending on schools, but at the same time the schools may be projecting a 5 percent increase in the number of students enrolling that year and another 5 percent increase in costs as a result of inflation (higher teacher salaries, utility costs, for example). The real effect of the governor's budget proposal would be that schools will fall behind rather than leaping ahead in terms of the "real" dollars available.

Politicians also use this number game—ignoring population growth and inflation—to overstate the growth in government spending in general.

A more accurate way to measure the growth in government spending, or
growth in a specific program, is to look at how much we are spending as a
percentage of our total incomes. This kind of comparison takes into account population growth and inflation and measures commitment to public services in comparison to our shared ability to fund them. For example, if over the past ten years
the aggregate income for all residents of New York State has doubled, but education spending has increased by just 50 percent, that means that Empire State residents are actually dedicating less of their resources to public schools.

Other Reasons Behind the Numbers

There are also other reasons that a quick look at the numbers, without deeper analysis, can miss the real story. During the recession and budget shortfall years of the
mid-1990s, then-California Governor Wilson sounded a public alarm about rising
welfare costs in the state. However, the increases in public assistance costs were not
because welfare recipients were getting bigger checks. In fact, as a result of Wilson-
sponsored benefit cuts these families were receiving nearly one-fourth less. The
higher welfare costs were the result of a severe recession when thousands of
people lost their jobs and needed public aid to make ends meet. This is the kind of
"reasons behind the numbers" that citizens should be aware of.

Bonds—Budgeting by Borrowing

State and local governments also use borrowing as a way of financing certain public projects and programs. Typically this is done by selling bonds, which are purchased by investors and paid back with interest using tax revenue over a set period
of years. In general, bond financing is used for construction projects such as
schools, water projects, and other programs that benefit taxpayers for a long period
rather than in just one budget year. However, many local and state governments also
borrow money to support public projects using what are called revenue bonds. As
a rule, these bonds are not supposed to be paid off out of taxpayer pockets but with
the revenue generated by the projects they finance. Sports stadiums are a common
example.

Here is where citizens must be extremely vigilant to avoid getting stuck
with the bill. San Francisco politicians, for example, proposed using millions of
dollars in local revenue bonds to finance a new professional football stadium and
pledged that the money to pay off the bonds would come from added sales tax revenue generated by an adjacent shopping mall that was part of the project. If those
mall revenues were to fall short, however, the remainder of the debt would have to
be paid either by raising taxes or cutting other city programs. In this case the stadium backers overestimated how much new sales tax revenue the new mall would
bring to the city. They projected that all the sales taxes generated would be new
money, when, in fact, much of the new mall's business would come at the expense

GLOSSARY OF TAX AND BUDGET TERMS

Actual Dollars: A simple count of the dollars allocated in a budget, unadjusted for inflation, population growth, and other factors.

Assessed Value: The value of a piece of property as set by local tax officials, for purposes of paying the property tax.

Bonds: Debt incurred by local and state governments to raise funds for public projects, with that debt repaid, with interest, out of tax or other public revenues over a set number of years.

Circuit Breaker: A property tax reform that reduces property tax bills for low-income taxpayers by limiting property tax bills to a fixed percentage of each family's income.

Earmarking: The practice of setting aside specific public revenues for specific projects or programs.

Flat Tax: A tax designed so that all taxpayers pay the same percentage of their income in taxes, regardless of how high or low their income.

Graduated Tax Rates: Tax rates that rise higher along with a person's income.

Progressive Tax: A tax designed so that the lower a person's income the smaller share of it he or she pays in taxes.

Real Dollars: A measure of dollars adjusted for factors such as inflation and population growth in order to allow for a more accurate comparison with dollar amounts from other years.

Refundable Tax Credit: A tax credit that can be received as cash back by taxpayers whose income is so low that they owe no taxes.

Regressive Tax: A tax designed so that the lower a person's income the larger share of it he or she pays in taxes.

Revenue Bond: A government bond paid back using revenues generated by the project that benefits from the bond.

Tax Credit: A tax benefit that reduces the amount of taxes a person owes by a specific cash amount regardless of the person's income.

Tax Deduction: A tax benefit that allows taxpayers to reduce the amount of their income subject to taxes, the value of which is worth more to people in higher tax brackets.

Tax Expenditures: Any type of special tax exemption, credit, or other exception to general tax rules that reduces funds available in the budget.

Tax Rate: The percentage used to calculate the amount of taxes owed, for example, a percentage of a person's income for income tax, a percentage of the sale price for sales tax, or a percentage of a property's assessed value for the property tax.

of existing stores, from sales tax revenue that the city already collected. In effect, stadium boosters counted the same tax dollars twice.

The Politics of "Guaranteeing Your Slice"

Frustrated by their inability to get the funding they want from local and state governments, many citizens groups have sought to guarantee their projects a specific slice of the budget pie. In California, for example, teacher unions sponsored and won a ballot measure guaranteeing that nearly two-thirds of all state general fund money will go each year to public schools. In San Francisco children's groups won approval of an initiative setting aside 2.5 percent of local property tax revenue each year for children's services. Similar "earmarking" of specific revenues for specific programs are in place in many states, on gas taxes, cigarette taxes, and many others.

This practice is a boon to programs that can win it but comes at a cost to everyone else. If new revenue isn't added and the size of the total budget pie stays the same, then money guaranteed to one program means that much less is available for other programs. The dollars guaranteed for children's services, for example, may come at the direct expense of funding for the public health clinics that serve those same children. Opponents of earmarking complain that it makes it even harder for local and state governments to craft budgets that balance competing needs. Supporters counter that sometimes raising new revenue is politically impossible or only possible if the public receives a guarantee of how the new money will get spent.

In the end, these issues of taxes and budgets come down to questions about how we want to balance our priorities. How much of our money do we want to keep in our personal pockets and how much do we want to invest in what we build in common? Among those projects that we do want to invest in together, which do we value most and what sacrifices are we willing to make as a community to fund them? The United States is a very wealthy nation, with more than enough resources at its disposal to build a public future and still secure our private ones. But to do that we need to take tax and budget matters out of the hands of economic and policy wizards by asking the questions and making the decisions that reflect the best of our values.

CHAPTER FOUR

Making Public Rules for Business and the Marketplace

"The art of economics consists in looking not merely at the immediate but at the longer effects of any act or policy; it consists in tracing the consequences of that policy not merely for one group but for all groups."

—HENRY HAZLITT, ECONOMICS IN ONE LESSON[1]

Throughout the 1980s and 1990s, in the United States and elsewhere, a powerful political voice has been raised against "big government." Corporate leaders and conservatives in particular have demanded increased economic freedom in the form of reduced government interference in the private marketplace. In response, many public rules and regulations governing business have been weakened or eliminated altogether.

As we look at our own lives and at the outside influences that affect us, however, what we see is that it is not government but the marketplace itself that determines much of our economic freedom. It is the marketplace, not government, that largely decides the jobs we have, what kind of health care we receive, what advertising and entertainment will be aimed at our children, the ingredients in the food we eat, and the quality of the air we breathe. Decisions made by private enterprise, outside the boundaries of our democracy, determine all this and much more, often subjecting us to great danger and abuse.

It is also a fact that private enterprise could not function without public rules to govern it. Who would manufacture widgets if there were not a law to keep those widgets from being stolen? Who would invest in widget factories without assurances that their investment will be used as promised? We make public rules for private enterprise for many reasons, to protect producers and investors, to protect all of us from being cheated as consumers or abused as workers, and to safeguard our personal safety and the environment. Clearly, we do not need rules for everything business does, but we do need rules for some things. Here again are a set of issues that we need to understand and be able to influence.

THE THEORY OF THE FREE MARKET

Every day all over the world millions of businesses and billions of consumers enter into voluntary exchange with one another, all without any centralized coordination or plan. The invisible force that pulls all this activity together is known as the free market. The modern champion of free market economics, Nobel Laureate Milton Friedman, uses a story to illustrate how the "invisible hand" of market economics makes the system work, a tale titled, "I, Pencil: My Family Tree."[2] The story begins, "Not a single person knows how to make me," and it explains the long process by which the wood, metal, rubber, and other ingredients come together through thousands of hands from disparate parts of the world to become a student's Number 2 pencil.

"No one sitting in a central office gave orders to these thousands of people," writes Friedman. The multitude of commands and actions involved in making the pencil was the product of prices and incentives. The wood for the pencil was cut because loggers could sell it at a profit to those who would turn it into pencils. The same is true for those who mined the metal and manufactured the rubber. Prices and incentives, according to Friedman, are the universal language that drives the whole marketplace. They tell consumers which products cost less and tell producers how much they can charge for a product before consumers will switch to a competitor. Prices and incentives tell companies how many workers they can hire and at what salary, and they tell workers at which company they can earn the highest wages. This is the theoretical magic of the market, millions of businesses and consumers all cooperating voluntarily to each one's mutual advantage.

According to Friedman and other free market boosters, this magic of prices and incentives not only stimulates efficient production but also, through competition, works to keep prices low and to keep products safe and of a high quality, making all of us better off. When government tampers with prices and markets, the theory goes, the magic of the market falls apart.

Friedman writes that the U.S. oil crisis in the 1970s is a clear example of the market falling apart because of government interference. Gasoline prices were spiraling upward. Consumers voiced their anger. The federal government then set limits on how much oil companies could charge for their product. Rather than produce more gasoline to meet consumer demand, the oil companies limited production, which resulted in shortages and long lines at the pumps. The price limits "did not permit the price system to function," he writes, and thus took away from U.S. oil producers the profit incentives they needed to boost production and make gas lines disappear.[3]

In many parts of the economy the free market theory does work as advertised. Where competition works well (the recent market for personal computers is an example), consumers benefit both in terms of better products and lower prices. There are, however, clear cases where the market does not work as claimed. In these cases competition alone does not keep prices low or products safe. The economically mighty are allowed to cheat the economically weak. Millions are denied access to the basics, such as health care. Manufacturers dump pollutants into our water and air. In economic jargon, instances such as these are called market failures, clear examples of where market theory doesn't fit real economic life.

Some of democracy's longest and most heated debates are about how to address these excesses and abuses in the free market system. At the heart of these debates are two essential questions. First, when is it appropriate for the public or government to intervene and make rules for the private marketplace? Second, when such rules are needed, what kind should they be?

BATTLEGROUNDS—WHEN IS INTERVENTION WARRANTED?

This debate about the marketplace—whether it is a place of magic to be left alone or a place of exploitation to be controlled—comes down not so much to dueling facts as to two very different worldviews. Conservatives, writes linguist George Lakoff, view government intervention in the marketplace as "interference with the pursuit of self-interest by people trying to make a living, people using their self-discipline to become self-reliant." Advocates of intervention, on the other hand, see government regulation "as the protection of citizens, workers, honest businessmen, and the environment against possible harm by unscrupulous or negligent businesses and individuals."[4]

These two dueling perspectives about public rules in the marketplace play out in a number of important policy battles, each with its own distinct flavor:

Protecting Access to the Basics

The theory of the free market suggests that everyone is free to go out and purchase the products and services they need and want, restricted only by what they can afford and by what producers are willing to offer. While that arrangement delivers to most of us much of what we need, the market left to its own devices also denies millions of people some of their most basic needs. One of the most heated examples is the crisis in consumer access to health care. Most producers of products or providers of services maximize their profits (the free market's cardinal rule) by selling to as many consumers as possible. Health insurers and HMOs, however, are a different case. They maximize their profits not by covering as many people as possible but by covering as many healthy people as they can and by excluding the rest.

This incentive to increase profits by excluding the sick has pushed health insurers and HMOs into a well-established record of excluding patients with preexisting medical conditions, canceling the coverage of patients with serious illnesses, and putting dangerous limits on the care their patients can receive. Rose Hughes, a founder of the group Parents of Kids With Cancer, recalled that when the parents first came together for emotional support in dealing with their children's illnesses they discovered that "we were just as traumatized by our insurance companies as we were by the cancer."[5] Consumer groups have fought for more than a decade to win public rules dictating what insurers and HMOs can and can't do to their patients, including prohibitions against discrimination and the exclusion of those who need care the most. When the marketplace breaks down and denies millions of people access to basic services or goods, such as health care, there is clearly a case for government intervention and public rules.

Protecting Our Wallets

The theory of the free market also suggests that competition between producers will automatically force prices down to the lowest point where it is still possible to make a profit. In many cases the theory works, but both history and the modern economy are full of examples of industries that have eliminated or reduced competition to the point where consumers have been left wide open to abuse. In the late 1800s U.S. railroads used monopoly controls over transport to charge farmers wildly inflated rates to move their crops to market. Modern fears about economic concentration range from bank mergers to high airline prices to Bill Gates's power over computer operating systems.

Utility monopolies are the textbook example of where only government price controls are needed to protect consumers. In many towns and cities there is usually only one company from which to buy home electricity or gas. Without public regulation of utility prices they could charge almost any amount they wanted. In 2001 Californians learned a hard lesson about abandoning price regulation in favor of the greener pastures of the open market. Soon after state lawmakers approved legislation deregulating the wholesale electricity market, consumers and businesses found themselves living a nightmare of skyrocketing energy rates and energy shortages as producers withheld power to boost prices even higher.

A similar market failure that gouges consumers is common in many big-city rental-housing markets. In San Francisco, for example, a city enclosed on three sides by water, there isn't a lot of room to build more rental housing, so supply is largely fixed. Heavy demand for rentals, matched with limited supply, allows landlords to charge exorbitant rents. Cities such as New York, Boston, Chicago, Los Angeles, and others face similar situations. A common political response is rent control, city ordinances that limit annual rent increases, usually to the local inflation rate.

Free market purists argue that prices must be set by the market alone, allowed to rise to whatever level consumers are willing to pay in order to give suppliers the incentives necessary to increase production to meet demand. Just as Friedman argues that government limits on gasoline prices caused gas shortages in the 1970s, opponents of rent control argue that limits on what landlords can charge discourages new development, keeping the supply of housing low and rents high, and giving a windfall to the lucky few who manage to move into rent-controlled apartments and houses. Energy producers argue that as prices rise energy production will eventually increase and prices will come down. All this may be true in theory, but when the normal rules of supply, demand, and competition don't work to keep prices down, government limits are the only protection we have against enormous abuse.

Protecting Safety

Another presumption of market theory is that, as consumers, we know everything we need to know about the products we buy. The theory assumes that we can make solid, well-informed choices without the need for government protection. But as economist Robert Kuttner counters, this is not always the case, "The consumer can't be expected to know with precision if her hamburger is poisoned, if the lawnmower will cut his foot off, if the water is safe to drink."[6] The debate over government rules to protect our health and safety began in earnest in 1906, when Upton Sinclair shocked the public with his account of squalid conditions in meatpacking plants in his book *The Jungle*. The resulting uproar led to creation of the U.S. Food and Drug Administration (FDA) and federal testing and regulation of food and drug products.[7] Similar public-safety regulations have been established over the years for products ranging from autos to amusement park rides.

Free-market fundamentalists argue that such rule making does consumers far more harm than good. They say that public rules stifle product innovation, especially in the development of new pharmaceuticals that could save lives.[8]

Instead of public rules to protect consumer safety, the fundamentalists argue that, here as well, we should let competition do its job. Businesses, they say, will enforce their own safety standards in order to protect their public good name. "It is in the self-interest of General Electric, or General Motors or Westinghouse or Rolls Royce," writes Friedman, "to get a reputation for producing dependable, reliable products."[9]

In too many instances, however, protecting one's public good name has taken a back seat to protecting profit, at deadly expense. In 1999 a California jury found General Motors guilty of ignoring a known manufacturing flaw that turned one of its cars into an exploding bomb when hit from behind. An internal GM memo reported that while deaths from potential fires would only cost the carmakers $2.40 per car (in potential legal claims), fixing the flawed gas tanks would cost as much as $4 to $12 per vehicle. Ranking profits first, GM chose to remain silent, putting thousands at risk, including the six people nearly burned alive who filed the anti-GM lawsuit.[10] Cases like this one make it clear that the market alone does not protect the public from hazardous products and that some form of public protection is critical.

Protecting the Environment

As Friedman argues, accurate prices are the key to market magic. Prices need to reflect all the costs involved in making a product so that we, as consumers, can make rational choices between different alternatives. But some products don't reflect all the costs involved in making them. The clearest example is the failure of companies to reflect the cost of environmental damage in their production costs and pricing. The costs of producing gasoline at a Shell oil refinery, for example, don't just include what the company pays for crude, for equipment, and for the salaries of its workers. The costs of that production also include the environmental damage caused by the tons of pollutants that the plant spews every year into the surrounding air and water.

Many of these environmental costs are simply passed on by Shell and other companies to those who live near that water and who breathe that air. Economists call these passed-on costs externalities, and the result is that polluters have little incentive to stop degrading the environment. In addition, because those costs are also not reflected in the price at the pumps, consumers are given a false sense of what that gasoline (or other products) really cost. If gas prices, for example, reflected the full cost of the damage that gasoline production and use cause to the environment, more of us would likely switch to more fuel-efficient cars.

Critics of environmental protection warn that too many rules reduce needed production and chase jobs to other communities or countries that do not have such rules. Nevertheless, even free market hard-liners agree that this is an area where leaving the market to its own devices does not protect our vital interests. Writes Friedman, "The preservation of the environment and the avoidance of undue pollution are real problems and they are problems concerning which the government has an important role to play."[11]

Protecting Workers

Public rules in the marketplace are also important to protect us as workers. The major battleground over worker rights is usually about salaries. The marketplace for labor is changing radically in the United States, leaving more and more low-wage workers farther behind relative to the cost of living. From 1973 to 1993, the number of work hours necessary for an average U.S. worker to earn an average household's expenses almost doubled.[12] At the same time the gap between the wealthy and the poor has also grown dramatically. From 1979 to 1993 the wealthiest fifth of the United States saw their real incomes grow by 18 percent, while the poorest fifth saw theirs drop by 15 percent.[13] Just a generation ago many families were able to live well on the income of just one parent. Today most families depend on two. Left to itself, the market is making it harder and harder for many workers to earn what a family needs to make ends meet.

The main government intervention to boost low salaries is minimum-wage laws. Free market purists argue that minimum wages hurt low-income people because when employers are forced to pay higher wages they hire fewer workers. These same theorists also claim that any costs imposed on businesses are just passed on to consumers. In that case, if McDonald's, Jack in the Box, and Burger King are all required to raise their minimum salaries by 25 cents an hour, the companies are far more likely to raise the price of their hamburgers, not hire fewer people to flip those burgers. It is also a fact that the money earned from those higher minimum wages is not just put in a charcoal broiler and burned. The increased spending power of those workers circulates back into the economy and often into many of the same businesses required to pay the higher wage.

Nevertheless, even minimum wages lag far behind what workers actually need to live. According to one study, three-fourths of the jobs with the most growth in the U.S. economy now pay less than what workers need to survive.[14] As a result, dozens of cities across the United States have either enacted or are considering enactment of "living-wage" ordinances. These mandate wages for city workers and those in nonprofit organizations and businesses with city contracts that reflect the actual cost of living in an area, often double the minimum wage.

As with the minimum wage, opponents argue that the result of a living wage will be higher wages for a few, but fewer jobs overall. This could be true if wages are raised too high too quickly. However, living-wage laws allow the poorest of workers to rise to a level of self-sufficiency, making them less dependent on government support and therefore less of a burden to taxpayers. Those higher wages also get circulated back into the local economy, benefiting everyone. The debate over government's role in setting wage floors is an important one; it is clear that, left alone, the market is creating a whole class of workers who can't make it without some form of public intervention.

Placing Limits on What Should be a Market and What Shouldn't

Finally, there is the question of what should be a market and what shouldn't. The marketplace is like a heat-seeking missile, always looking for new areas of our lives and our culture that can be converted into an arena for profit making. Centuries ago the Catholic church made a market out of entry into heaven, through its sale of papal indulgences. Today the market encroaches further and further into other areas of our lives once considered off-limits. Not only are our children pummeled with manipulative advertising during their Saturday morning cartoons, but in many school districts that advertising has also invaded the classroom, as schools sign a Faustian bargain with Channel One. The company offers classes a free TV and "educational" programming in exchange for requiring students to watch paid advertisements. Public broadcasting, once a safe haven from corporate messages, now runs lengthy corporate promotional clips and claims they aren't ads.

Every year more parts of our culture are being converted into vehicles for advertising and commercialization—sporting events, movies, even the time we spend on hold while making phone calls. Left to its own devices, the market imposes no limits on what it will convert into an opportunity for profit making. If we believe that there ought to be limits, such as restrictions on advertising aimed at children, we can only have them by establishing public rules.

PUBLIC RULES FOR BUSINESS—WHICH PATH TO TAKE?

Where market failures, excesses, and abuses do warrant some form of public rules and protections, what kind of rule is the most appropriate given the circumstances? A wide variety of actions are possible; the challenge is to find the most effective and fair, yet least costly way to change the production habits of thousands of businesses or the consumption habits of millions of individuals.

Regulation

The most traditional form of public rule making in the marketplace is "command and control" regulation, specific rules that businesses must follow under threat of public penalties. On the one hand, this is the most direct way to command an action in the marketplace—be it banning dangerous products, setting caps on energy prices, forcing polluters to clean up the damage they cause, or prohibiting health insurers from canceling coverage for the seriously ill. In many cases, unless there is a rule governing all the potential businesses involved in a certain problem, those businesses that might act voluntarily (to clean up their pollution, for example) could easily decide not to do so because it would put them at a disadvantage against competitors who don't adopt those same practices.

However, the command approach to regulation can also have serious weaknesses. First, such regulations may suffer from a "one size fits all" problem. It is virtually impossible for one national or state rule to be the best approach in every single case. One factory might do a more efficient job of pollution cleanup with one type of technology, while a different plant might do better with another. Opponents of business regulation also criticize its high cost, which some antagonists argue add as much as $100 billion per year in extra charges to businesses and consumers.[15]

In response, government regulation is moving away from "command and control" and more toward an approach called "performance standards." Government agencies mandate specific outcomes rather than the specific steps businesses must take to achieve them. A factory might be required to reduce its pollution output by 30 percent, then left to decide for itself whether it is more efficient to do that by buying a new smokestack scrubber or by financing carpools for its commuting employees.

In either case, it is important to keep in mind that cost estimates for regulation are sometimes inflated by regulation opponents for political purposes, and these estimates also often ignore the economic value created by regulation. Auto emission controls, for example, in addition to producing cleaner air, are also a $7 billion per year industry that contributes mightily to the overall economy. U.S. environmental protection technology, developed in direct response to government rule making, is becoming a lucrative export as other nations begin to address the same kinds of environmental problems.

One other weakness of regulation is the potential for industries to use their political might to win influence or outright control of the government agencies assigned to regulate them (something economists call "industry capture"). A century ago the railroads won political control over the agencies created to oversee them. Today doctors use state medical licensing laws to keep nurses and other medical professionals from carving into their practices. Consumer activists in California thought they had won a permanent victory over insurance companies when state voters converted the office of insurance commissioner into an elected post in 1988. Within just six years, however, the insurance industry used its campaign contribution clout to elect an unabashed champion of the industry's interests.

Regulation is the use of the government's coercive power to force the marketplace to act in certain ways. In some cases it is the best approach, often the only one that can truly protect us. In other cases, however, it can be overused, creating whole new industries dedicated to escaping those rules. Regulation is best treated as a scarce resource, to be used on important matters and only when less costly, less intrusive methods won't work.

Financial Incentives

An alternative to regulation that is becoming increasingly popular is the use of government financial incentives, such as tax breaks, to encourage businesses to take actions deemed to be in the public interest. These actions include tax credits for reducing pollution, subsidies to insurers who agree to cover people with long-term illnesses, and tax breaks for businesses that locate and employ people in economically depressed neighborhoods. Brookings Institute economist and former Carter administration economics advisor Charles L. Schultze calls the incentive approach, "harnessing the 'base' motive of material self-interest to promote the common good."[16]

There are many instances in which incentives may be more effective and less costly than regulation. Incentives avoid the assumption that government regulators know the best solution to every problem. They can encourage innovation and they force us to put a clear price on what we are willing to pay in order to get certain results. The incentives involved are not free, however. They usually come directly from tax dollars needed for schools, libraries, public clinics, and other services. They are often given away with no clear accountability to assure that what they cost is really matched by the actual public benefits. Many also argue that businesses should not be paid to do things they ought to be doing anyway, such as, in the case of Shell Oil, cleaning up its refinery pollution.

In cases where paid incentives are used in the marketplace, we must be careful to calculate what the public is getting in return. One important model is the "responsible corporation" legislation proposed in Congress. The law would give a very specific package of tax breaks and regulatory relief to businesses that in turn deliver a very specific package of employee protection, training, labor rights, and health and retirement benefits.[17]

Disclosure and Empowering Consumers

Another approach is the development of vigilant, active consumers, equipped with strong public disclosure laws, who can monitor the claims and practices of businesses and force them to be accountable. Sometimes this vigilance takes place at an individual level, as consumers make use of independent information, such as *Consumer Reports* magazine's highly regarded product testing. Access to independent information must also be matched with organized consumer action, such as the consumer education campaigns, boycotts, and other tactics that have forced industries into granting labor rights to farm workers, stopping fishing practices that killed dolphins, lowering meat prices, and other victories.

Consumer advocate Ralph Nader proposes the creation of new institutions designed to ensure corporate accountability to consumers. One proposal is to create a universe of "consumer utility boards" linked to specific utilities, banks, HMOs, and insurance companies. Consumers of those companies would elect people to represent them and would fund advocacy on their behalf through ballots and contribution forms enclosed in their monthly bills and statements. This would give consumers the same sort of collective bargaining and advocacy rights with companies that workers have through labor unions.

Government-required disclosure rules are an essential part of this consumer empowerment. At the local, state, and national level government rules require manufacturers to make public the ingredients in their products, require polluters to disclose what chemicals they've used and where, and require lenders to report what communities they have cut off from access to credit. With the marketplace wielding so much power and influence over our health and well-being, the public has a right to get a clear look at what corporations are up to so it can take appropriate action. These disclosure rules must be protected, and additional ones must be added.

Simply educating consumers and organizing them is not a substitute for government rules, however. The world's corporate giants have amassed such power that only government has the clout to provide the counterbalance needed. Even organizations such as Consumers Union, which actively work to educate consumers, also aggressively advocate government regulation (of car safety, health plans, bank practices, and many other areas) when such public rule making is needed.

Civil Liability

Where inadequate government rules have left the public unprotected (such as with the sale of dangerous products), one of the other main recourses left is to take businesses to court. Business groups bitterly oppose the use of consumer lawsuits to police them, complaining that such litigation drives up the cost of doing business. Yet, in many cases, it is the lobbying efforts of these same corporations that have left the public unprotected and left the public with no other choice but to sue. As economist Robert Kuttner writes, "The exploding Ford Pinto gas tank and the Dalkon Shield intrauterine device, which rendered many of its users infertile, slipped through the regulatory net because conservative administrations had weakened enforcement. It turned out in both cases, that manufacturers had known of the risks but had marketed these products anyway. These facts came to light only through litigation."[18]

Certainly, both consumers and businesses would be better off if these hazards were averted through safety regulation before any deaths and injuries occurred. However, in the absence of adequate safety rules, lawsuits provide justice to those harmed and communicate a financial threat to offending corporations.

Unfortunately, the threat of a lawsuit is the only language some companies are able to hear. In cases where corporate negligence is especially severe, many juries also impose "punitive damages," penalties as high as hundreds of millions of dollars, sending a powerful warning signal to other companies that might contemplate such abuses.

Criminal Liability

In other cases, even the threat of expensive civil suits is not enough to make some corporations protect consumers or other public interests. Potential penalties or jury awards are treated as one more cost item to add to the ledger. Most of us, on approaching a red light, do not make an economic calculation in our heads about the benefits of running the light versus the costs of getting caught. Yet, according to University of Illinois Law Professor Cynthia Williams, some legal experts argue that corporations should do exactly that. In the words of one conservative legal doctrine, "Managers have no general obligation to avoid violating regulatory laws, when violations are profitable to the firm."[19] It was exactly this cost/benefit approach to consumer safety that led General Motors to ignore the exploding gas tank problems that left six plaintiffs badly burned.

In response, a number of lawmakers and consumer groups are pushing for personal criminal liability for corporate managers who knowingly expose the public to such risks. Dubbed, "be a manager, go to jail" by its critics, the criminal liability approach is important because by the time civil suits or government penalties catch up with offending corporations, the managers responsible have left the company.[20] Criminal convictions face a stiffer burden of proof than civil suits and are often hard to win. Nevertheless, somewhere in the complicated web of the modern corporation, responsibility needs to be placed firmly on people who make the decisions, giving them a solid reason to err on the side of the public interest rather than pure profit.

PRIVATE ENTERPRISES VERSUS PUBLIC ONES

Finally, there is the debate over whether certain services are better provided by private corporations or as public services financed through tax dollars and made available to all. In the United States primary and secondary education has long been considered a public responsibility. Public enterprises are also how we move the mail, build highways, and provide health care to the aged. The inequities of the marketplace may be acceptable as a way to buy cars, clothes, and furniture, but for the basics that we need to survive, the natural inequities of the marketplace are often too much.

Today this debate over public versus private plays out most loudly on the issue of health care reform. In a health care market dominated by private coverage, more than thirty-six million people in the United States have no coverage. Among them, eight out of ten are working people and their families.[21] While most reform proposals focus on regulating the actions of private insurers, a strong alternative view argues that the public would be better served if much of our health care system were reformed into a public service, as is the case in virtually every other wealthy nation. Supporters of public health care argue that corporate health care wastes up to thirty cents on the dollar on marketing and administration (up by 500 percent in just thirty years), far in excess of what government programs such as Medicare spend.[22] They cite evidence from the General Accounting Office and others that a Canadian-style, publicly financed health care system using private health providers operating under public contracts would allow the United States to extend coverage to all of the nation's uninsured at no extra cost.[23]

Opponents of state-run health care contend that such a system would stifle the innovation present in U.S. health care and increase access only by giving everyone "equally bad" or "equally delayed" care. They also raise concerns about the bureaucracy, inefficiency, and political meddling that can burden government-run programs. However, private health insurers, who often cancel or deny coverage and services just when people need them most, are themselves huge bureaucracies, but without the options for recourse and public accountability characteristic of public agencies. When the evidence suggests that a publicly financed and governed system can deliver a better product at less cost, whether for health care, electricity, or a university education, it is time to look at how to move those services from private hands into public ones.

THE CHALLENGE OF GLOBALIZATION

The relationship between a free market and government protection is about balance. When the market is too free, the door is open for serious abuse. When government protection is too rigid, innovation and freedom are stifled. In the United States over the course of the last century, that balance has been fought for through battles on issues from child labor to protection of the environment. The result is a market left essentially to itself but with many of its worst excesses checked by government policy and negotiated settlements with organized labor. Today, that balance is under serious threat from economic globalization. Corporations that were once based in a single nation have been transformed into global webs. Billions of dollars in capital and thousands of jobs move easily from one country to another. The old national systems that served to check the dangerous excesses of the market have been or are being outgrown.

On the one hand, economic globalization is inevitable. The world is knitting itself together, both economically and culturally. To argue against globalization is like arguing that we shouldn't have earthquakes. It also important to recognize economic globalization's benefits—new products and lower prices for many consumers, new opportunities for many workers and businesses. That said, it is even more critical that we recognize the potential dangers of a global marketplace in which all the main rules are being written by the world's wealthiest, to their direct advantage at the expense of everyone else.

Workers, consumers, and the environment face the same kind of abuses globally that have been fought against so hard domestically, not just in the United States but in many countries. Global corporations have a big incentive to move where they can find the cheapest labor, the weakest environmental rules, and the least government interference. To compete, local, state, and national governments bend over backward to give companies what they want. Developing countries face not only these pressures but also coercion from international financial institutions like the World Bank and the International Monetary Fund, which link their financial assistance to government rollbacks of labor rights and privatization of their public enterprises. Author Jeremy Brecher has called this politics of bowing to corporate demands, "the race to the bottom."[24]

The boosters of unrestricted economic globalization trumpet these changes. Says a former Reagan administration Treasury Department official, "Now the challenge is to demonstrate to the world that the loss of sovereignty by governments to capital is a new paradigm that will reward governments with good policies and punish those with bad ones."[25] Under this view of corporate sovereignty, "good" policies mean rolling back labor, consumer, and environmental protections while "bad" policies mean trying to keep those protections in place. Former Mexico City Mayor Cuauhtémoc Cárdenas warns, "The exploitation of cheap labor [and] lax environmental protection [should not be] the premises upon which Mexico establishes links with the U.S., Canada, and the world economy."[26]

The architects of economic globalization are also busy writing a whole body of international law aimed at eroding public protections against the marketplace's worst abuses. Trade agreements such as NAFTA and GATT take local, state and national laws (such as California's antitoxics law, Proposition 65, approved by voters in 1986) and make them subject to repeal by international trade panels as "non-tariff barriers to trade."[27] Ralph Nader warns that the current round of trade agreements, "formalize a world economic government dominated by giant corporations, without a correlative democratic rule of law to hold economic government accountable."[28]

The democratic challenge of the new century will be to build, on a global basis, the same kinds of rules, institutions, and campaigns that were used to limit market excesses within nations during the twentieth century. After World War II, world leaders agreed to an international Declaration of Human Rights that set ground rules for how governments must treat their people. Today we need a set of international standards governing how corporations can treat consumers, workers, communities, and the environment. We also need international institutions that can enforce those limits on corporate behavior. Finally, just as it has taken organizing efforts among workers and consumers within the United States to win and protect rights here, that organizing and campaigning must be replicated an international basis.

If democracy is our right to determine the course of events that shape our lives, then the marketplace as well must be subject to democratic choices. While it is true that the market is largely a place of individual decisions and actions, its excesses, abuses, and cruelties are also evident in abundance, and we have a right to control them with public, democratic action. What we need is a marketplace that is neither overly controlled nor allowed to serve solely the interests of those with the most money and power.

In thinking about this balance between economic freedom and economic protection, we can borrow a piece of wisdom from the science-fiction master Isaac Asimov. In his writings, Asimov imagined a future society that had created a race of robots with both the physical and intellectual power to dominate humans. To prevent that domination each robot was inscribed upon creation with a descending order of rules that it could not violate. They were, essentially:

FIRST, do no harm to any person.

SECOND, do not, by inaction, allow a human being to come to harm.

THIRD, protect your own existence.

The modern corporation is the robot of our age, machines of enormous physical and intellectual power, able to control human lives but not automatically subject to human morals. Among business leaders there are certainly many fine women and men who do look for ways to keep the public's broader interests at heart. In case after case, however—decisions by auto makers to let families drive around in exploding cars, Dalkon's decision to let women become sterile from a flawed birth control device—we have seen that some corporations too often follow Asimov's rules in reverse. Profit and expansion are paramount, preventing harm to our health, environment, and livelihoods secondary.

Public rule making in the marketplace is about reversing that order of priorities. The marketplace is a complex beast and no magic wand of regulation or public rule can automatically make it behave the way we would wish. However, by agreeing that there can and should be public rules and by making them sensibly, we can have both economic freedom and the public protections that are so important.

CHAPTER FIVE

Civil Rights and Criminal Wrongs

Society's Rules for Individuals

We hold these truths to be self evident; that all men are created equal; that they are endowed by their Creator with certain inherent and inalienable Rights; that among these are life, liberty and the pursuit of happiness.

—UNITED STATES DECLARATION OF INDEPENDENCE

The United States was born with a promise "that all men are created equal" and that all who lived here would be afforded the opportunity for "life, liberty, and the pursuit of happiness." The nation's history in the more than two centuries since those words were written has been one of struggle and controversy over how we live up to that promise.

In the beginning, the founders' commitment to individual rights was expressed in the safeguards they erected against the abuse of those rights by the national government, a reaction to the tyranny of the British monarch against whom they had just fought and won a revolution. In the new Constitution they ratified a "Bill of Rights" that protected freedom of religion, speech, assembly, and trial by jury and established barriers against self-incrimination, unlawful searches, and cruel and unusual punishment.

In the centuries since, protection of individual rights has turned toward others who would violate them. States, local governments, and school districts have been forced to abandon direct practices of racial and other discrimination. Businesses and the marketplace have had rules imposed on their employment and other practices to prevent discrimination in these areas as well. We also continually debate what rules against individual acts and crimes that would deny life, liberty, and pursuit happiness to others we should place on individuals. These debates over rights that are guaranteed and the rules by which we must abide, have always been and will continue to be among the most emotional our nation faces.

RIGHTS: WHICH ONES AND FOR WHOM?

Over the centuries, the subjects of our debates about civil and individual rights have changed dramatically, from the abolition of slavery to the question of gays in the military. Two basic questions have remained constant, however. To what rights are we entitled? To whom shall these rights be granted? Slowly, and only with great struggle and in the face of great resistance, answers to these questions have broadened to include a wider reach and additional groups who had been previously denied.

Our keeping of the national promise has been extended to include the right to not be owned; the right to vote; the right to attend school and use public facilities regardless of race; the right to marry regardless of race; the right to not be discriminated against in employment or housing. Each of those rights and others has been, in stages, extended to women, blacks, the disabled, the aged, and others. Each these extension of civil individual rights was bitterly controversial in its day. Today's civil rights battles are no less controversial, but in looking at these issues through the lens of history, it is clear that what begins as heated controversy often slowly evolves into national consensus. Once, whole states were pulled apart over whether black children and white children should be allowed to sit down together in a school classroom. Today only the most bigoted few would argue that point.

It is also true that contemporary civil rights struggles almost always echo with those that have come before. Take, for example, the cyclical eruptions of fear and anger in the United States over immigration. In 1921, Representative Lucian Walton Parrish of Texas warned his House colleagues that Jewish immigrants from Europe were not like the familiar faces of days past. "[Previous immigrants came] with the sincere purpose of making true and loyal American citizens . . . but that time has passed now . . . the true spirit of Americanism left us by our fathers will gradually become poisoned by this uncertain element."[1] While today's anti-immigrant voices raise new concerns about the impact of rapid immigration on the nation's environment, the familiar strains of racism and fear are there as well. In a more recent condemnation of immigration, an editor at *U.S. News and World Report* writes, "The newer immigrants differ from earlier generations, which were largely from Europe. Latinos, Asians and immigrants from the Caribbean now constitute 80 percent of the yearly influx; many find it hard to leave their own cultures behind and do not easily assimilate."[2]

Two issues at the forefront of the contemporary civil rights debate—gay rights and affirmative action—illustrate the struggle with how to keep the promise made at the nation's birth.

Gay Rights

While women, ethnic minorities, the disabled, the elderly and others all certainly still face various forms of discrimination, they do not face it backed by the authority of law. Gays and lesbians in the United States, however, do face legally sanctioned discrimination. In fact, in thirty-eight of the fifty states it is legal to discriminate against gays in employment, housing, and public accommodation.[3] As U.S. gays struggle for their legal rights, two battles are drawing the most attention—gays serving in the military and gay marriage.

The controversy over gays in the military hearkens back to the earlier debate, which took place more than half a century ago, over whether to allow black and white soldiers to serve in the same units of the U.S. Army. Then, as now, opponents of integration argued that the army should not be used as an instrument to force people to associate with others against whom they had strong, emotional prejudices. "The settlement of vexing racial problems cannot be permitted to complicate the tremendous task of the War Department and therefore jeopardize discipline and moral," argued General George C. Marshall, chief of staff of the U.S. armed forces during World War II.[4] That same argument finds life again today in the debate against gays. During his campaign for President in 2000, GOP candidate Steve Forbes, expressing a view voiced by many conservatives, declared, "The military is not an institution for social engineering, it has a very real role of protecting us."[5]

Some argue that allowing gays to serve along side straights is not the same issue as mixing of blacks and whites. "The appropriate analogy is not black/white but male/female. The military does not require men and women to shower or to sleep together," explained one antigay advocate in a national TV interview.[6] Yet, in many countries, gays and straights do serve together in the military, without undermining "order, discipline, and morale." The argument against integrating gays into the military today parallels that made against blacks: "You can't make people mix who don't want to." In fact, it is the argument that has been employed time and time again, against racial integration in housing, schools, the workplace, and the armed services. Gays are just the contemporary target.

An even more controversial battle, this one over "gay marriage," also echoes back to history's battles over race. From the 1660s and stretching forward nearly three centuries, the United States has had active laws on the books prohibiting marriage between the races, most notably between white and black. In 1958, Richard Loving and Mildred Jeter (a white man and a black woman) crossed the border from their home in Virginia, which banned interracial marriages, into Washington, D.C., to be married. Soon after their return to Virginia, the local sheriff entered their home and arrested them. The trial judge sentenced them to a year in jail, suspended on condition that they leave the state. In his ruling the judge declared, "Almighty God created the races white, black, yellow, Malay and red, and he placed them on separate continents. And, but for the interference with his arrangement, there would be no cause for such marriage. The fact that he separated the races shows that he did not intend for the races to mix."[7]

Today, religious opponents warn that marriage between gays runs counter to God's plan. In the words of the conservative Family Research Council: "[Gay marriage would] deny the procreative imperative that underlies society's traditional protection of marriage and family as the best environment in which to raise children."[8]

If the "procreative imperative" were the sole basis for marriage, then a good many childless heterosexual couples might well be denied the right as well. Today, throughout the United States, there are thousands of gay families who are clearly doing a wonderful job of raising their children, in many cases a better job than some straight couples. As with the opponents of interracial marriage, opponents of gay marriage have translated their personal discomfort and prejudice into the denial of a basic right to millions of people. Whether it is in ten years' time, or twenty or thirty, the bias and legal discrimination against gays in the United States will be looked on just as we now look back at legal discrimination against people based on race a generation ago—a narrow-mindedness outgrown by struggle and time. Already, the door to gay marriage has begun to crack open with Vermont's "civil union" law, which allows gay couples to establish a state-recognized bond.

Affirmative Action

While the debate over gay rights is a familiar one about extending to another group the same rights enjoyed by everyone else, the debate over affirmative action is more complicated. Affirmative action extends preferences and advantages to certain groups of people as a method of remedying past discrimination, a tipping of the scales to counterbalance prejudices that antidiscrimination laws alone cannot eradicate. Affirmative action programs have existed in the United States for more than thirty-five years, beginning with a 1965 executive order by President Lyndon Johnson requiring government contractors and subcontractors to actively solicit minority-owned firms for government business. In the decades since, outreach efforts and preferences for women and ethnic minorities have become a common feature of both college admissions and government and private sector hiring practices.

Advocates of affirmative action cite the large gaps that still exist for women and minorities in college admissions, professional placement, income, and other important areas of opportunity. "If one looks at the composition of various professions such as law, medicine, architecture, academics and journalism, or at corporate management, or at higher-level government positions or if one looks overall at the average income levels of white men one immediately notices that people of color are still significantly underrepresented and underpaid in every category," writes civil rights author Paul Kivel.[9]

Supporters argue that not only is more progress needed toward equality but that much of the progress that has been made is directly attributable to affirmative action and preference policies. As one advocacy group writes, "Affirmative action has been an essential pressure on employers and school administrators to break down the sexual partition in the various fields of work and education."[10]

Affirmative action is now under increasing attack, including the University of California's (UC) repeal of affirmative action in its admissions, the victory of a 1996 anti-affirmative-action ballot measure in California, and similar reversals under way in Florida and elsewhere. "In the long term a color-blind public policy is the only one consistent with the principles of the Declaration of Independence, and the only workable foundation for a multiethnic society," writes affirmative action opponent, Dinesh D'Souza, of the American Enterprise Institute. "The law should pursue equality of rights, not of condition."[11]

Ward Connerly, the African American UC regent who has championed the anti-affirmative-action rebellion, argues that preferences are no longer needed and that their real result is to taint the accomplishments of women and minorities and

...ake them the targets of white resentment. "But those of us who are in that group called 'minority and women,' if we are performing in any role that is not seen as being a traditional role, the impression is that we did not get that by reason of our own accomplishment. We got that because of somebody giving it to us, because of affirmative action. On the other hand, a lot of whites blame affirmative action for something that had nothing to with it. They lost a job because somebody better got it."[12]

Supporters of affirmative action counter that equality-minded preferences based on race and gender take place in a world where college admissions and employment are tainted by all kinds of preferences that work against women and minorities. The National Organization for Women points out, "Veterans often get preferences in workplaces and on campuses—which usually benefit men more than women. The children of alumni get preferential treatment over others in admission to college. Friends help friends and acquaintances get jobs. Affirmative action helps open doors for women and people of color who often don't have those connections."[13]

To some degree the current controversy over affirmative action is the result of shrinking opportunities that affect all people. The battle over UC admissions, for example, takes place against a backdrop of an exploding population of college-age Californians with virtually no expansion in the elite UC system to meet the demand for enrollment. If some of the energy being devoted to both the demise and the defense of preference programs were devoted instead to expanding the university system for all students, some of that debate would be far less urgent.

In the face of challenges to affirmative action in Texas, Latino and African American legislators pushed through a new approach to university admissions. It skirts direct racial preferences but accomplishes many of the same goals. Under a new Texas state law, any student in the top 10 percent of his or her high school class automatically becomes eligible for admission to the state's most selective public universities, the University of Texas at Austin and Texas A&M (regardless of SAT scores). Because the 10 percent rule covers all high schools, rich, poor, white, and minority alike, the result has been a dramatic increase in opportunities for students who had been previously excluded. Civil rights scholar Lani Guinier, writes, "[S]even percent more black and twenty one percent more Mexican-American applicants were eligible for enrollment under this system than under the old affirmative action guidelines. And access to public education has increased for white high school graduates in rural parts of Texas—students who also tend not to do well on the SAT and so had been refused admission to the most competitive public colleges under the old system."[14]

Although debates over direct discrimination stand a good chance of moving from controversy to consensus, the policies of racial and gender preferences will likely be controversial for as long as they exist. How long are such preferences? Harvard Law Professor Christopher Edley argues, "When race is of no more social and economic significance than whether you're a Protestant or a Presbyterian, then there will be no need for affirmative action."[15]

RULES: WHAT IS A CRIME AND HOW SHOULD IT BE PUNISHED?

On the flip side of the rights we are guaranteed are the rules we must abide by. No society can survive without boundary lines for individual behavior. "Thou shalt not kill." "Thou shalt not steal." These are rules that have served us for the ages. Public debates about individual behavior are also rooted in two fundamental questions. What personal behavior is so damaging to society that it must be classified as a crime? What sanctions and punishments do we impose on people who commit those crimes?

For the most part, identifying actions we consider to be crimes is straightforward and simple. Such actions do harm to another either physically (murder, assault, rape) or materially (theft, embezzlement, burglary). Then there are places where the question of what is a crime are less clear and more hotly debated. Should prostitution be a crime if it is an act between two consenting adults? Should smoking a marijuana cigarette be a crime when drinking a six-pack of beer is not? Should sleeping on the sidewalk be a crime if you have nowhere else to go?

On the question of how to deal with those who commit crimes, the conservative side of the debate employs a logic that is straightforward and simple: We have a right to be safe from all crime. To dissuade people from committing crime we need penalties that are clear, certain, and stiff. People who are not dissuaded by such penalties need to be locked up and kept away from society for as long as needed and at whatever the cost. Their rights and those costs are less important than our safety. In the words of one conservative lobbying group, "To ensure that law-abiding Americans feel safe in our streets, criminals must be punished not pampered."[16] The counterview is more complicated. It makes distinctions between violent and nonviolent crimes. It considers the rights of those accused, the cost of punishment, alternatives to incarceration, and strategies for prevention. The debate between these two points of view is sharply drawn on two major issues that symbolize the crime debate as a whole—the "war on drugs" and the movement for tougher sentencing in general.

The War on Drugs

The issue of illegal drugs in the United States is a complicated one that runs the gamut from the grandmother who uses medicinal marijuana to relieve her nausea from cancer treatments to a pregnant mother addicted to crack cocaine to a heroin dealer smuggling large quantities of drugs in from abroad. In the view of many, drug use is a crime, plain and simple, one that undermines the physical and moral health of our culture and should be punished like any other crime. To others, drug use is part a personal choice in which government does not have a right to intrude, part an addiction problem for which criminal penalties are neither helpful or appropriate.

There is no debate, however, over which direction the United States has actually chosen in its approach to drug use. According to a report by the Justice

Policy Institute, the number of people imprisoned in the United States for drug offenses increased eleven-fold from 1980 to 1997. Nearly half a million people are now in U.S. jails because of some drug-related charge, more than the number jailed for violent crimes. Among these numbers are thousands jailed for simple possession of marijuana and others whose main crime was an addiction they could not break. The cost of incarcerating these half-million people now exceeds $9 billion each year.[17] The national addiction to jailing drug offenders is also deeply slanted by race. While African Americans make up just 13 percent of the regular drug users in the United States, they represent 62.7 percent of the drug offenders sentenced to prison.[18]

Advocates of the "criminalization" policy for drugs contend that it has led to important reductions in drug use in the United States. Testifying before Congress in June 1999, U.S. Drug Czar General Barry McCaffrey trumpeted the crackdown's success. "We are making strong, steady progress in reducing drug use and preventing young people from turning to drugs," proclaimed the general, citing statistics that drug use in the United States had fallen by half and cocaine use by three-fourths since 1980.[19]

Many others question whether the huge increase in jailing really deserves so much of the credit, suggesting that education, treatment, and other prevention efforts are both more effective and more humane. Criticizing the criminalization crackdown, the conservative news journal *The Economist*, wrote, "That misguided policy has put millions of people behind bars, cost billions, encouraged crime and spread corruption while failing completely to reduce drug abuse."[20]

In response, a growing number of organizations and public officials are calling for an alternative approach. While those who commit violent crimes in association with drug use would still go to jail, drug users who do not commit violence would be treated differently. Certain drug use, such as medicinal marijuana with a doctor's prescription, would be made legal. The personal use by adults of lesser drugs, such as marijuana, would be decriminalized. For more serious drugs (crack, cocaine, and heroin) the approach suggested is called "harm-reduction," featuring strategies such as clean-needle exchanges to reduce HIV infection among heroin addicts and diverting a small part of the billions spent on jails to expand under-funded drug-treatment programs.

Tougher Sentencing

When people violate the law, society has a wide variety of options it might use as a sanction or punishment. In extreme cases, such as murder, the penalty could be death; the United States remains one of the only democratic nations to use death as punishment for a crime. More commonly, the penalty for a crime would be time in jail. The sentence could be an indeterminate one, for example one year to ten, with the judge making the decision based on the facts of the case, or giving prison officials the option to authorize an early release based on good behavior. Or the sentence can be a determinate one, for example, ten years based on the crime charged, regardless of the circumstances. A defendant could also be given a suspended sentence, conditioned on their compliance with certain obligations, such as reporting to a probation officer.

Those convicted can be ordered to pay a fine to the state or restitution, such as repayment for items stolen, to those they have victimized. For drug offenses, convicts might be diverted out of the criminal justice system into a drug-treatment program. Finally, a person convicted could be sentenced to do community service (such as cleaning up local parks) or to some alternative activity specific to the crime (such as forcing slumlords to live in their own buildings or requiring drunk drivers to install breathalyzer devices into the ignition system of their cars).[21]

Amidst all these various options it is very clear which among them has become the most often used in the United States over the last two decades—prison sentences of ever-increasing length. The United States is in the midst of an unprecedented long-term prison building and incarceration explosion. Between 1980 and 1995, the U.S. population behind bars grew from about 330,000 to more than 1.5 million.[22] The number of prisoners jailed on drug-related charges alone (23.7 percent of the total) is more than the total number of people in prison for all offenses combined just twenty years ago.[23]

Societies imprison people for many reasons. For some the goal is retribution, making people pay the price for the crimes they have committed. Others see jail as a deterrent, a threat that will dissuade people from committing crimes in the first place. In the words of Pete du Pont, former governor of Delaware, "What criminals need most is evidence that their crimes do not pay. Bad decision, bad consequences."[24] Putting people in prison is also seen as a way to keep dangerous criminals off the streets and away from potential victims. A few still see imprisonment as an opportunity for rehabilitation, though the reality is that exposure to prison usually only makes those inside more adept at being criminals once they get out.

The prison boom underway in the United States today was sold to Americans as a way to deal with violent crime. Fear of crimes such as murder, assault, and rape are legitimate, and thousands of people in the United States are victims of these crimes every year. On the other hand, a lot of that public fear may have less to do with actual crime statistics, which have been falling, then with the perception of crime levels created by the media. As one study concluded, "Between 1992 and 1996, while the homicide rate in America dropped by 20 percent, coverage of homicide on the ABC, NBC and CBS evening news increased by 721 percent."[25]

Sensational media coverage aimed at boosting ratings ("if it bleeds it leads"), combined with politicians promoting crime fears to win votes, along with powerful lobbying efforts by prison guard associations, have all helped sell the public on the idea that more prisoners and longer sentences are the answer to violent crime. However, the real effect of the prison boom has been to put more nonviolent offenders behind bars.

While the benefits of longer sentences for nonviolent criminals are questionable, the costs are very real. According to California statistics, the cost of incarcerating one prisoner for a year could send two students to the University of California, three students to the state university system, or seven students to a local community college.[26] The tradeoff between prisons and education and other programs is a real one. Over a ten-year period, the South Carolina increased its prison spending by 20 percent and decreased its spending on the state university system by 15 percent. It built nine new prisons and not a single new state university campus.[27]

Much of the increase in prison population is due to increases in mandatory minimum sentencing and reforms such as the "three strikes and you're out" laws that keep prisoners in jail for longer periods of time. California's "three strikes" law, for example, mandates a life sentence for those convicted of a third felony, even if that felony is a nonviolent offense. The Justice Policy Institute cites the example of Duane Silva, a mildly mentally retarded man who also suffers from hallucinations. Silva broke into the home of a neighbor whom he believed owed him money and who was away from home on vacation. He stole some coins and a VCR. Later Silva called the neighbor, told him where his belongings were, and was arrested. As a teenager, Silva had set fires in some garbage cans and in the glove compartment of a pickup truck. For the fires he pled guilty to two felony counts of arson and was sentenced to probation and mental health counseling. When those teenage offenses were combined with the robbery of his neighbor under the state's "three strikes" law, Silva drew a twenty-six-years-to-life sentence in Folsom Prison, at enormous taxpayer cost.[28]

The problem, according to a Rand Institute cost/benefit study of the law, is that the "three strikes" approach "ignores first-time serious offenders and instead expends large amounts of money keeping older criminals—including many convicted of minor offenses—locked up well past the time when they might have given up on crime anyway."[29]

People have a right to be safe, and incarcerating criminals is an important tool in achieving that. At the same time it is important that sentencing rules be based on logic rather than fear, taking into account the tradeoffs and alternatives. When we spend billions of dollars to add years of prison time to the sentences of nonviolent offenders, we sacrifice the resources for other programs—education, recreation, job development, drug treatment—that may have a better chance of preventing crime to begin with. No parent dealing with an errant child would want to be left only with the choice of doing nothing or grounding the child in her room for a year. Sanctions need to fit the offense and have a chance of accomplishing something positive, whether in a family or in a criminal justice system.

These debates, about the rights and rules for individuals, may be our most emotional and heated because they are so personal. They are about safety and liberty. They are about whether we will be judged by the content of our character or by some magnet for prejudice (race, disability, gender, sexual preference). They are about government telling us who we can employ, or sell our home to, or with whom we will share a barracks. In situations such as these it is human nature to place what we believe are our own rights above those of anyone else.

The heart of the American promise is equality for all. The guarantee we demand for ourselves is only as strong as what we protect for everyone else. With so much emotion packed into these issues, the cold light of history may be our most useful guide. In the heat of debate we might ask ourselves, Are we walking in the footsteps of those who have fought for the American promise, or against it? Do we echo the voices that have demanded equality over the ages, or do we echo the voices of discrimination?

PART TWO

Tools

for

Democracy's

Activists

CHAPTER SIX

Developing a Strategy

Advocacy's Road Map

If you have an hour to chop a stack of wood, spend the first half hour sharpening your axe.

What is an advocacy strategy? Being an activist, taking on the challenge of pushing social change, is hard work. One of the hardest parts of that work is staying on track in the midst of political battle—staying clear about your objectives, undaunted by the moves of your opponents, steady in your message, and unified among your allies. Advocacy campaigns are like a long journey across strange, often hostile terrain. Strategy is the map that keeps you focused and guided along the way.

When I teach workshops on developing advocacy strategy, I begin by giving people a short length of rope tied into a tangle of tight knots. Then I give everyone two tasks: first, untangle the knots, and second, observe the methods you use for doing so. People's observations are always remarkably similar:

"First I took a good look at it."

"I worked at it one step at a time."

"It would be easier if I could use some tools."

"Sometimes I had to work the knot hard, sometimes very softly."

"I had to be sure to protect the progress I made along the way."

These are also some of the most important lessons about developing advocacy strategy. Each advocacy situation, like each knot, is different. The best way to approach each problem is to break down the tasks involved and apply some basic common sense.

It is remarkable how often advocates, even experienced ones, don't take time to think strategically, to first, take a good look at it. Many suffer from the "when you have a hammer, everything looks like a nail" syndrome. Instead of looking at the situation with a careful, strategic eye, they rely on what's familiar. If they know how to hold a news conference they hold a news conference. If they know how to organize a protest they organize a protest. If they know how to write reports they cook up a new one. Each of these tactics may be useful to the campaign at hand, but not necessarily so. They might, in fact, be exactly the wrong way to go.

A good strategy, like a good route through new terrain, doesn't just rely on the roads you know. It starts where you are, ends where you want to go, and provides a good, plausible route in between. What do you want? Who can give it to you? What do they need to hear? From whom do they need to hear it? What actions can deliver that message effectively? With a solid strategy, one that answers each of these questions well, you might change the world. Without a strategy, or with a poor one, you are more likely to get lost and accomplish very little.

WHAT DO YOU WANT? DEFINING YOUR OBJECTIVES

Most people begin their advocacy efforts knowing what their general goals are: better schools, a cleaner environment, justice for the poor, better health care. These big goals are good long-term beacons for your work, but advocacy campaigns have to be organized around shorter-term objectives that are clear, specific, and attainable. As the saying goes in Spanish, "¿Adónde estamos caminando?" "Where are we walking?" If you want people to walk together toward some public goal, it helps a lot if they can see the destination.

The Different Types of Objectives

There are many different kinds of objectives that an advocacy campaign might choose. Before deciding which is the right one, it's worth considering the full menu of possibilities. Some groups pick initial objectives where the main goal is really to prepare for a larger campaign that you're not quite ready for. Groups do this by researching the issues, educating and organizing their base of supporters, working on the messages they will use, and generating some initial public interest in the issue.

Ultimately, however, advocacy campaigns take aim at some specific change that advances the cause forward. Sometimes that is a change in public behavior, such as encouraging more people to recycle. Other times the objective is to pressure a corporation to change the way it does business, such as the campaign that forced Starbucks to pay a farmers a fair price for their coffee. In most cases though, advocacy is aimed at changing government policy—winning more money for local schools or getting a law passed that prohibits health insurers from canceling people's policies. In all cases, advocacy objectives need to be clear and specific. How much more recycling do we want? What coffee price is a fair price? How much more money for schools? What should happen to health insurers who cancel their patients' policies?

It is also true that sometimes the political winds are strongly against you, and the change you seek is unlikely to happen any time soon. In these situations your objective may be, in the words of religious activists, "to bear witness." It is what thousands did through protest in the earliest days of the Vietnam War and again through much of the 1980s against U.S. support for right-wing militaries in Central America. It is what thousands do today in protest against the death penalty. Bearing witness means engaging in public actions, in spite of contrary public opinion or political obstacles, to remind the public and those in power that there is a dissenting view and to keep alive the hope that public opinion and the politics of the issue one day might change.

Picking the Right Objective

The art of picking the right objective is half policy analysis, half political intuition. The first questions are, What will actually solve the problem and what are the costs and practicalities of each alternative? Potential alternatives also need to be evaluated politically. Is the fight one you can win? How does it position you politically and organizationally to help advance your larger aims? These are questions that advocates and advocacy coalitions should sort through together at the start. When evaluating potential objectives there is a set of important qualities to look for.

First, advocacy objectives need to be dramatic and compelling. They need to be able to attract the active involvement of people busy with other priorities and attract the interest of the media and the public, both of which have many other issues demanding their attention. When a national coalition of health and consumer groups set out in the mid-1980s to warn expectant mothers about the risks of drinking during pregnancy, they needed something more engaging than a once-a-year public awareness week on the issue. Instead, they mounted a national campaign for legislation requiring birth defect warning labels on every alcoholic beverage container in the nation. That objective sparked the interest and involvement of hundreds of groups and thousands of citizens, enough to win a landmark law from Congress mandating such labels.

On the flip side, your objective should also be small enough to achieve something of value within a reasonable time, in most cases one to two years. This doesn't mean you have to win a total victory that quickly, just something substantial enough to give those involved a sense of momentum and hope. There are many different smaller wins you can mark along the way—a boost in media attention, new coalition partners, new support from policymakers. Campaigns that start out with huge expectations but have little to show for their efforts find their participants drifting away to other work that seems more compelling and productive.

Finally, your objective should also lay the groundwork for future advocacy campaigns by creating a political climate that works to your longer-term advantage. Campaigns do this by drawing public attention to the larger issues, by bringing together the kind of support base you'll need over the longer term, and by putting your long-term opponents in the harshest public light possible. In the mid-1980s, California health care advocates waged a fight against the lethal practice among private hospitals of turning away critically ill patients who didn't have health coverage—a practice they labeled "patient dumping." The antidumping campaign drew broad support and huge media attention, culminating in a new state law prohibiting hospitals from turning away patients in critical condition.

However, the campaign against patient dumping also accomplished much more. It assembled the coalition of consumer, health, and labor groups that would go on to win larger victories on issues such as access to prenatal care and consumer protections from HMOs, and it became the spark for a vibrant new movement for access to care. "The patient dumping campaign laid the groundwork for everything we did for the next ten years," says campaign leader Maryann O'Sullivan. "It put the issue of access to care on the political map and it put pressure on powerful opponents like the state medical association to become advocates of reform rather than obstacles to it."[1]

How Much to Ask For

Shoot for the moon

One of the hardest decisions in defining an objective is how much to ask for or demand. On the one hand, it is generally a good idea to start out asking for more than you're willing to settle for or expect to win, because along the way you will need something to trade away in compromise. Alcohol labeling advocates started out demanding not only written labels but also a picture label of a pregnant woman next to a drinking glass with a slash through it. Advocates never expected lawmakers to agree to put the image on bottles, but it gave them something to negotiate away when alcohol makers and legislators sought to water down the proposal. It is also true that in some cases having a more extreme proposal can make political room for a more moderate one that otherwise wouldn't have a chance. In the 1930s, a national campaign was waged for the so-called Townsend Plan, a radical Depression-era proposal to give every senior citizen in the United States a $200 per month pension (big money in those days). While the free pension plan never got off the ground, it did create the spark under Congress to approve a less radical alternative, Social Security, paid for by employee contributions.[2]

However, when advocates stop listening to public opinion and stake out positions too far beyond what current politics will allow, the results can be disastrous. Following the 1992 election, the new Clinton administration made health care reform its number-one priority. Ecstatic health care advocates became overconfident and made the strategic error of demanding too much. In California, the activist group Neighbor to Neighbor qualified a ballot measure (Proposition 186) to establish a single-payer health care system in the state; the system would have shifted nearly all private health care into government hands, a proposal that had consistently polled miserably in state voter surveys. "We were intoxicated," remembers one campaign leader. "We believed our own bumper stickers."[3] Insurers spent millions branding the plan as health care by government bureaucracy, and on Election Day the initiative was crushed 73 percent to 27 percent. Sabin Russell, who covered the campaign for the *San Francisco Chronicle,* called the campaign, "a disaster for single payer," a move that converted a serious policy idea into a political joke.[4] It is one thing to aim for objectives that broaden the public's vision, but when advocates force a public choice on an alternative that is clearly unpopular, the result is to marginalize that alternative and make it less viable, not more.

Sometimes Your Objectives Get Picked for You

Advocates do not always have the luxury of selecting their objectives. Sometimes objectives are forced on you by circumstances beyond your control. Gay rights advocates, for example, did not pick "gays in the military" to be their first political fight under the Clinton administration; in fact, most gay rights groups would have preferred a more winnable battle over employment discrimination. It became the leading national gay issue only after a reporter asked Clinton about it just days after he was elected. From that moment on it became an unintended litmus test, for Clinton and others, on the issue of gay rights. Immigrant rights advocates did not choose to fight a California ballot initiative battle (Proposition 187) over whether the children of undocumented immigrants could attend public school or receive public health care. Rather, it was forced on them, in this case by their opponents.

Circumstances not only confront advocates with surprise threats but also surprise them with unexpected opportunities. In 1997, Congress approved legislation to provide matching funds to states that set up health insurance plans for low-income families with children. Children's advocates and health care advocates around the nation were sent suddenly scrambling to organize state level campaigns to take full advantage of the unexpected political gift.

When circumstances beyond your control offer an opportunity, the challenge is to move quickly to get the most out of it. When you're handed a threat, the challenge is a harder one—to make the best out of a fight you may not win. Emily Goldfarb, a leader in the immigrants' rights battle, advises advocates in these circumstances to ask themselves two questions: "What do we want things to look like when it's over? What can we do to make ourselves in the best shape possible afterwards?"[5] Even losing battles are opportunities to strengthen your cause, by learning new political skills, building your base, or reaching out to new allies. Gay rights advocates working on the military-service issue were able to recruit conservative icon Barry Goldwater to their cause. Immigrant rights groups used the ballot campaign, which they lost, to forge new alliances with teachers groups, health care workers, and business and political leaders and to establish important new relationships with the media.

WHO DO YOU NEED TO MOVE?
TARGETING YOUR AUDIENCES

Advocacy is about getting someone to move, to do something they wouldn't otherwise do. The question up front is, Who is it you need to move in order to get what you want? I once asked a group of health activists I was working with in South Africa, "Who has the power to make health care available for everyone?" They responded with strong democratic sentiments, "We have the power, the people." Ultimately, it is to be hoped this is true, but someone is vested with the official authority to make the actual decision. That might be your school board, city council, or mayor. It might be state lawmakers, Congress, or the President. It could also be the head of a corporation or some anonymous official buried away in a government agency. Somebody will make the actual decision to implement or not implement the change you want, and he or she is your "primary target." Everything you do should be aimed ultimately at that target and his or her decision.

These people and these institutions are by no means your only target. They won't be making their decision alone in a closed room with all the windows shut. What they decide will be influenced by the actions of many others. What will their key allies and supporters be telling them? How will the media report the issue? What position will be taken by various community and political organizations? All these people and institutions are your "secondary targets," and influencing what they think, say, and do about your issue is just as important. An effective advocacy strategy requires a clear list of both these targets and who can influence them, along with a clear plan for how to reach and move each one.

WHAT DO THEY NEED TO HEAR?
CREATING YOUR MESSAGES

Once you know who you need to move, the next question is, What do they need to hear in order to be pushed in your direction? That is, what is the advocacy message? Once developed, this advocacy message becomes your campaign's mantra, repeated over and over again every chance you get. Effective advocacy messages have two sides. First, they must make your case on the merits; second, they need to make it clear to your main targets that it is also in their self-interest to do what you are asking. On the merits, an advocacy pitch should lay out, in a clear, compelling, and concise way, the problem you are trying to solve and the solution you are suggesting. For example, "Our elementary school classrooms are crammed full with as many as thirty-five children, one main reason that we have one of the poorest educational records in the nation. By reducing our elementary classes to a maximum of twenty students, we can give all of our children the kind of one-on-one teacher attention they need to excel." On the self-interest side, messages need to be subtle, but with the point made clear that there are rewards or consequences ahead for your political target depending on how she or he performs. For example: "Senator, the PTA has one million members in the state and twenty-five thousand just in your district. This class-size-reduction bill is our number-one priority and our members are looking forward to hearing what you decide."

FROM WHOM DO THEY NEED TO HEAR IT?
PICKING YOUR MESSENGER

Saying the right thing is important, but so is making sure that your message is delivered by the right people. Advocacy campaigns need a mix of messengers, people who can give their points a combination of human sympathy, expert credibility, and political clout. Messengers who put a human face on the issue help ground campaigns in compelling reality, making the message difficult to ignore. The tragedy of alcohol-related birth defects was brought home to California lawmakers when a nurse named Amy Casey testified about an infant in her intensive care unit whom hospital workers called "the button baby," so deformed by fetal alcohol syndrome that nurses stitched a button to his tongue to prevent him from swallowing it and choking. "If you spent eight hours with this child last night, as I did," she testified, "this would not be a controversial bill."

Messengers like these, who make an issue human, need to be matched with others who give the effort rock-solid credibility on the facts—researchers, academics, or others whose credentials can match those speaking for the other side. A successful campaign also needs people and groups who have direct political clout with their specific targets. These could be campaign contributors, key constituents, business associates, personal friends, or organizations that are a part of your target's support base. Immigrant rights advocates in California lobbied the state assembly speaker by recruiting his barber to talk to him while he got his hair cut. Advocacy campaigns also make themselves strong by having diverse messengers, making it difficult for opponents to pigeonhole and dismiss them. Alcohol warning advocates had both Planned Parenthood and leading right-to-life advocates on their side, giving the campaign an image that spanned the ideological spectrum.

TAKING ACTION

With your objective, your targets, your messages, and your messengers clear, it is time to settle on the concrete actions that will make you heard and get the powers involved to move. As one of the workshop participants untangling the knot noted, "It would be easier if I could use some tools," and there are many different tools that advocates can use to take action. These range from gentle to in-your-face, from lobbying to media work to protest. Which one to pick depends on the situation, but as a rule, it's best to take those actions that involve the least work and the least confrontation but still get the job done.

The Conventional and Courteous

Sometimes you can move your targets simply by putting your information on the table, such as by sending a letter to a public official or making your case in a private meeting. The next step is to communicate that same information, but this time in public through the media. When Consumers Union wanted to draw attention to the inflated prices that some California supermarkets were charging for milk, it released a comparative price survey that told the story. The media attention was enough to alert consumers to shop elsewhere, putting pressure on the supermarkets to lower their prices and catching the attention of policymakers in a position to force prices down by law or regulation.

Flexing Your Political Muscle

When gentle communication isn't enough, the next step in building the pressure is to demonstrate the breadth of your support and to make it painful for your target to be on the wrong side. Initially, advocates do this with letter-writing campaigns or coalition visits to the officials involved. When making your case and demonstrating your support isn't enough it may then be time to put a hard public spotlight on your target. In 1993, activists put the public spotlight on President Clinton's lack of action in the fight against AIDS by confronting him directly at a Georgetown University public forum on the disease. "You promised during your campaign that you would establish a 'Manhattan Project' for AIDS, and all we got was another task force," challenged one audience member. The confrontation made national news and pushed Clinton to take more aggressive action against AIDS.[6]

Protest and Direct Action

Sometimes public pressure and embarrassment aren't enough to move officials, and the next step is direct confrontation—through protest, direct action, and civil disobedience—all tactics with an honored tradition in the United States dating back to the Boston Tea Party. There are occasions when nothing short of massing in the streets or violating the law and risking arrest will force the issue. As Martin Luther King Jr. explained in his "Letter from the Birmingham Jail," "The purpose of our direct-action program is to create a situation so crisis-packed that it will inevitably open the door to negotiation."[7] It is also possible to combine actions, with some parts of a movement waging direct confrontation to apply maximum pressure while others focus on maintaining decent relations with the authorities involved, trying to reach the best compromise possible. As in the example of the knot— "sometimes I had to work the knot hard, sometimes very softly"—the challenge in taking any of these actions is to know how hard to push and when.

UNDERMINING YOUR OPPOSITION

While you are working hard pushing in one direction there is almost always someone else (often far stronger) pushing in the other. Knowing your opponents and how to undermine them is also a key part of advocacy strategy. There are times when it is possible to negotiate with a foe and avoid political battle altogether. If you can gain through negotiation something as good or better than what you are likely to win by confrontation, settlement may be a better option than fighting. In the end, it may be better to save your advocacy resources for a different battle. In most cases, however, up-front agreements aren't possible, and there are some well-tested methods for weakening your opponents as you strengthen yourselves.

Pick Battlegrounds Where You Have the Advantage

First, know your opponents' strengths and pick the battleground where you have the best advantage. This is exactly what proponents of the California health care initiative failed to do. They carried their fight into an election contest where the insurance industry's oversimplified attacks, backed by millions of dollars in TV advertising, were far more powerful than what activists could counter. Health advocates have fared far better when they've picked incremental battles popular with the public, such as specific patient rights, and fought those battles in the legislative arena where a dedicated network of activists, organizations, and sympathetic lawmakers have been better positioned to counterbalance industry cash.

Use Your Opponents' Weaknesses Against Them

Just as important as knowing your opposition's strengths is understanding your opponents' weaknesses and taking advantage of them. The most devastating political weakness is unpopularity with the public; the image of unchecked power is especially unpopular. When your opponent is a wealthy interest using its financial clout to win its political way, wealth and power themselves become their biggest weakness. Framing your issue as a David-and-Goliath crusade against big oil, big business, big polluters, or big developers helps define the sides to your advantage. Using public campaign or lobbying reports to highlight your opponents' lavish spending is a good way to make that image stick.

Another common weakness is internal division. If your opponents suffer from it, find a way to exploit it. Antitobacco activists finally broke through the tobacco industry's impenetrable political armor after they were able to get just one manufacturer to break publicly from the industry line that "cigarettes do no harm." It is also possible to use your opposition's most outlandish statements against them. Community groups opposing Christian Coalition efforts to take over local school boards highlighted the declaration by one candidate that "[p]ublic schools serve as a vehicle to promote atheism by teaching evolution."[8] Publicizing statements like these paint opponents with the label of political extremism and help turn the public against them.

Don't Let Them Hide

If your opponents are unpopular, don't let them hide, however hard they try. Former Christian Coalition Executive Director Ralph Reed once explained his group's stealth strategy in this very Jesus-like way: "I want to be invisible. I do guerilla warfare. I paint my face and travel at night. You don't know it's over until you're in a body bag."[9] The Christian Coalition was engaged in a behind-the-scenes effort to elect candidates to local school boards nationwide without revealing them as conservative activists with a religious agenda. Community groups used letters to the editor, public candidate forums, phone banking, and other tactics to unmask these covert campaigns.

Make the Fight Against You Too Costly

In the end, victory against stronger opponents sometimes comes not because you have overpowered them but because you have made the battle so painful or costly that it is no longer worth fighting. Alcohol makers finally gave in on birth-defect warnings because the public relations damage they suffered from the battle of the liquor industry versus healthy babies became too high a price to pay. Making the issue personal turns up the heat even more. Clothes designer Jessica McClintock finally gave in to demands for workers' rights in her factories after protesters picketed her house and embarrassed her in front of her neighbors. Advocates should ask themselves, if we can't beat them, how can we make it too painful for them to keep fighting?

COMPROMISE—YES, NO, OR MAYBE?

One of the hardest questions that arises in advocacy strategy is about compromise. Should you compromise? If so, when should you? When is a potential compromise better or worse than winning nothing at all? Some people treat compromise as a theological question—a half loaf is always better than no loaf at all, or always worse. In reality, the challenge of compromise is much more complicated than that.

When I worked as a health care advocate in California, our coalition was always thrown into its worst conflicts over the strategic question, If we can get lawmakers to approve a bill giving health benefits to some of the uninsured but not all of them, is it a deal we should agree to? Inevitably, some people would make the case against compromise. "As soon as we agree to a solution that leaves some people out, the political heat will be off and the rest will never get included." Then someone else would counter, "How can we in good conscience stop passage of a law that would give millions of families health care that they wouldn't get otherwise?" Both these perspectives have value, so how do we decide between them?

The one piece of genuine wisdom I have heard on the question of compromise comes from Richard Brown, a professor of public health at UCLA. In the midst of one of these health reform debates, he offered the observation that a compromise is worth having if it puts in place the programs you want in the long run and creates incentives that, over time, will move the people and institutions you want into those programs. More generally, that advice could be translated to this:

Does the compromise move you closer to where you want to go, or does it move you farther away? The answer to that question will be different in every situation. In addition, if there are sacrifices to be made in accepting a compromise or in rejecting it, the people who will actually be making those sacrifices must have a strong role in making the choice. During those debates over compromise on health care for the uninsured, the advocates who objected to compromise most loudly always had health insurance themselves.

ADVOCACY STRATEGY IN A NUTSHELL

EXAMPLE: "Fix Our Parks"

Objective

We want our local parks to have safe playground equipment and organized recreation programs for our children and teens.

Target Audiences

- The decision makers: parks and recreation commission; mayor; city council
- The influencers: local media; PTA; neighborhood associations

Messages

- "Our local parks are full of dangerous equipment and have virtually no organized recreational programs. Better parks will keep our children safe, give them something constructive to do, and build a stronger community for all of us."

Messengers

- Children, teenagers, parents, local sports figures.

Taking Action

- A survey of local parks, released to the media, showing how many unsafe playgrounds there are, how many recreation programs, and other pertinent facts.
- A walking tour of local parks with the news media.
- A lobbying visit by kids and parents to local officials.
- A kids-and-parents protest at City Hall demanding action.

Note: This example is based on an actual (and successful) campaign waged by Coleman Advocates for Children in San Francisco.

EVALUATION AND AFTERMATH

Even the best advocacy strategy cannot predict every change of political wind that will happen. Events change, new opportunities emerge, and so do new threats. Advocates need to take stock and see if what they're doing is working. If you've hit a brick wall targeting the mayor of your city, would you be better off going after the city council? If you can't get media attention holding news conferences, would you get more attention if you picketed or held a candlelight vigil? If going on the attack is only making you more isolated, would you be better off putting your energies into winning a new ally or two who can open some doors? If traditional lobbying isn't working, is it time to become more confrontational and combative?

No advance is safe forever. As the knot experimenter in my workshop noted, "I had to be sure to protect the progress I made along the way." Winning a change in law or corporate practice is only as permanent as the public attitudes behind it. Czech president and champion of democracy Václav Havel has written, systemic change is "something superficial, something secondary, something that in itself can guarantee nothing."[10] Immigrant rights advocates in the United States thought they were protected because they had secured their rights in court, only to see those rights come under attack as public opinion shifted against them. On the other hand, health care advocates made progress because their "patient dumping" campaign helped awaken the public that their personal health care worries required political solutions. In the end, the best strategy for change is to have public opinion on your side. That, more than clever tactics, is what wins advocacy victories and protects them.

CHAPTER SEVEN

Research and Analysis

Advocacy by Fact, Not Fiction

Knowledge will forever govern ignorance, and a people who mean to be their own Governors must arm themselves with the power which knowledge gives.

—JAMES MADISON

Public decisions affect the lives of millions of people in deep and lasting ways. For this reason it is essential that these decisions be based on accurate information and solid analysis, not assumptions or half-truths. Far too often, this is not the case in public life. Important public debates become driven by misconceptions that take on the power of truth only because they have been repeated so often. As citizens, it is important for us to be able to evaluate public debates critically. When we become advocates and assume public leadership on an issue, our obligation to be informed and accurate becomes even more important. Ultimately, advocacy is about pushing public change. Solid, reliable information helps us understand in which direction we ought to be pushing that change. It also strengthens our political credibility and clout along the way.

Research and analysis are often the part of public advocacy that intimidates people most. We are unnecessarily afraid of numbers, enormous reports, the language and arrogance of so-called experts. At its heart, policy analysis and research is about common sense, breaking down public issues into a sequence of questions that allows us to think clearly about them. What exactly is the problem? What are the possible alternatives that could be used to solve that problem? How do we evaluate those alternatives and decide among them?

Sometimes policy research and analysis are used to predict the likely effects of policies being proposed. If we expand public prenatal care for poor women, what improvements might we expect in the health of their newborns? At other times analysis is used to evaluate the actual effects of policies that have already been implemented. In the aftermath of welfare reform, what has actually happened to the families cut off from public benefits? In both cases the goal is to help make the public make choices based on facts and to bring together the stories and experiences of separate individuals to bring into focus the story of the whole.

POLICY ANALYSIS—A PRIMER

Public policy debates are concerned primarily with two basic questions: What is the problem, and what is the solution? Policy analysis is a step-by-step method for answering these questions.

Step One: Define the Problem

What do we mean by a "public problem"? By saying it is a problem, we mean that a situation exists that some people are unhappy about. By saying that the problem is public we mean that the action required is not something that an individual or even a small group can do on their own. More likely, it is a matter of changing some government policy. If I spill a can of motor oil on the floor of my garage, that's my personal problem to deal with. If a tanker ship spills millions of gallons of oil into the ocean, that is a problem requiring public action.

The first step in defining the problem is to state it in a very basic way. For example:

Finding parking at our university is a nightmare.

Child poverty rates are rising.

Pollutants are seriously damaging our rivers.

Then the work begins of adding some detail and specifics. First, add some facts about "how much." How many students can't find parking? How many children in your state are living in poverty now versus ten years ago? How many tons of pollutants are being dumped in the local river? Second, put together some "why" facts about the problem. Why is parking such a problem—is student enrollment increasing, was a parking garage shut down? Why are there more poor families now than before—is the economy in decline, have government benefits been cut? Why is there so much pollution—are there new factories nearby, are some factories ignoring environmental rules? Third, put some "so what" facts on your statement of the problem. Does the parking problem make students late for class? Do family poverty rates create health and educational problems for their children? Is river pollution contaminating the drinking water supply? Defining the problem as specifically as possible helps draw public attention to it and begins to point the way to possible solutions.

With these facts about how much, why, and so what added in, it is possible to define each of these problems in a much more specific way:

> As a result of increased enrollment at the university, there is a serious shortage of parking that causes many students to arrive late to class on a regular basis.

> Even though the U.S. is experiencing one of its most significant economic booms in history, a higher percentage of children are being raised in poverty than a decade ago, harming their health, their education, and their prospects for the future.

As more and more factories locate along the Ohio River, pollution levels have increased and are beginning to contaminate local drinking water supplies.

In most cases, writes University of California at Berkeley Professor Eugene Bardach, public problems are defined in terms of having too much or too little of something—too much pollution, too little parking, for example. It is also important, he adds, that we not define the problem in a way that it presumes the solution.[1] For example, if we define the problem as "there aren't enough parking spaces," that assumes that the solution would be to provide more parking when, in fact, a better option might be to increase public transit.

Finally, in advocacy especially, it is important to define the problem not just in terms of aggregate numbers but also with specific examples that put those larger facts into human terms. HMO reform advocates, for example, have used not only national and state data to make their case but also well-told personal stories that make those data real for people. In testimony before Congress, an HMO physician explained how, following her health plan's policy, she denied a patient a heart transplant. "I caused the death of a man," she explained. "Once I stamped 'deny' across his authorization form, his life's end was as certain as if I had pulled the plug on a ventilator."[2]

Step Two: Get the Information You Need

With the basic problem defined, the next challenge is to begin gathering information, to educate yourself and your allies, to develop your ideas about what solution to propose, and to build the case in support of that proposed solution.

What to Look For

Begin with some calm, careful thinking about exactly what information you need. If you are looking for a needle in a haystack, it helps to know you are looking for a needle. Start by looking into the "bigger picture." Get some information about the history and context of the issue. On child poverty, for example, What are the longer-term trends for child poverty rates? What are the basic methods and strategies the government has used historically to address the issue?

Next, start assembling your inventory of specific facts. What income is the estimated poverty level in your state? How many children are estimated to live below that income level? What are the trends in recent years—is poverty up by 5 percent, 15 percent, 100 hundred percent? What specific problems do children living in poverty experience? How much more likely are they to become sick or to drop out of school? What about ethnicity—what percentages of poor children are Latino, African American, Asian, white? A basic collection of facts will help you to both understand the problem and talk about it effectively.

Then, look at some of the specific strategies being proposed to address the issue. Some states and communities might be focusing on passing living-wage laws

---

THE FREEDOM OF INFORMATION ACT

The Freedom of Information Act (FOIA) gives the public the right to information that is in the hands of the U.S. government. Any person may request that a federal agency make its records available, and, by law, federal agencies and departments are required to respond to that request (saying that they will comply or that they won't) within ten working days. An agency or a department can deny the request based on certain exceptions, such as the material being classified, certain personnel matters, tax files, trade secrets, and a few others. Denials of information can be appealed, first within that agency and, if needed, in federal court. To obtain information under the FOIA, submit a letter of request, clearly describing the information you are seeking, to the agency or department.

For an excellent source on using the FOIA see: http://www.aclu.org/library/foia.html.

---

to boost the incomes of low-income families. Another strategy may be to increase publicly provided services such as housing vouchers, expanded health benefits, or education tutoring. Collect information about the widest variety of approaches possible, including data about their costs and their effectiveness in solving the problem.

Finally, take a careful look at the politics of the issue. What proposals seem to have political momentum and support, which approaches seem stalled? What are advocates, politicians, editorial writers, and others saying about potential solutions? Are there public opinion polls available that indicate how the public feels about the issue and potential solutions?

How to Find Information

An important rule of policy research is this one: never waste time creating information if someone else has already created it in a reliable way. There is usually a huge amount of very good information already available about the issue you're investigating. Most policy research is about finding that information, judging its credibility, interpreting it, and repackaging it to meet your specific needs. Why, for example, undertake complicated research about the costs of different types of parking structures if a local transportation agency has already done something similar? Potential sources of good information include:

Government agencies (national, state, and local)
The offices of members of Congress, state legislators, city council
    representatives
Congressional, legislative, and city council committees
Advocacy groups (on your side and on the other)
Think tanks (like Rand or the Brookings Institution)
Universities
Business groups and corporations
Newspapers and magazines

PORTRAIT OF AN INTERNET SEARCH

As an example of using the Internet for policy research, I sought the answer to a simple question: How many children in New Mexico have no health insurance?

Step One: "www.yahoo.com" search: "uninsured"

Links to everything from insurance brokers to hospitals to banks. Nothing related to policy, data, or advocacy.

Step Two: "www.yahoo.com" search: "uninsured children"

Less insurance brokers, more hospitals and one program that provides free health care for children. Still nothing related to policy, data or advocacy. Yahoo is one of the Internet's most popular search engines—great if you want to buy something, but for research, you'll have better luck with others (especially www.google.com).

Step Three: "www.infoseek.com" search: "uninsured children"

Bingo. The first link is "Children's Defense Fund . . . key state statistics . . . number of uninsured children." I hit the link.

Step Four: "www.childrensdefense.org . . ."

I come right to a page with a long chart listing, among other things, the number of uninsured children by state in alphabetical order. "New Mexico-126,000." I scroll down to the bottom to see if they list a citation, which they do, a March 1997 study by the U.S. Census Dept., a solid source.

Step Five: The "links" button on the same page

I move to a page that lists dozens of groups that work on all aspects of children's issues, some national, some state specific, some local. Here is a portal already created by someone else which can provide me with connections to just about all of the facts, sources and data I might ever need on the topic.

Keep in mind: Don't waste time on search engines or sites that don't immediately get you what you need. When you find a site that's useful, "bookmark" it for future reference. When you find a page that is especially useful, print it out or save it in your computer.

Policy journals
Your local library
The Internet

There is a strategy for getting what you need, one I call "Paper, People, Produce Your Own." Always begin with paper. Gather whatever you can in terms of reports, articles, memos, advocacy alerts—anything in which someone has put together some worthwhile information about your issue. These days one of the best ways to start is with a search over the Internet. This will give you a sense of who is gathering information about your issue and what information they have. You can download the information that seems most useful. You can also obtain written information from most of the sources listed in this chapter by calling them on the phone and asking to speak to the person who covers the topic you are researching.

In all of this paper research you are looking for three things: ideas, facts, and leads to other information. Start keeping files so you can find what you need later, and be careful to record all of your sources so you can cite them properly. Once you have all this paper in hand, look it over, figure out which of your questions you have answered, which remain, and what new questions or in-depth investigating you want to pursue.

The next stage of your research involves making direct contact with experts, officials, advocates, journalists or other people who have important information to share. Most of them will be busy, so you'll want to think beforehand exactly what you hope to get from each person. You may have specific information gaps you'd like to get them to fill—"How much would it cost to build a parking garage for five hundred cars?" You may be contacting them to deepen your understanding about a specific aspect of the issue—"Given that your organization opposes higher minimum wages, what strategy do you support for raising the incomes of low-income workers?" Usually, you will identify the people you want to talk to from your paper research, someone you saw quoted in a news article or an advocate whose material you read on the Internet. To get access, be polite, be as clear as possible about what you are looking for, and fit into their schedule. Take good notes (if you are not tape recording) and always ask at the end, "What should I have asked you that I didn't?" If you are recording, ask permission first.

When your paper and people investigations still haven't given you what you need, you may want to attempt to produce some original information on your own. This could include surveys (interviewing students to see how many would stop driving if there were more public transit options); case studies (looking at the results of a specific health program for low-income children); or creating models (if a specific factory used technology X or Y to reduce pollution, what would be the likely costs and effects).

In Washington, D.C., for example, groups concerned with youth smoking organized a team of sixth- and seventh-grade girls to count how many storefront ads and billboards for cigarettes they passed on their way to and from school. Not only did the survey give them solid information about cigarette advertising aimed at children, it also gave the media a compelling angle from which to cover the story.[3] In order to be credible and accurate, information gathering must follow methods that are accepted and sound. Surveys need to include a representative sample. Case studies and models should include all the relevant facts, not just those that paint the picture you'd prefer.

Step Three: Interpreting the Information You Get

Much of the information used in policy research is about data—raw counts of people, dollars, things, occurrences, and so on. For many people, work with numbers can be intimidating. Here again, the challenge is to think clearly and to understand what public story the numbers actually tell.

The Story Is in Comparisons

Numbers begin to shed light on an issue when you use them to make comparisons: this versus that; now versus before; here versus there; with or without; this group versus that one. Comparisons such as these turn raw numbers into new, valuable information about public problems, giving broader perspective and important insight into possible solutions.

One method is to compare raw totals: "Last year the number of deaths from cigarette smoking exceeded the number of deaths from auto accidents and AIDS combined." Another is to compare percentages: "Last year in Indiana 27 percent of African American high school students dropped out, compared to just 5 percent of white students." You could compare ratios: "New York City has a student-to teacher-ratio of thirty-five to one, while in Buffalo that ratio is twenty to one." You could also compare spending: "This year Ohio will spend $7,500 per pupil in education, ranking highest among the fifty states, while California will spend $5,000 per pupil, ranking lowest." All these comparisons help illuminate the story behind the numbers. [*Note:* Unless otherwise cited, the examples used in this chapter were created for illustration only.]

The preceding examples are all about comparing one population group or community to another. You can also use numbers to make "before and after" comparisons for the same community or population in order to judge the effects of some change in policy: "Before antipollution standards were implemented for auto engines, Los Angeles experienced an average of fifty nine 'smog alert' days per year. Afterward, that number dropped to twelve." Similarly you can make "with and without" comparisons: "The students who received after-school tutoring scored an average of A- on their math work this year. Those who didn't have after-school tutoring scored a C+." The purpose of making comparisons like these is to make some informed predictions about the potential effects of certain policies based on real experience with them. For example, if certain antipollution standards substantially reduced air contamination in Los Angeles, might they have the same effect if implemented in Houston?

Tips and Traps

When you work with data and numbers there are some important rules to keep in mind. Again, don't waste time creating original information when you can recycle it (with citation) from existing credible sources. However, do use sources as close to the original as possible. Like the old game of Telephone where people pass a message from one to the other to see how it winds up at the end, the farther you get from the original source of data, the less reliable the information becomes. Try to use the most recent data available on the issue. Finally, check your math and check it again. One slip of a decimal or other wrong calculation can undo the credibility of a whole report and even an entire organization.

The evaluation method called "cost/benefit analysis" comes with its own special cautions. On the one hand, this type of analysis can be very useful. For example, if leaders in your city are proposing to spend $1 million on new streetlights that they claim will save electricity, it is very useful to calculate exactly how much electricity (and money) the new fixtures will save and how that stacks up against the expense of buying and installing them. On the other hand, beware of those who would apply this cost-benefit formula to everything. Not all things can be so easily calculated. If new auto safety features might save one hundred lives per year, how do we calculate the dollar value of those saved lives? Similarly, how do we calculate the dollar value of a child transformed from dropout to graduate, or an infant born healthy instead of ill? The risk of relying too heavily on cost-benefit analysis is that some things that can't be counted or calculated end up getting discounted or excluded.

Step Four: Developing and Judging the Alternatives

Ideas for policy solutions can come from many sources. One thing to look at is how other people in other places have addressed the same problem. How have other universities dealt with parking, other regions addressed river pollution, other states addressed the problems of child poverty? These experiences can provide both ideas and some concrete experience by which to predict the potential results of trying the same thing in your own situation. You can find alternatives by looking at how your own community or state has addressed a different problem that has some similarities to the one you are working on. How, for example, did your city try to address its downtown parking problems? You can solicit ideas from experts who have researched or worked on the issue. Finally, you can brainstorm among yourselves. It may well be that the best solutions have yet to be tried by anyone.

The Basic Menu of Policy Options

Most public policy alternatives follow a fairly standard menu of approaches. When the objective is to reduce something we don't want (such as pollution or smoking), one option is flat-out prohibition, such as prohibiting the spilling of pollutants into public waters. In some cases, prohibition may be justified and the most effective approach. In other cases (such as the U.S. experiment with alcohol prohibition), resistance is so high that the approach creates more problems than it solves. An alternative is to give people or businesses a financial disincentive to change behavior (charging polluters heavy fees to be used for cleanup, charging students who drive more for parking). In this case, the main issue is whether those disincentives actually get you the results you want and whether the costs are fair to those who must pay them. A third option is to seek to change individual behavior through public relations efforts, such as marketing campaigns against smoking. Here the main question is, How effectively does this approach actually work and how much will it cost?

In the reverse case, when we are trying to increase the supply of something we want more of (such as health care or public transit), one common approach is for government to step in, to both finance and provide the service. This is usually how governments fund public education and public transit, raising the funds through tax dollars and also assuming responsibility for running the schools or the trains and buses. Some argue that only through public services can we assure equal access to certain things (such as education and health care). Others think the marketplace meets consumer demands more efficiently. Another option is for government to finance the program or project, but to contract out the implementation to private firms. This is typically how government carries out the construction of public works projects such as highways. Some governments also provide public contracts to nonprofit groups to provide certain social services (such as assistance to the homeless). Advocates of this approach say it still allows for equal access to the services involved, but in a more efficient way than if government did the work directly. Skeptics warn that contracting out is sometimes a device to transfer work from unionized and higher-paid public employees to unorganized and lower-paid private-sector workers.

In other cases, governments use tax or other financial incentives to push businesses or individuals toward certain behavior (such as tax credits for employers who provide health coverage to their employees). Advocates of this approach say it leverages private resources and action to help solve the problem and at a lower cost. Skeptics of this approach argue that it just gives away public resources for what businesses and others ought to be required to do anyway. Some policies use advertising and public relations to encourage certain behavior, like the big signs posted off congested urban freeways beckoning traffic-plagued drivers to switch to mass transit. In some cases this type of public nudging is enough, but in others people must be given real incentives (such as lower train fares) to get them to move. Finally, there is the choice of doing nothing, of staying with things as they already are. Standing still may not be the best option, but including it in your analysis provides a useful point of comparison.

Policy Analysis Applied: The Example of Teen Smoking

Taking into account all these possible approaches, consider how they might be applied to the following problem: "Teen smoking is on the rise, addicting our youth to tobacco at an early age and promising major health problems for them, and major health costs for all of us, in the future."

One option would be to raise taxes on cigarettes. The evidence is very clear that when we raise taxes on cigarettes, thus pushing up the price, the number of cigarettes sold drops dramatically. On the one hand, this option looks great—you raise the tax, consumption declines—a simple, proven formula. It also raises millions of dollars for health or other programs and comes out of the smokers' pockets rather than anyone else's. On the other hand, given that smoking is addictive and many smokers can't quit, then a tax on cigarettes is also a tax on that addiction, as well as being highly regressive by falling hardest on those with the least income.

Alternatively, we could place limits or an outright ban on cigarette advertising. Proponents might argue that this approach is cost-free to the general public. Yet will an advertising ban alone make enough of a difference? There are also potential constitutional free speech issues involved.

A third approach might be for government to finance a major advertising campaign discouraging teens from smoking. While this might work with some teens and be less intrusive than taxes or an advertising ban, there are still questions about whether it would make much difference. Such a program would also cost money, potentially a lot of money. Finally, government could do nothing. Policymakers could decide that the most important force against teen smoking has to be parents talking to their kids.

Step Five: Making a Choice

Deciding which alternative is best is based on many considerations First, there are policy questions. What is most likely to solve the problem? How much will it cost, is it worth it, and who will pay for it? What other problems will it solve or create? Can it be implemented? There are also political considerations: Who will support and oppose each alternative? Which ones could attract enough political support to be adopted?

Looking again at the teen smoking example, which alternatives have the best chance of actually getting young people to quit or never start smoking? What does each option cost and who pays those costs? Which can survive legal challenges? Which can muster the political support needed? Weighing policy options takes all these questions into consideration—looking for the right balance of effectiveness and political viability. In the end, you might mix and match the options. For example, you might combine a ban on cigarette advertising near schools with a modest cigarette tax hike, dedicating the revenues to a public relations effort aimed at young people. There is no automatic formula for making the best choice, but the choice you make is likely to be much wiser and more easily accepted if you conduct an analysis that is clear, gets the facts right, examines a diverse list of alternatives, and decides between them with a solid eye to both policy and politics.

LOOKING AT ANALYSIS WITH A CRITICAL EYE

Most people involved in advocacy actually spend much more time using or critiquing research and analysis done by other people than they do conducting their own analysis. The political arena is a snowstorm of competing numbers, predictions, evaluations, and conclusions about public policy and its effects. Policy research and analysis comes from think tanks, government agencies, private consulting groups, politicians, and advocacy organizations of all stripes. It is important to be able to look at all this information with a critical eye, to sort out what is solid from what is pure baloney.

Advocates develop that critical eye by focusing on several questions. Is the source a credible one? Who did the research or analysis? Do they have a credible track record of work in the area? Does the analysis seem based on facts or on rhetoric? Are the conclusions consistent with, or extraordinarily different from, most other research on the same issue? Who funded and carried out the work? An analysis, for example, about the best ways to clean up air pollution, funded or carried out by Shell Oil, would especially warrant close scrutiny.

How transparent is the methodology used to get the information? Does the analysis clearly explain the sources of the information used, or does it merely summarize conclusions without giving the source? If the authors are using numbers or other information (surveys, case studies, interviews) developed especially for that analysis, do they show how that information was put together so you can check its accuracy? If they are relying on the work of others, do they document those sources clearly so you can check their credibility?

With numbers, does the analysis count the right thing and count it correctly? Numbers are often used to make a study sound authoritative, but those numbers should rarely be accepted at face value. Albert Norman, a Massachusetts organizer involved in blocking the spread of the Wal-Mart stores, offers an example of what he calls "Wal-Math," the chain's rosy predictions of what communities can expect in new tax revenue and employment when a store moves in. "Wal-Mathematicians only know how to add. They never talk about the jobs they destroy, the vacant retail space they create or their impact on commercial property values. Dollars merely shifted from cash registers on one side of town to Wal-Mart registers on the other side of town."[4]

Is the analysis based on facts or assumptions of fact? Many candidates in the 2000 presidential primaries tried to outbid one another over how deep a tax cut they would give voters if elected, arguing that the cuts could be easily financed, without harm, from the nation's growing budget surplus. Those promises were made on assumptions that the nation's economic boom would surge on uninterrupted, an assumption often contradicted by history. Citizens and advocates alike need to question this kind of analysis, watching for assumptions and conclusions that go well beyond what the facts actually support.

COMMUNICATING ANALYSIS

All the good research, number crunching, and analysis in the world comes to nothing if you can't communicate it effectively to the audiences you want to reach. Even as you are gathering and compiling information, keep those audiences in mind. What piece of information might your city council person be particularly interested to know? What trend or comparison might be an especially appealing news hook for the reporters you will eventually be pitching to?

Match the Level of Detail to the Audience

The challenge with each audience (policymakers, reporters, activists) is to strike the right balance of enough information to be credible and not so much as to overwhelm them. Begin with a simple, clear rendition: "Our research shows that children in smaller classes learn better and behave better." Then add on more specifics as appropriate to the audience: "A study conducted in the Tennessee public schools showed that students in classes with a maximum of twenty students scored 25 percent higher on math and reading and experienced 25 percent fewer discipline problems." If your audience is the general public or the media, a simple and basic message, essentially what you can fit into a short news release or a one-page fact sheet, may be enough..

For policymakers, you may want to add more detail, perhaps a two- or three-page summary of your findings or something in a questions-and-answers format. When your audience includes policy experts or others whose interest and knowledge in the issue runs deep, you'll likely want to lay out all your findings, with a clear explanation of your research methods and sources. Usually, you'll want to prepare your information in a mix of formats—a fact sheet, a brief executive summary, and a full report, letting people pick and choose which they want. If you are dealing with large quantities of numbers or statistics, put them into graphs, charts, or tables that make the information absorbable and clear.

Making Your Analysis Compelling

Finally, amidst all the investigation, interpretation, and data gathering, do not forget that, in the end, good analysis is also about good storytelling. When crafted well, policy analysis synthesizes facts, numbers, patterns, and personal stories to create a compelling, factual, understandable public story about what is happening and about what should be done. Three rules are key: talk about time frames that people can relate to; always make your data as local as possible; and use comparisons and stories that capture the imagination.

A national antismoking group used a simple time-frame technique to give more punch to national statistics about deaths from cigarettes. Instead of talking about 400,000 deaths per year due to smoking, they talked about 1,100 people dying every day, 46 deaths every hour. In a national campaign by Citizen Action, aimed at mobilizing public support against corporate polluters, advocates used pollution disclosure data to make the issue local. Citizen Action leader Heather Booth explained, "We can knock on a door and say 'in your neighborhood these are the corporations that are polluting; this is how it stacks up across corporations in the rest of the country; this is how your neighborhood stacks up by different kinds of pollution."[5] Another group of antismoking advocates, who wanted to demonstrate how cigarette advertising reaches children, released the results of a nationwide survey which found that six-year-old children in the United States were just as likely to recognize Joe Camel as they were Mickey Mouse.[6]

All policy analysis and research work should aim at the same goals: to highlight and synthesize the stories and numbers about individuals to make apparent the public issues involved; to cut through assumptions and misconceptions and get straight to the facts; and, finally, to provide the tools necessary to discuss the issues intelligently and factually, making our democracy both smarter and more participatory at the same time.

CHAPTER EIGHT

Organizing

Bringing People Together to Make Social Change

Organizing is providing people with the opportunity to become aware of their own capabilities and potential.

—FRED ROSS[1]

Organizing is the foundation of public activism. It is the bringing of people together, out of their isolation from one another, to create something larger and more powerful. It is a dozen neighbors joining forces to demand a stop sign on a dangerous corner. It is hundreds of immigrants in a city coming together to demand their legal rights. It is tens of thousands of mothers forming a movement to demand controls on the guns that bring violence into their communities. This coming together in pursuit of public change is deeply rooted in U.S. civic culture, which has a long and proud history stretching back centuries. Alexis de Tocqueville wrote of it in the 1830s, "In no country in the world has the principle of association been more successfully used, or applied to a greater multitude of objects, than in America."[2]

WHY ORGANIZE?

We organize for many reasons. Most typically, we come together to fight some public battle that can only be won when people join forces—to win passage of a new law, to secure public funding for a local project, to force a corporation to change some harmful practice, to stop a war. For issues like these, organizing is about creating, with numbers of people, the kind of political clout that other forces buy with piles of cash. In other instances, organizing is about educating or empowering ourselves to address a problem directly—public housing residents organizing to fix up their own homes, or parents organizing to provide tutoring at their local school. At other times the goal of organizing is to educate the larger community—about crowded classrooms, neighborhood crime, or global warming and what can be done to address problems like these.

Organizing is also an important end in itself, showing people their own potential and capacity for making social change. As the leaders of the Midwest

Academy organizing training center wrote, "Giving people a sense of their own power is as much a part of the organizing goal as is solving the problem."[3] Organizing empowers people and releases their knowledge and experience into the field of public ideas. Often, it does this in a way that is very personal and can last a lifetime. Francisco Herrera, a longtime organizer in California's Latino community, recalled how the simple act of being listened to by his parish priest turned him into an organizer. The priest was organizing in Herrera's boyhood town of Calexico, on the California/Mexico border. "So here I was this kid and this gringo was listening to me. Honestly, there were times when I thought, 'God, who is this guy? What's he doing listening to me? Gringos are really naïve.' It made me feel my thoughts counted and it was a key ingredient in my commitment to work for the community."[4] When we organize we have no idea how far and for how long those small ripples of empowerment may continue forward.

EFFECTIVE ORGANIZING: THE KEY INGREDIENTS

Effective organizing requires a mix of ingredients: strong people skills to bring people together and keep them inspired and working well; capable organization, to assure that the work involved actually gets done; and strategic savvy in order to pick the right objectives and the right public actions to win them. Learning how to mix those ingredients together is the first step of effective political action.

The Organizer

At the heart of any organizing effort is the organizer, the person who takes chief responsibility for putting all the pieces together and keeping them together. Cesar Chavez, the legendary organizer and leader of the United Farm Workers Union (UFW), once compared the job of the organizer to that of a juggler, trying to manage a half-dozen plates spinning wildly on top of thin poles. The organizer has many different tasks to manage—from recruiting people to the cause to coordinating the work at hand. Organizing is also carried out with as many different styles as there are organizers. Some believe that organizers belong mostly behind the scenes, always putting others in the lead. Fred Ross, who trained and led organizing for the UFW and other social justice causes for decades, said, "An organizer is a leader who does not lead but gets behind people and pushes."[5] For others, the organizer needs to be out front and visible, a public symbol of the movement she leads.

Regardless of style, the most critical ingredient in organizing is relationships. The quality of the connections made between the people involved is the glue that holds an organizing effort together. The organizer's connections with people must be genuine and human. If not, organizing becomes just a calculated manipulation of people and tasks. "It's an attitude," says Francisco Herrera. Through simple acts like thank-you notes and follow-up calls the organizer keeps the work

---

THE WORK OF "THE ORGANIZER"

✓ Recruiting people to the cause.
✓ Helping the group define its goals and strategies.
✓ Keeping people motivated.
✓ Managing the work tasks involved.
✓ Managing conflict.
✓ Teaching skills to newcomers.
✓ Protecting against attacks by opponents.
✓ Being the organizing effort's external symbol and spokesperson.

---

moving forward and solidifies the personal connections that keep people involved. Adds Herrera, "That's the invisible work that isn't glamorous."

Organizers also win people's trust and involvement by genuinely including them in decision making and strategy. Skilled organizers give people opportunities to increase their involvement, to broaden their connections in the community, and to learn more both about the issue and about the art of making social change. A good organizer needs to be a good teacher, including by the example she sets with her own competence, perseverance and strategic skill. Like a compass in a storm, the organizer needs to keep the effort on track, regardless of the distractions, challenges, and doubts that arise along the way.

Finally, strong organizers also need a good sense of self-awareness. They need to know their own strengths and weaknesses. They may be skillful at recruiting people and motivating them, but if they aren't also skilled at dealing with the media, they need to know this and make sure that work is handled by someone who is. Taking on work you can't do well is of no help to anyone, except perhaps the opposition. In fact, the best organizers are those who know and are open about their weak spots, empowering those around them by giving them a genuine role in the leadership of the organizing effort.

Outreach and Recruitment

The starting point of an organizing campaign is recruiting people to the cause. In some cases the issue and who ought to care about it are local and very clear—such as the neighborhood in search of a stop sign. Most issues and campaigns, however, are not so local. Recruiting begins by approaching those with a direct self-interest or personal stake. If the issue is improving the public schools attended by immigrant children, then immigrant parents are the first people that organizers need to approach. If the issue is gun violence, or drunk driving, or abuse by health insurers, it is often families who have suffered that violence or abuse who are most willing to step forward and get involved. Rose Hughes, a California mother, became an activist for health care reform as a result of her son's childhood cancer and her battle with her insurer to get him care. "We want to alleviate that burden on other families," says Hughes. "We want them to know they have someone to go to."[6]

Another important group to recruit and involve are people who work in direct service with those affected by the issue involved—nurses, teachers, pastors, social workers, and others. Their personal experiences give them not only a strong motivation to get involved but also powerful stories and wisdom about potential solutions. Explains Laura Ware, a social worker with the homeless in San Francisco, "Advocacy is important to me because it keeps me aware and involved in the larger issues facing homeless people while working with individual families on their immediate concerns."[7] Anyone touched by an issue is a potential recruit to an organizing campaign for change. When children's advocates in San Francisco were gathering signatures for a ballot measure earmarking city funds for youth and children's programs, they were joined by local members of the teamsters' union, newspaper-truck drivers moved to action by the local paper's elimination of paper boys' jobs.[8]

The most direct way to find people for an organizing effort is through the organizations and institutions in which these people are already involved—such as unions, schools, PTAs, neighborhood organizations, service programs, and churches. Through these connections, people may already feel a commitment to the issue (union members and labor rights, for example), and these groups present ready-made networks where the involvement of just a few people could lead to the involvement of many more. The best person to talk to first, rather than the leader, is more likely to be someone you already know, ideally, someone you already know to be interested and sympathetic. You want to find someone who carries some clout within the organization, an ally who is willing to make your case on the inside and give you sound advice about what it will take to win support. It is important, first, to ask questions and try to understand how the issue might be seen within the organization—"How do you think your union members would feel about labor protections for immigrant workers?" The key is winning people's trust. Eventually, you want to have the chance to make a formal presentation to the group, after you know you have people in the organization ready to support you.

A lot of organizing, however, is not done with existing organizations but is carried out the harder way—one-on-one with individuals. At the most local level, this is often door-to-door, neighbor-to-neighbor. In a broader neighborhood or in a city, organizers might try to identify interested people by circulating a flyer ("Parents, come to a meeting to learn what you can do to reduce class size in our schools") or by setting up a table in front of a local store or mall. Another important organizing technique is the "house meeting," which taps into the social, friendship, and employment networks of existing supporters. These meetings can pull anywhere from five people to fifty into someone's home for an evening, to hear about an organizing campaign and how people can get involved. Some meetings make a fundraising pitch and pass a hat. Others give people an opportunity to take action right on the spot by writing a letter to a local official. Organizers work closely in advance with the sponsor of the house party, helping them identify potential invitees and ways to get them interested in coming.

Outreach efforts to diverse groups of people—of different ethnicities, ages, classes, or cultural backgrounds—requires special attention and approaches on the part of organizers. When organizers for Direct Action for Rights and Equality (DARE) first began organizing child-care workers in Providence, Rhode Island, in the early 1980s, most of the workers were African American. By 1990, because of rising immigration, an equal number were Latino, requiring a different strategy for organizing. DARE initiated its organizing efforts among Latino child-care workers by conducting outreach in Spanish and by forming a "Comité Latino" allowed these workers to carry out their meetings in their native language and among others with whom they felt most comfortable.

Gradually, African American and white DARE members began attending and participating in Comité activities, building connections across cultural and ethnic lines. Eventually, based on these connections and with the use of simultaneous translation equipment, DARE was able to hold meetings that linked together all child-care workers, setting the stage for important joint victories on issues such as health care coverage.[9] This same approach, organizing first within an ethnic community and then making other links, is used successfully by many other groups.

 Regardless of whom you are organizing, outreach and recruitment must hit people emotionally, not just intellectually. Recruitment has to take people's personal experience and redefine it as a political issue requiring public action. People have to believe that the organizing effort is urgent and has a real chance of making a difference. Ultimately, getting people interested is about helping them see the links between what is happening to them and what is happening in their larger community, their state, the nation, or the world:

"There are no recreational programs for our teenagers in the local parks. Will you help us lobby the city council to start some?"

"Our children are crammed into overcrowded classrooms where it is harder to learn. Will you help us pass a state bill to reduce class size to twenty kids?"

"A new study says our tap water isn't even safe enough to brush your teeth with, because of dumping at the local oil refinery. Will you help us force them to stop?"

Once you do have someone new interested in getting involved, don't wait. "When you find 'live wires' put them to work immediately," advised Fred Ross, "Find something they can do—any little thing—get them started and ready to do more or you will lose them for the cause."[10] Above all, help people see that their involvement is meaningful and worth the effort, so that they recognize their own potential as a force for public change.

Meetings and Decision Making

It is no surprise that a lot of organizing work takes place in meetings. Organizing people to work together also means organizing them to think and plan together, and meetings are where that happens. Effective meetings move quickly, allow for genuine exchanges of ideas and opinions, and get real work done. Ineffective meetings move like molasses, are unfocused, leave participants frustrated, and leave the organizing effort in big trouble. It is important for organizing campaigns to put time and careful thought into assuring that their meetings and decision making are carried out well.

Agendas

Meetings are supposed to be an organized discussion. Agendas are the agreement among the participants about how that discussion will be carried out. Through the agenda, the group agrees on what it will talk about, which issues are most important, and how much time it will allocate to each item. These choices are all important to bring some discipline to the conversation. A well-crafted agenda should follow some basic rules:

The meeting should start and finish so that there is some informal time at both ends, to welcome newcomers, give people time to greet one another, and organize any follow-up that needs to happen at the end.

The agenda should be put in writing, either on individual sheets for each participant or written out on a large sheet or blackboard for the whole group.

The discussion items should be limited to those that the group can actually cover in the time allowed for the meeting. A meeting that tries to cram in too many items will only leave participants frustrated by the hurry and inattention given to each one. The group should prioritize the items that are on the agenda according to their importance.

There should be specific time allocated to each item listed, with the group disciplining itself to honor those times. However, it is also useful to leave some wiggle room in the agenda, knowing that some discussions will inevitably take longer than expected.

For more formal meetings, which are longer (a full day or more) or involve large numbers of people, it is useful to have a subgroup plan the agenda in advance.

Often, the best agendas are those organized as a series of questions to focus the discussion—What is our main goal for the year? What should we do to mobilize parents for the public hearing next month?

Specific time should be allocated at the end to identify and note items for follow-up and who is responsible for each.

The agenda should be reviewed and agreed to at the start of the meeting and there should be time allocated at the end for announcements and for a brief evaluation of the meeting itself. Longer meetings should also allocate appropriate time in the middle for breaks.

The start of the meeting is especially important. The facilitator or leader of the group should set the tone, explaining the purpose of the meeting and going over the agenda, with an opportunity for input from the group members. Some larger meetings open with some form of icebreaker to get people animated or at least talking to one another. These range from the staid (simple introductions) to the wacky ("If you could be any animal . . . ?"). What's appropriate depends on the group. Finally, it is important with longer meetings to take account of how people's energy ebbs and flows during the day. Immediately after lunch, for example, when people tend to get sleepy, is a terrible time for a presentation and a good time for discussions and small-group work that is especially interactive or animated.

Facilitation

In addition to thoughtful agendas, effective meetings also need skillful facilitation. Even with the clearest of agendas, group discussions wander off track or get bogged down in detail. Someone needs to take clear responsibility for keeping an eye on the goals at hand and keeping the group moving forward. Another important job is to look for potential consensus in the group and try to put that forward. Strong facilitators do this by listening carefully and, at a ripe moment, suggesting a potential description of consensus. "It sounds like we want to focus our efforts on media work, with an event that gives youth a chance to speak out about the lack of recreation programs." Then the facilitator lets the group react to that, listening for how the suggestion is on or off the mark. Later, at another ripe moment, the facilitator can restate that possible consensus, modifying it based on the additional comments. "Okay, it does seem clear that we want to do a media event with youth speaking out, but first we want to release a study which documents the lack of recreation programs in the city." These suggestions about consensus should not just be the facilitator's own ideas (though he or she may have input), they are the facilitator's efforts to articulate back to participants a summary of the group's own ideas so that they can be refined and agreed to.

The facilitator has other important jobs to do as well. He or she needs to make sure newcomers are introduced and made to feel welcome. He or she needs to keep track of the time and keep the group on schedule. "Just a reminder, we have fifteen more minutes to wrap-up this discussion so lets try to come to closure on this." It's also important to keep the discussion focused and on track. "That's a really good point, but let's come back to that later when we talk about next steps." If the group is a large one, the facilitator should keep a speakers' list, making sure that air time is allocated fairly and paying attention to who in the group is not actively participating, using breaks or some other opportunity to check in with them. The facilitator must also manage conflicts that arise in the group.

Facilitation is hard work, and facilitators need the help of everyone present. Someone other than the facilitator needs to be taking notes, ideally on paper or a blackboard so that the whole group can see them and offer any corrections or additions that are needed. A separate person might also be assigned the task of keeping track of time. This help the facilitator to focus on managing the flow of the discussion. The participants need to help as well, by also looking for points of consensus and helping to keep the discussion focused and on track. For larger or longer meetings, it often works best to divide the task of facilitation between two or more people, giving individual facilitators a rest and giving the group a chance to be led by different perspectives (by gender, age, and ethnicity especially).

Discussions, Decision Making, and Resolving Conflict

Ultimately, the purpose of a meeting is discussion and making choices about how to move forward. Both are about striking a right balance—between participation and closure, between one point of view and another. Groups use a variety of discussion techniques to strike that balance and to reach decisions that reflect the participants' best collective wisdom.

One question to consider up front is how small or large a group can handle the discussions you need to have. Ten people can get into some detail and still leave room for real participation; fifty people can't. If participation is important and the group is large, it may make sense to break into small groups, each one focusing on a specific piece of the work (such as media strategy, logistics planning for a rally, outreach to new communities) and allowing time for reporting back later to the full group.

At the start of a discussion, especially one about general objectives or strategy, brainstorming is a common technique for generating the widest possible range of ideas and allowing the broadest participation. The rules of brainstorming are simple: participants can offer up any idea, but without much detail; no criticism is allowed of the ideas presented; quantity of ideas is good and diversity of ideas is good. Then the group can look over the entire list of ideas and decide which ones to prioritize for real consideration. A variation on the technique, which sometimes draws out people who are more reluctant to speak up, is to have people write their ideas on index cards. Those cards are then passed around for people to look at. and participants are asked to read aloud the card they end up with in their hand.

As groups get to the task of deciding what to do, conflicts inevitably develop. Disagreements over priorities, strategies, and tactics are not bad things in a group. No single person in a group has a monopoly on wisdom. As the saying goes, "The opposite of one profound truth may well be another profound truth." Again, the trick is balance. Too much conflict in a group makes it hard to move forward in a common direction. Too little may mean that the group isn't diverse enough in its thinking and won't run into the downside of its ideas and plans until it is too late.

Some groups use the rules of formal consensus, in which no decision is final until every single participant has signed off 100 percent. In its extreme, enforced consensus can be a huge problem, can even be antidemocratic, giving one person the right to overrule dozens of others. Other groups use straight voting, talking out disagreements up to a point, then making a final choice by majority. While more efficient than formal consensus, strict majority rule runs the risk of alienating members caught on the losing side. In the ideal, the best way for groups to make decisions is by informal consensus, where ideas are suggested and hashed out until the group is in general agreement about what to do, with those most in objection compromising or ceding to the overwhelming majority. In all cases, the best methods of resolving differences involve listening, trust between the participants, and careful compromise.

In group discussions, whether large or small, tensions and conflicts may arise that have to do with race, gender, class, or other differences between people. It is important not to ignore or silence these tensions. They may reflect real differences in the way people see the organizing effort and its goals, with real implications for strategy, for the way the work is carried out, and how to help people be included. Some members of the group, precisely because of their race, gender, sexual orientation, or other factors, may feel excluded or marginalized in ways that others aren't noticing or can't fully appreciate. When someone is the only woman present, or the only African American, it may have a huge effect on his or her comfort in participating. Ethnically or sexually tinged comments, even the use of "insider' references and language, can have the same effect. These are all things groups need to pay attention to.

Sometimes race, gender, and class issues can become just about the only things the group talks about, at the direct expense of discussing the organizing work to be done. Some people feel so strongly and personally about these issues that they insist of making them the focus of the group's discussion, well past the point where it is constructive and useful. When these issues arise, create a clear time to talk them through, but also decide how much time and stick to that limit.

Summaries

In the end it is important to capture, in writing, a summary of the meeting, which keeps important decisions from being forgotten and allows for clear follow-up. Some groups record notes on poster paper, others enter a running summary into a laptop computer. In fact, long and detailed summaries of meetings (such as who said what) are rarely very useful. What is valuable is to glean from all these notes a brief summary that can focus people's thinking. It should lay out the key points of discussion and agreement, along with the main items requiring follow-up, including deadlines and who is responsible. Ideally, a summary like this is created soon after the meeting and sent out to participants for comment and revision (e-mail makes this far easier).

Other Things to Consider

To assure that meetings allow for genuine participation, keep a few other suggestions in mind. Make sure meetings are held at times and locations that are convenient and accessible. If the participants are there for reasons related to their work, then a daytime meeting as opposed to evenings or weekends avoids pulling them away from their families. If the meeting is about something outside people's work,

---

RESOURCES THAT ORGANIZING CAMPAIGNS NEED

Things

✓ Research	✓ Computers	✓ Money
✓ Written Materials	✓ Telephone	✓ Contacts
✓ Flyers	✓ Fax	✓ Office Space
✓ Copying/Printing	✓ Postage	✓ Office Supplies

People

✓ Researchers	✓ Organizers	✓ Fund-raisers
✓ Writers	✓ Speakers	✓ Contributors
✓ Phoners	✓ Experts	✓ Envelope stuffers
✓ Artists	✓ Canvassers	✓ Media spokespeople

---

then meetings during the day may exclude a good many people who can't take time off from their jobs. Consider the importance of providing child care so that people with children can easily attend. Consider also whether the meeting location is accessible by public transportation for those who don't have cars, easy to find, and accessible to the disabled.

At the meeting, have people sit in a circle. This communicates in a physical way that everyone there is considered an equal. It also lets people see and hear one another better. Depending on the diversity of the group, it may be important to provide for translation, either foreign language or signing for deaf participants. This kind of assistance is not always easy to arrange, but if groups get into the habit of doing so it opens the doors to broader participation, making the group wiser, stronger, and more inclusive.

Coordinating the Work to Be Done

After taking time to decide what to do, organizing campaigns need to get down to the real work of doing it. Since effective organizing has a lot to do with being organized, the first step is careful planning. All the projects you have decided to take on need to be divided up into the specific tasks involved in getting them done. What needs to be researched? What needs to be written? Who needs to be called? What people need to be brought together, when and where? What material needs to be sent out, and to whom? What resources will you need and where will you get them? Lay all this out in specifics, with firm, realistic deadlines, and designate who has the responsibility to get the job done. Each task should also be prioritized according to its immediacy and urgency.

Organizing the work to carry out that plan also requires careful matchmaking, delegating the right kinds of work to the right people. An organizing team needs to assess its diverse talents. Who is a good writer? Who is good at reaching people on the phone and recruiting them? Who works easily with the media? Who knows how to lay out a great-looking flyer? Who has the chutzpah to ask other people for money? Who is a good speaker to send out to community meetings? If the needs of the organizing effort are matched well with people's interests and talents, that work gets done competently and with joy. If those needs and talents are matched poorly (if you delegate a writing project to someone who hates to write), you'll get excuses and missed deadlines.

What comes next is follow-up—in abundance. In the words of one veteran activist, "Reminding is the essence of organizing." The person in charge of coordinating the effort needs to know all the pieces of work involved, who has responsibility for getting it done, and what the deadlines are. She or he is the keeper of the plan and must constantly be checking in with people: "How is it going?" She or he needs to look for early warnings that people seem overwhelmed or off track and help them get back on track. If major tasks are behind schedule, the organizer needs to find that person help or jump in and help get the job done.

Motivating and Caring for People Along the Way

Since organizing work is fundamentally about people, supporting them and motivating them should be built consciously into the campaign at every step. One important way to do this is to set clear goals and give people an opportunity to see their steady advancement. Big visual charts that show how many signatures have been gathered on petitions, how many lawmakers have been lobbied, how many doors knocked on, or how much money has been raised—all these give participants a constant reminder of being a part of something bigger on its way to victory. In the words of veteran health care organizer Martha Kowalick, "Nothing is as motivating as progress."[11] Another way to keep motivation high is to help people see how the work they are doing contributes to the larger effort. During the 1996 initiative campaign on health care reform in California (Proposition 186), volunteers worked hard organizing fund-raising house parties. A campaign memo reminded volunteers, "Remember, every $100 raised will allow us to reach 16,900 people with one of our TV spots!"[12]

Having food, taking time out to honor and recognize people for their contributions, making sure that credit is shared and spread around, injecting humor and some playfulness into the work, these are all ways of making the atmosphere of an organizing effort enjoyable for people. "The culture has to be motivating and fun and appreciative," notes Kowalick. "We always had bagels." Organizers at Senior Action Network in San Francisco take dozens of snapshots at every activist event, then post the pictures on a bulletin board in their office for volunteers to take home as souvenirs. Take time to celebrate all victories, no matter how small. People want to feel they are a part of something positive and winning.

Another way to keep people interested and to encourage people's capacity as activists is to build training opportunities into your organizing effort. Training is something tangible you can offer volunteers in exchange for the work they offer.

It could be something as simple as a morning-long workshop on "How to Work With the Media" or "Lobbying Your Local Officials." You can invite a local representative or reporter to open such a workshop with a brief presentation, giving people an "insider's" view, as well as showing the representative and the reporter that you have a base of active supporters. Take advantage of the experience of the most seasoned activists in your group and turn them into trainers who share what they know.

When organizing campaigns take on powerful opponents, they also need to prepare supporters for the inevitable backlash that those opponents can engineer. As a young advocate, I had the opportunity to hear this lesson firsthand from Caesar Chavez. The Farm Worker leader explained to me how important this lesson was during the UFW's grape boycotts in the 1960s, '70s, and '80s. Knowing that their corporate opponents would sling powerful mud and intimidation in the union's direction to undermine public and political support for the boycott, they equipped their supporters with fistfuls of information to be ready to state the facts clearly when the mud flew. The success of an organizing campaign is not necessarily measured by how far it advances the cause when it first goes public, but by how well it maintains its strength once its opponents strike back. Often, this is determined by how carefully the campaign prepares its volunteers and supporters to withstand that backlash, something it must plan for from the start.

There is one other aspect of supporting people during an organizing effort that is very personal and can't be overlooked. In advocacy, frequently, the most powerful voices are those with a personal story to tell, and often a hard one—the mother who has lost a child to a drunk driver or a bullet, the daughter of a parent abused in a nursing home, a formerly homeless woman ready to tell her tale. These stories are powerful and advocates are often anxious to use them—in a public hearing, a legislative visit, or in a news conference. But with such stories comes a special responsibility to the teller. When I worked in the 1980s with MADD mothers, it was important to take time to listen to them and be prepared for their tears. When I worked on health insurance reform in the 1990s, with a father who had to go on TV to plead for funds to pay for his dying son's care, I had to make a connection with him that wasn't about being an advocate. Involving people who come to the issue out of a difficult personal experience carries with it a responsibility to prepare them well for what to expect and to be with them throughout in a way that is caring and not manipulative.

Fund-Raising

"Money is like sex. Everyone thinks about it, but no one is supposed to discuss it in polite company."[13] Advocacy and organizing campaigns need money—sometimes a little, sometimes a lot—to get the job done, but few people relish the job of raising those funds. Fund-raising is a piece of the work that has to put on the table early. Campaigns that are going to need cash (for printing, mailing, advertising, office space, staff, or other needs) do best when they make a clear budget and a fund-raising plan to come up with the money required. Activist campaigns use a wide assortment of methods to raise funds. Here are some of the basics.

Membership Dues

For established organizations, having a paid-dues requirement, even a modest one, provides a base of funding that can be depended upon from year to year. These dues can be individual, with a price break for people with low incomes, students, and seniors. Dues might also be organizational, based on each group's size or budget.

Events

Campaigns use everything from rummage sale, to house parties to expensive formal dinners to nudge their broadest network of supporters into contributing financially, and in many cases to increase the group's visibility in the community. Depending on the type of event, it can take an enormous amount of work to pull off. Groups who go this route should be sure the work involved is worth the effort and plan the event with as much attention as any other aspect of the campaign.

Door-to-Door Canvassing

A number of groups use door-to-door solicitation to raise funds, sometimes carried out by volunteers and sometimes by people who are paid a percentage of what they raise. This kind of fund-raising requires careful organization. Neighborhoods are usually targeted for solicitation based on the likelihood that people there would be willing to give; affluent neighborhoods that vote progressively are a special favorite. Fund-raising canvasses usually focus on a specific issue that is hot at the moment (passing a "bottle bill" for example), and canvassers are trained in a carefully crafted "rap" for how to talk about that issue. Financial controls are also important for canvassing, including careful tallies and oversight of the monies raised.

Direct Mail and Phone Solicitation

For advocacy campaigns that have a large and enthusiastic base of supporters, direct mail and telephone solicitation can be a very effective way to raise funds. However, for these methods to work, you not only need to have a popular base you also need to have those addresses or phone numbers on a list. Usually such lists take a long time to develop. Whether the pitch is made in a letter or by phone, the message should be the same—explain why the issue is crucial, why there is a special opportunity at just that moment to do something important, and explain exactly what that person's contribution will buy that makes a difference (a newspaper ad, buses to bring people to a rally, the brochures needed for a major leafleting campaign). Organizations that publish newsletters can also include solicitations like these in those newsletters.

Major Donors

Some organizing efforts also go after "major donors," a small group of more affluent supporters who can afford to write sizable checks. In 1990, California environmentalists were able to persuade multimillionaire Hal Arbit to give nearly $5
million to qualify an initiative aimed at protecting the state's ancient redwoods.
Arbit explained to the *Los Angeles Times*, "I have the choice of buying a $2 million
painting and looking at it on the wall . . . or I could spend $2 million and have a
chance of saving the last five percent of California redwood forests."[14] Huge donations like this one are obviously very rare, and even more modest major donations
don't just fall from the trees. They require a long process of meeting and wooing
potential donors and someone dedicated to doing that.

Foundation Grants

A number of foundations, especially some of the smaller and more progressive
ones, provide grant support for organizing and advocacy efforts. The easiest way to
find them is to ask other groups doing related work what foundations they've been
able to tap for grant funding, or to look through a foundation guide at the local library. Wooing a foundation is much like wooing a major donor: you need to take
time to understand what they are interested in and find a way to make contact and
establish a relationship. I'm sure that some groups get funded by sending in grant
proposals cold without a contact first, but that kind of success is rare. To receive a
grant your group will need to be a 501©3 charitable nonprofit, or be sponsored by
one. Foundations are prohibited from providing grant support for direct lobbying
of public officials.

For more about the lobbying restrictions imposed on nonprofit groups see
Being a Player—A Guide to the IRS Regulations for Advocacy Charities, published
by Alliance for Justice in Washington, DC.

Organizational Contributions

Depending on the campaign, it is sometimes possible to raise support money from
established organizations that have a close interest in the same objectives. Labor
unions, for example, often give seed funding to progressive grassroots efforts that
address the needs of their members. Here again, relationship building is important,
and it helps a great deal if members of the organization are actively involved in
your organizing drive.

Sale of Publications and Materials

For groups that produce well-regarded publications and materials (usually advocacy groups that are also known for their research), the sale of this material is also
a source of funds. The groups who do this best usually try to build up a subscriber
base of people who pay annually to receive all the materials (such as newsletters
and reports).

In-Kind Support

It is also worth paying attention to opportunities for in-kin" support, donations of services or materials instead of cash. Advocacy campaigns can often persuade supporting organizations to make photocopies, pick up printing and postage costs, or provide a phone, an office, or a computer. In larger efforts some organizations will dedicate a staff person to the work of the campaign.

In the midst of all this fund-raising it is important to ask the question—is there cash we wouldn't take? Should an organizing effort in a Latino community take money from Phillip Morris tobacco at the same time the company is targeting its smoking advertising at Latino youth? Should a consumer group accept funds from a large bank that it later may attack publicly? There are differing views on this question of "dirty money." Some organizations take the stand that taking financial support from the wrong groups compromises your credibility and isn't worth it. Kim Klein, author of the book, *Fundraising for Social Change*, writes that the issue is how you use the money, not where you get it. "Money is a tool. Similarly a hammer is a tool. A hammer can be used to help build a house or it can be used to bludgeon someone to death, but we never talk about dirty and clean hammers."[15] Each group needs to consider where it will draw that line.

Building a Formal Organization

Some organizing campaigns are ad hoc and short term (like the campaign for that stop sign). That's all they need to be. Other organizing efforts last longer. The issue may be one that won't get solved overnight—such as health care reform or protecting the environment. In those cases, the effort must make the often difficult transition from being something ad hoc to something lasting and permanent. "Building a strong, lasting and staffed organization alters the relations of power," writes the Midwest Academy. "Once such an organization exists people on the 'other side' must always consider the organization when making decisions."[16]

Creating a formal organizational structure is a tradeoff. Structure gives the effort stability and allows for longer-term planning and division of the work to be done. However, creating that structure also requires a good deal of attention and effort and opens the door to a whole new set of conflicts over strategy and power. Who will lead the group? What officers should it have? What will the bylaws be? Will it have a paid staff? Should there be dues and how much? What long-term objectives will it commit itself to? Who should be in and who should be out? These are all critical questions, each of which can create enough argument to torpedo the coming together at the very start.

As a rule, I advise groups to adopt only the level of structure they need to get the work done, and no more. With too little structure, important work and choices can fall through the cracks. Too much structure diverts energy away from the actual work at hand and into needless debates over detail. Typically, an organization will form an unpaid board of directors, with a president, other officers, and committees that deal with specific issues such as personnel and finance. The staff will be led by an executive director who runs the day-to-day operations and reports to the board. It is important that the organization decide early on what decisions rest with the executive director and staff, which need to be made in consultation with the board president or executive committee, and which require action by the full board.

In whatever size and with whatever structure, a permanent organization becomes the long-term embodiment of certain ideals, principles, and goals. Board and staff people may come and go, but the mission remains constant, creating a lasting structure in which people who subscribe to that vision can come together, again and again, to shift the balance of political power on an issue and take concrete action.

WHEN ORGANIZING TAKES ACTION—THE OPTIONS

Taking action is what organizing is all about. But what should that action be? What are your objectives? Whom do you need to move in order to win them? What messages and actions will move them? Answering these questions carefully is essential to developing an action plan that can win.

As you develop that plan there are some important principles to keep in mind. First, your action has to have a real chance of delivering the goods. Organizing is hard work, involving people who have a lot of other things to do. People want to be involved in something that can have a real and positive impact in their lives—opening a new neighborhood clinic, cleaning up a local dump site, or some other goal worth fighting for. Generally, it is also better to bring people together around a specific and modest objective and win it (the right to see a specialist at your HMO) rather than to target an objective that is huge—"health care for everyone"—that offers little chance of victory any time soon. In fact, usually the best way to win something big is to build toward it with a series of smaller victories that create momentum.

It is important as well to pick an action that genuinely involves those you have organized. Deciding to take on a local polluter by going to court puts all the power and action in the hands of one or two lawyers. Picketing the CEO's house puts power in the hands of regular people. Even if litigation does make strategic sense on the issue, it is still important to build in real actions that can be taken by the people you have organized. Finally, give careful consideration to the reaction you are likely to provoke from your opponents. Does it help you or does it push you backward? Can your people handle it? Will it move the people and institutions you are targeting in your direction or just make them more intransigent? Will it get you the media attention you want, or just the opposite? Will it move a wealthy opponent into spending huge amounts of money on public relations, wooing the public to their side? In direct-action situations, are your people prepared for the arrest or even violence they might be subject to? None of these questions is a reason not to act, but merely a call to take whatever action you do with your eyes wide open.

In reality, there is virtually no civic action or tactic that is new. From letter writing to lobbying, protests to vigils, it has all been done somewhere. Look at what other people have done, what actions they have used, and how they have worked. Look at all of them and figure out which ones makes sense given your objective, your community, your opponents, your resources, and your people. As organizer Francisco Herrera observed, "Why did David use a sling? It's what he knew."

Organizing for Self-Education and Public Education

Sometimes the main goal of an organizing effort is self-education and self-help, bringing people together to learn their basic rights or to address directly the problems they want to solve. Parents of Kids with Cancer first came together to share information and support related to their children's illness. In cities across the United States, America's newest immigrants have organized themselves to learn and to teach one another about their legal rights. What does your employer have to pay you? What papers do you need to file to bring your parents here? In New York City, the group Community Voices Heard, which organizes welfare recipients and low-wage workers, holds twice-a-month Worker/Welfare Rights Clinics at which people share and receive information about finding work and solving problems at their workplaces.

In many cases this self-education awakens people to the fact that the problems they are experiencing are not just personal but are issues that must be taken to the larger community. Immigrant organizers have moved from holding self-help workshops to holding community speak-outs on immigrant rights, aimed at political leaders and the media. Parents of Kids with Cancer started addressing the abuses of the insurance industry. Community Voices Heard marched in the streets of Manhattan to spread the message that workfare in the city was forcing forty thousand low-income New Yorkers to work in unpaid jobs.

For these types of public education organizing campaigns, the essentials are these: a clear message; having that message delivered by people with strong credibility, individuals who can speak from personal experience; and delivering that message using the resources you have available. Where the issue is local and you have substantial people power, it may be possible to get your message out using grassroots methods such as door-to-door leafleting or setting up information tables in public places. However, most broader public education work relies on media—television, radio, and print—to get the messages across.

Organizing for Advocacy and Lobbying

In many cases, addressing your concerns takes more than self-help or even general community education. It requires political action, a decision by someone in authority to change or to enforce the rules. Immigrants win the right to public prenatal care only if legislators pass the law and fund the clinics. Children with cancer keep their coverage only when government lays the law down on insurance companies. Low-income workers don't win their employment rights until public officials enforce those rights. The next step in organizing is advocacy, the strategic application of public pressure on those with authority. The strategy of organizing for advocacy and lobbying revolves around two main considerations: Who are your targets, and what tactics will you use to bring pressure on them?

Targets

In establishing your targets the first question is, Who makes the decision? Is it the president, your school board, state lawmakers, the head of the local parks department, the corporate CEO? It is important to make your primary target the person or institution with the direct authority to deliver what you are demanding. When Parents of Kids with Cancer wanted to win new rules against the cancellation of health benefits, they targeted state lawmakers and the state insurance commissioner.

In addition, there will be secondary targets, other people or organizations that hold a heavy influence over what your primary target will decide to do. When AIDS activists wanted to put heat on the Burroughs-Wellcome company over the huge prices it was charging for the drug AZT, they took their protests to Wall Street, to the company's investors and corporate peers. Constituents, shareholders, financial contributors, political supporters, even people's barbers and neighbors are all audiences you can approach to get your primary target to move in your direction. In virtually every case, the most important secondary target of all is the media, the chief tool for manipulating the public images of public official or corporate leaders.

Tactics

Many different kinds of organizing actions, ranging from the mild to the fierce, can be used to put pressure on public or corporate officials. As a rule, it is best to pick the one that involves the least effort and the least confrontation but still gets the job done. At the mild end is putting together a long list of endorsements, a broad coalition of groups who may do nothing more than sign onto a joint letter. That broad support can also be expressed by gathering large numbers of names on petitions. Petitioning can be an effective organizing action, giving people something very concrete that they can do by taking the issue to their friends and neighbors. To be effective, however, petitions have to be delivered in big numbers. Politicians and other targets know that it takes very little commitment and effort to sign your name to a petition. Unless the volume is huge, the impact is probably very small.

More ambitious, and more effective, is a well-organized letter-writing campaign. Personal letters that recount real-life stories related to the issue are attention-grabbing. As with petitions, volume is critical. Organizing campaigns that do letter writing well don't just ask people to write a letter and then give them the address, they get people to write a letter on the spot, at a PTA meeting, a protest rally, in the lobby of the hospital, or in the campus cafeteria. Then they take those letters and mail them for people.

The next level of pressure is holding a face-to-face meeting with the officials involved, preferably on your turf—in your school, your clinic, or your neighborhood. The Industrial Areas Foundation (IAF) uses a very specific model for community hearings, at which local officials are invited and put on the spot to respond to a community organization's demands. These events are preceded by months of careful work to get the right groups involved and to turn out big numbers of people. The actual meetings follow a consistent basic agenda. They open with a prayer by a local religious leader—rooting the meeting in moral authority and highlighting the involvement of local churches and synagogues. The invited officials sit alone in chairs at the front (the "hot seats"), as leaders of the group present a brief report summarizing research they have done that frames the issue and backs it up with hard facts. The issue may be the rise of drug crime in their neighborhood, the lack of jobs, or some other community concern around which people have organized. Following this report on the research comes the personal side, testimony by witnesses, the people directly affected. Then the officials (local mayors, department heads, legislators) are given a brief opportunity to respond to what they have heard, and the group's leaders and the audience are given a chance to ask questions of the officials. Before the meeting ends, group leaders put forward a set of specific requests for action. Overshadowing it all is an active effort to get the media to attend, letting officials know that the numbers of people watching go well beyond just those actually in the room.

Though a great deal of work to organize, hearings like this remind the officials that they are public servants accountable to members of the community. They give people a direct opportunity to address those with the authority to take action. A Portland, Oregon, organizing campaign to address violence aimed at girls used the community-hearing tactic to gain the attention of officials and the local media and gave teenage girls a powerful public voice on a concern that had long been ignored. An August 1996 speak-out at a Portland church drew a huge audience of girls, public officials, and members of the media and members the community. Not only did the girls mesmerize local officials with their stories, but they also directly challenged how local funds were being spent. "Everyone at the speak-out, especially the officials, were amazed by it all," said John Ashford, one of the organizers. Within a year, Portland had established the first local task force in the state on preventing violence against girls, and local school officials began to track and report such incidents and started a series of violence-prevention projects based on the girls' testimony.[17]

Election Work

Election campaigns, both for candidates and for ballot measures, are an important opportunity for making a difference through organizing. Election organizing is usually aimed at one clear goal—maximizing political support for your candidate or cause on Election Day. Organizing efforts do this through a very specific set of actions.

Voter Identification

The first step is usually figuring out where voters already stand on your issue. You want to be sure that the ones who are already with you turn out to vote. You want to ignore the ones who are firmly opposed to you. You want to work on persuading the ones who are on the fence. In large-scale campaigns, this voter identification is usually done through expensive polling techniques. Smaller campaigns, in towns or small districts, can do the same thing by going door to door with voter lists and asking people what they think about a candidate or ballot measure. In either case, what you want to end up with is a strong sense of where voters stand so that you can target your campaign appropriately.

Voter Persuasion

The next step is to work on educating and persuading the group of voters you have identified as your swing vote, the people who could just as easily vote either way. Like most advocacy work, voter education and persuasion comes down to several questions. What is the message that will move them? What messengers (people and organizations) delivering it are likely to have the most influence? What activities can you use to get that message delivered? In big campaigns (for president, governor, senator, statewide initiative), voter education these days has virtually nothing to do with organizing and everything to do with media. At the local level, however, organizing work is still key. Grassroots campaigns can carry that message through leafleting at shopping centers, door-to-door precinct work, coffee klatches, visits to people's workplaces, speaking to neighborhood groups, any opportunity to carry the message to persuadable voters in an effective way.

Voter Registration and Get Out the Vote

In terms of voters you know are definitely on your side, election organizing is about making sure they are registered and that they show up at the polls on Election Day. Registration laws vary by state, but in most places anyone old enough to vote can use a simple voter registration form to register new voters. Effective voter registration efforts are carefully targeted, usually going door to door in neighborhoods or setting up registration tables in areas with heavy foot traffic—in both cases only in areas where your political support is very clear. You do not want to end up registering large numbers of people who will vote against you.

Get out the vote (GOTV) activities on Election Day are also aimed very carefully at voters you know are on your side. GOTV activities at a local level include calling or visiting voters a few days prior to the election to remind them to vote and where they need to go to vote; offering people rides to the polls if they need one; leafleting key neighborhoods with doorknob hangers early on election morning; and checking the afternoon postings at polling places to see which voters haven't shown up and then calling or visiting them. Many campaigns work in advance of an election to have their supporters vote by absentee ballot, making sure even earlier that these people have voted.

Using Elections as an Opportunity to Influence Politicians

From an organizing point of view, elections are also an important opportunity to influence and pressure politicians. Organizing efforts of this sort might host a candidate debate on their issue, send out candidate questionnaires, show up at candidate forums and debates to raise their issue, or work in the campaigns of supportive candidates.

Protest and Direct Action

Confrontation, including breaking the law, is an honorable tradition in U.S. political life. It has, in fact, provided the nation with some of its most noble moments. Direct-action protest was present at the birth of the republic, as every school child knows, when the Sons of Liberty dressed as Mohawk Indians and dumped British tea into Boston Harbor to protest "taxation without representation." It is the method that civil rights protesters used in the 1950s and 1960s to tear down the walls of segregation. As Dr. Martin Luther King Jr. wrote to his critics in 1963, in his "Letter from the Birmingham Jail":

> You may well ask: "Why direct action? Why sit-ins, marches and so forth? Isn't negotiation a better path?" You are quite right in calling for negotiation. Indeed, this is the very purpose of direct action. Nonviolent direct action seeks to create such a crisis and foster such a tension that a community which has constantly refused to negotiate is forced to confront the issue. It seeks so to dramatize the issue that it can no longer be ignored.[18]

Protest and direct action, like all public advocacy, must be carefully strategic, with a clear eye on what it seeks to achieve and what actions are most likely to do that. There are some important principles to keep in mind here as well.

Deny Your Target Something It Wants

One important way to get public officials, corporations, or other institutions to move is to deny them something they want. Protest and direct action can deny a target its decent public image, its livelihood, and even its ability to function, all in the interests of forcing that target to negotiate or change its ways. King targeted his 1963 Birmingham protest at local merchants during the Easter season, denying them one of their most valuable shopping seasons and putting pressure on them to end their segregationist practices.[19] Labor and environmental protesters blocked entrance to the December 1999 meeting of the World Trade Organization in Seattle, denying the WTO the ability to carry out its business and drawing unprecedented international attention to the issues of economic globalization. The organization INFACT forced the international food giant Nestlé to change its practice of marketing unhealthy baby formula in poor countries by engineering a successful consumer boycott against Nestlé products around the world. When workers and activists picketed the home of designer Jessica McClintock in San Francisco to publicize her poor labor practices, their aim was to deny her the friendly public image she wanted.

Go Outside Your Opponent's Experience, and Stay Close to Your Own

Saul Alinsky, the legendary organizer, offered this advice about how to apply maximum public pressure on your target: "Whenever possible go outside the experience of the enemy. Here you want to cause confusion, fear and retreat."[20] While helping press for local civil rights demands in Rochester, New York, in the 1960s, Alinsky used this approach by targeting the pride and joy of the city's elite, the Rochester Symphony:

"I suggested [to white community leaders] that we might buy one hundred seats for one of Rochester's symphony concerts. We would select a concert in which the music was relatively quiet. The hundred blacks who would be given the tickets would first be treated to a three-hour pre-concert dinner in the community, in which they would be fed nothing but baked beans, and lots of them; then the people would go to the symphony hall—with obvious consequences."[21] According to Alinsky, the threat of mass flatulence was way beyond the experience of the marches, sit-ins, and other protests that Rochester's leaders had seen before, and it was perfectly legal. The threat itself was enough to get action moving on the group's demands.

Similarly, Alinsky cautions that you don't want to pick tactics and actions that go too far outside the experience and comfort zone of the people you are organizing. Some people feel quite comfortable standing arm in arm to block the entrance to a military base, others don't. Some people are comfortable delivering testimony to a legislative hearing, others are petrified. The tactics and actions you choose have to match what the people you are organizing are able to do, and those tactics need to leave people inspired and empowered.

Make It Personal

A lot of protests are aimed at large institutions such as corporation or government agencies. To make a protest effective, make it personal, name names, and bring it close to home. The protest action against designer Jessica McClintock worked because it focused on her personally and embarrassed her in front of her own neighbors. When I was involved in mobilizing public action against the Bechtel Corporation for the unconscionable price hikes its subsidiary was charging poor people for water use in Bolivia, I arranged for Bechtel's CEO, Riley Bechtel, to be bombarded by personal e-mails and to be pinned personally with the blame for the price hikes in the local press in San Francisco, where Bechtel is headquartered. These actions forced a previously mute Bechtel Corporation to respond. Always target a person, not an institution.

Be Creative

To get noticed, protests and actions need to be more than the typical rally with a bullhorn and placards. During the 1980s, during the wars in Central America, religious peace groups in San Francisco would, as a protest against continued U.S. funding of those wars, hold an annual December 2 candlelight vigil in memory of four religious women from the United States who were killed on that date in El Salvador. With a slight change of plans, the annual downtown protest was converted from a little-noticed vigil in a small park to a huge and visible event. Instead of gathering in a concentrated group, we stretched out, with candles and banners, ten feet apart, in a mile-long line through the downtown shopping district. This converted the protest into an inescapable and solemn presence during the height of the busy Christmas shopping season.

Be Wary of the Potential Backlash

Think very carefully about the kind of public reaction you are likely to provoke. In fall 1994, immigrant leaders in Los Angeles set out to organize a massive preelection protest against California's sweeping anti-immigrant ballot initiative, Proposition 187. Less than two weeks before the election, a crowd of more than 70,000 immigrants, mostly Latino, marched through the streets of Los Angeles, one of the city's largest protests ever. Unfortunately for organizers, the march took place just weeks after the World Cup soccer finals in Los Angeles, in which Mexico had been a finalist, leaving behind a huge supply of Mexican flags. On the morning of the protest, thousands of marchers decided to bring the flags along. That image, of thousands of Latinos marching under a sea of Mexican flags, sparked exactly the kind of public resentment the initiative's promoters were aiming for. It was the lead on all the evening news shows and on the front page of the next morning's *Los Angeles Times*. "The YES vote shot through the ceiling, boom, overnight," recalled "No on 187" consultant Karen Kapler, who was tracking voter polls.[22] Think very carefully about the images and messages you will project and what effect they will have on those you seek to influence.

Be Well Prepared

Protests and actions also need clear and thoughtful advance preparation, taking into account all the possible situations that might develop. Organizers are taking enormous responsibility for hundreds, if not thousands, of people. Some considerations relate to logistics. How will people get there? Will there be parking for people who drive? How will people know where to go when they arrive? Are permits needed? Are there bathrooms? It is important to have basic supplies and assistance on hand, everything from walkie-talkies to banners, to water to first aid equipment.

Public actions of this sort also need clear leadership. Who is in charge? Someone or some small group of people needs to be in position to make snap decisions as they come up, about everything from a change in protest route to delicate negotiations with police over arrest issues. Someone or a group of people should be delegated to deal with the media, and only they should speak officially with reporters, using clearly agreed-to messages and the right materials (such as news releases).

If the action involves some people getting arrested, be prepared for that. There should be a clear line of communication with police, and lawyers on hand to provide legal assistance. People who might be arrested should be trained in advance about what to expect and how to deal with it. A whole host of logistical arrest-related details should be planned for in advance, including bail, child care, access to medications in jail, and calls to family members or friends.[23]

Keep People Inspired

Amidst all the strategy, logistics, media work, confrontation, and other parts of putting together a protest or action, pay attention to keeping people inspired. At the start, someone should deliver a speech that gives voice to why people are there. What is the issue, why does it matter? Such inspiration comes not only from recounting the lofty ideals or statistics involved but the sharing of personal stories. That inspiration can also come from organizing opportunities for people to speak in smaller groups about what the action means to them. Successful public movements do not forget to take time to move people.

Organizing in all its forms—from public education to advocacy to public protest—is a process of discipline, of methodically channeling enthusiasm and resources into concrete action. It requires homework and research, strategy and planning, dividing up the work and staying on track. It also requires strong doses of creativity, daring, and inspiration. At its best, effective organizing not only produces real and immediate improvements in people's lives, it also gives people a sense of their own power that they will carry forward for a lifetime, into other issues and other battles. It has the potential to alter the long-term relations between those who typically have power (by virtue of wealth or social or political position) and those who traditionally don't. Organizing, carried out well, is how the small Lilliputians come together to tie down mighty Gulliver and issue their demands and achieve their goals.

CHAPTER NINE

Building and Maintaining Advocacy Coalitions

A single bracelet does not jingle.

—CONGOLESE PROVERB

Organizing is about bringing individuals together to make public change. Coalition building is about bringing together organizations to work toward a public goal. Time spent in coalitions can be the best or worst of times in an advocacy campaign. When they work well coalitions can add great power to your cause. When they work poorly, coalitions can be a gut-wrenching exercise in organizational and personal infighting. In the words of one advocate, "Coalitions are an unnatural act between partially consenting adults done with the lights on."

WHY COALITIONS ARE VALUABLE

Most often, coalitions are made up of organizations that are long-term allies, sharing a common philosophy and having an affinity for one another that brings them together on issues. In other cases, coalitions bring together groups that have very little in common and, in fact, disagree on many other issues. In either case, there are many solid reasons to undertake the challenges of doing advocacy work in a coalition.

Developing a Stronger Public Image

As the late Speaker of the House, Tip O'Neil, observed, "Power is the appearance of power." In advocacy, the image of a campaign is crucial. By bringing together a diversity of organizations with different public images and different bases of popular support, coalitions can capture that rare and valuable resource in politics— looking like a cross-section of the public—a characteristic that helps to win media attention as well as public and political support.

Bringing Together Diverse Resources and Ideas

No one organization, on its own, possesses all the tools and resources necessary to carry out a full-scale advocacy campaign. Some have a grassroots base, others have experience with lobbying or the media. Some have expertise in the policy issue involved, others have good political connections. Strong advocacy coalitions unite all these resources under one tent. It is also true that no one organization has a corner on good ideas about how to solve a public problem or how to advance an advocacy

120

strategy. Coalitions also allow groups to pool their ideas, letting the best ones emerge from debate and discussion.

Avoiding Needless Duplication of Effort

Organizations working on the same issue can't afford to waste time duplicating work on research, educating reporters, organizing communities, or lobbying policy makers. Coalitions allow groups to divide up that work, matching the tasks involved to each group's specifics talents.

Linking Groups that Work Locally, Statewide, and Nationally

In coalitions, groups that work at the local level can link up with groups working on those same matters at a state or national level, providing them with an opportunity to work on issues that reach well beyond their communities (international human rights work, for example). Coalition work also allows state and national advocacy campaigns to link with local groups, giving them the kind of grassroots base that is often critical to making change at the state and national level.

Giving Your Opponents a Way to Negotiate With You

Many advocacy victories come by negotiating concessions from your opposition. However, to win these concessions your opponents must have a way to negotiate with you, something that is hard to do when your side is a collection of two dozen disorganized groups. Coalitions give you and your allies the vehicle you need to carry out such negotiations.

Allowing Exchanges Between Experienced Advocates and New Ones

Coalitions that include a mix of experienced advocates and newcomers to the issue (or to advocacy altogether) create opportunities for an exchange that goes both ways. Newer advocates can learn the lessons that more experienced advocates have to share. Long-term advocates can benefit from having their ideas challenged by newcomers and by picking up some of their fresh enthusiasm and idealism.

Providing Moral Support During Tough Fights

Advocacy work can be very hard, and often those who carry it out can become dispirited and ready to give up. Coalitions that work well create a community spirit of action that helps the people involved make it through the tougher moments.

These are all the positive reasons for building and acting in coalitions. There are also some serious downsides to coalition work. Coalitions move slowly, their action can be cumbersome, and they require a great deal of time and energy to build and maintain. There are some issues, where the fight is easy enough and where coalition clout is unneeded, when it may be simpler and smarter for one group to act alone. When the advocacy battle is a tough one, however, because the opponent is strong or public opinion must be changed, the strength of a coalition may be the campaign's only hope.

FORMING COALITIONS

The most important decisions that a coalition makes are in the beginning. What goals will it set for itself? Who will it seek to include and who won't it include? What kind of structure will it create to facilitate its work? How the coalition answers these questions at the start will determine most of what will come later.

Setting Your Goals

Coalitions are based on a set of shared basic concerns and goals that must be clear from the very start among the core group of organizations. Those basic goals form the basis for the more specific objectives the coalition will set for itself later. If those basic concerns and goals aren't clear from the start, the coalition is inviting a host of internal disagreements and confusion down the road, which will make the coalition ineffective and make participation in it a nightmare.

Among the core group that begins a coalition, the definition of these goals may start out big, broad, and long term—health care for all, a clean environment, better schools. Those big-picture goals then need to be defined more specifically in terms of concrete and winnable objectives—providing health insurance to children under age five, banning a specific pesticide, reducing class size to twenty children in the primary grades. With those objectives clear among its founders, the coalition is ready to expand and recruit a broader membership. Many coalition efforts are actually based on two sets of objectives. The first is the specific policy or public change that the campaign is seeking to win in the short term. The second, and often equally important, is to build up a larger movement on that issue for the long term.

For all coalitions, three questions are important to ask up front. First, is the objective big enough to matter? The organizations and people you are trying to recruit are busy, and the objective needs to be ambitious enough to catch their interest. Second, can you win something meaningful in the short term? If the coalition campaign doesn't produce something of value within a year or two, and in some cases sooner, people and groups will start to abandon ship. Third, does the initial objective lay the groundwork for the coalition's larger goals in the future? Coalition campaigns do this by engaging the public with the symbols and messages they will need for the bigger fights ahead, by solidifying the long-term alliances they will need, and by building up the grassroots base and the skill level of the people and groups who are involved.

Recruiting Coalition Members

As a rule, coalitions don't emerge out of thin air but rather out of existing organizations or campaigns that already have credibility with potential coalition members.

RESOURCES THAT GROUPS CAN BRING TO
ADVOCACY COALITIONS

✓ Public Credibility   ✓ A Large Membership Base   ✓ Access to Decision Maker
✓ Staff Time   ✓ Advocacy Experience   ✓ Media Contacts/Expertise
✓ Funding   ✓ Space/Equipment/Postage   ✓ Volunteers
✓ Diversity   ✓ People Directly Affected   ✓ Contacts With Potential Allies

---

For example, the coalition that led the winning campaign to block Robert Bork's nomination to the U.S. Supreme Court was born out of a core group of national civil rights organizations.

Coalition recruitment begins with a wish list of resources, skills, and connections. These include public credibility, money, a broad membership base, and other political resources. The ability to influence the authorities you are targeting is especially important. For example, during the public movement in the 1980s aimed at cutting off U.S. assistance to the wars in Central America, the involvement of religious organizations and churches was critical to coalition building. The moral authority held by temples and churches was a public force that even the Reagan administration found hard to deal with. "Taking on the churches is really tough," admitted one State Department official. "We don't normally think of them as political opponents so we don't know how to handle them."[1] Effective coalition building looks for these strengths not just in the organizations it recruits but also in the individuals who represent those groups, in order to bring together an assortment of leaders with the right mix of gifts—passion, experience, knowledge, a devotion to detail, and more.

Diversity is also an important priority in coalitions, as well as being a major challenge. Strong coalitions bring together a blend of people and organizations that cross all kinds of traditional boundary lines. Lee Cridland, an activist who helped lead a Colorado voter registration coalition, notes, "We had conservative women from the suburbs and we had leftist activists from the cities. It was a bizarre collection of people who would never even have been in the same room otherwise."[2] A coalition may begin with the groups that the organizers know best, but then has to be expanded beyond those "usual suspects."

"It is a great strength in a coalition to have as a partner someone or some group who is an enemy on all other issues," says Michael Pertschuk, co-director of the District of Columbia–based Advocacy Institute. "First of all it makes you interesting. You've got people saying, 'that's an interesting and curious assortment, we better take a fresh look at it."[3] In the 1970s, when immigrant rights groups were battling against national legislation to prohibit the hiring of undocumented immigrants, they teamed up with the Western Growers Association, a major agribusiness lobby.[4] When the League of Women Voters and Common Cause, two traditional

:formers, were sponsoring a 1996 California political reform initiative,
ed the pro-business California Taxpayers Association as an ally. You
.o agree with allies on every issue, just on the specific objective you've
joined up to win.

Diversity within coalitions also has its limits. Each of the groups in the
coalition must be in agreement with the coalition's fundamental objectives. Recruiting organizations that don't share those objectives or aren't completely sold
builds in an ongoing source of conflict that will drain the coalition's energy at every
turn. Keeping groups like these in your coalition can water down your objectives
until they are so vague as to lose all real meaning (for example, "health care for all"
without any definition as to the specific policy approaches to be advocated). It also
leaves the coalition wide open to having one or more of its members picked off by
the opposition, causing serious damage to the coalition's public image and political momentum.

Coalition members also need to be in basic agreement about the main tactics the coalition will use to pursue its goals. If one coalition member believes
that the only viable tactic is to take over legislative offices and get arrested
while the bulk of the coalition is committed to the standard lobbying approach,
the marriage may not work and the conflict over tactics may be more than the
coalition can handle. An alternative is for those groups to maintain close connections with the coalition, and even coordinate activities with it, while remaining formally outside.

Recruiting organizations into a coalition begins with a clear sense of what
those groups are interested in and how those interests relate to the coalition's
objectives. In some situations, the case for joining the coalition will be clear to potential. In other situations the connection between a group's goals and the coalition's has to be pitched carefully. Gun control advocates in Lafayette, California,
for example, seeking unusual allies for their efforts to prohibit local gun sales, were
able to recruit real estate brokers to their side by talking about the effects that gun
violence has on local property values.[5]

A key element in coalition building is turning personal connections into
organizational ones. Both at the leadership and grassroots levels, it is up to individuals to push an organization from the inside, toward joining and actively
participating in a coalition effort. For larger groups, that wooing needs to take
place at all the different levels of the organization. Having an organization's formal support through its leadership does not necessarily mean you have the
support of the organization's popular base. Leaders of the 1994 battle
against California's anti-immigrant initiative (Proposition 187) had endorsements from scores of large statewide membership groups (including the PTA
and many labor unions), virtually none of which translated into votes on Election Day. Said one campaign leader, "We had their leaders but very few of their
people."[6]

Creating an Effective Coalition Structure

Coalitions also need an effective structure that will allow them to carry out their work. Coalitions have a natural anatomy. At the center is the leader or leaders, the people who carry the ultimate responsibility for the coalition's work, the ones who lie awake at night worrying about whether that work got done. Beyond the leaders is a core group of others who, while not assuming as much responsibility as the leaders, are actively involved in setting strategy and carrying out the coalition's work.

Beyond the core are the active members, groups and individuals who participate regularly but who follow direction rather than taking leadership themselves. Other groups will drop in and out of active involvement at different times, and another set will support the coalition by lending their endorsement but never participate actively. The size of each category of support will vary along with the size of the coalition. A large national campaign might have a core group of two dozen organizations that meet regularly. A local campaign might have a core of just two or three groups.

This natural anatomy of a coalition needs to be captured into some form of organized structure that fits appropriately. Coalition structures vary from loose to formal. At the least formal end are networks, simple lists of organizations that don't meet together or have a specific campaign, but do share information (through newsletters, for example). More formal are ad hoc coalitions, in which one organization may take the lead, pulling together a support coalition that has no formal membership or structure but does takes some coordinated action.

As coalitions get more organized and structured, they may formalize membership and eligibility criteria, begin holding regular meetings, develop joint letterhead, elect their leaders formally, and even raise some joint funds to cover expenses. When a coalition becomes even more formal, it might add bylaws, form an executive committee with special decision-making authority, create other committees that deal with specific aspects of the work, levy dues, and may hire staff. With more formality than that, coalitions themselves may become legally incorporated organizations.

As a rule, it is best to adopt a structure with the least formality necessary to get the job done. Each step toward becoming more formal adds another layer of issues to deal with and another set of logistics to be managed. In some instances, when the number of groups actively involved is large or when the objective of the coalition is broad and long term, making the coalition formal and structured may be necessary to make clearer decisions and to take effective action. In other cases, however, the added structure and formality are unneeded and only makes things more complicated and bureaucratic, diverting attention from the coalition's actual advocacy work.

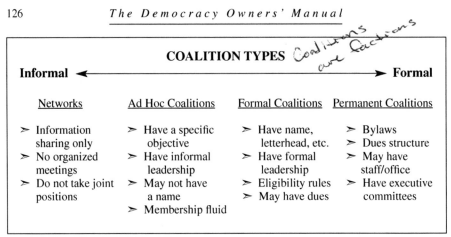

FIVE IMPORTANT ELEMENTS THAT
MAKE COALITIONS WORK

After a coalition is in place and its basic membership, goals, and structure are decided, it must begin to go about its work, perhaps for a short period but in other cases for years. Five key elements help coalitions to do their work effectively:

Leadership

Effective leadership is essential in a coalition. Leaders are the glue that holds a coalition together, managing the work, so that it doesn't fall through the cracks, and the chemistry, so that it doesn't fade out or explode. In some coalitions that leadership responsibility falls on just one person's shoulders, in others it is handled by a small core group or executive committee.

There are many different styles of coalition leadership. Some believe that coalition leaders should merely be facilitators, supporting the work of the coalition without intervening with any strong opinions of their own. Others argue that coalition leaders need to take charge, seizing control of the work at hand and giving the rest of the members someone to follow. The best models fall somewhere in the middle, with leaders taking clear responsibility for getting the job done, but with ample participation and democracy within the coalition regarding how that work gets carried out.

Coalition leaders need to play a number of important roles all at the same time. They need to be strategists, helping the coalition design its path forward and keeping the coalition on that path. They need to be coordinators, keeping track of all the work to be done and making sure it gets done. They need to be advocates, speaking publicly on behalf of the coalition and modeling effective advocacy for the other members. They need to be listeners, for consensus, common ground, and tensions. Finally, they need to be motivators, getting people involved and keeping them inspired.

The leaders of a coalition need to be dedicated both to the issue involved and to the coalition itself as a vehicle for advancing that issue. This means that coalition leaders must have the strong backing of their own organization, given the sacrifices of time and resources required. They also have to be willing to make those same sacrifices personally, letting their own interests take a back seat to that of advancing the coalition.

Decision Making

Making key decisions can be one of a coalition's toughest chores. It is a part of the work that is ripe for misunderstanding, avoidance of tough issues, heated conflict, and domineering by a few members. Coalitions use several strategies to make decision making run more smoothly. One strategy is to have a clear, well-understood process for how decisions get made. In smaller, like-minded coalitions this may be by simple consensus reached through occasional meetings or telephone calls. For larger and more diverse coalitions, the decision-making process must be more structured. Who is authorized to decide what? What questions are left to the leader's discretion to decide? What matters are left in the hands of an executive committee? What questions are so important that they must be brought to a vote of the entire coalition? Who controls the funds if there are any? Who decides how the coalition will respond quickly to a delicate media call, a proposed legislative amendment, or a compromise offer from an opponent? By having a clear understanding of all these issues in advance, coalitions stand a better chance of avoiding divisive misunderstandings about decision making in the midst of their work.

Coalitions also need to be keenly sensitive to the internal politics and needs of each of the member groups. Some organizations can make decisions fast. Others, which have a broad membership base (the PTA, League of Women Voters, labor unions) may have a long and cumbersome internal decision-making process that makes it difficult or impossible to can't move quickly. Coalition members have to be sensitive to all the constraints their partners must deal with, including the messages, images, and tactics with which they can be associated.

As the leader of a consumer/health coalition campaign in California in the 1980s, working to win birth-defect-warning labels on alcoholic beverages, I wanted desperately to take public action against state lawmakers who had pledged their support for our bill during election season and then reneged on that promise later under direct pressure from the liquor lobby. I tried in vain to persuade my coalition allies that we should make use of a new public relations prop we had just purchased for Consumers Union, a six-foot-long, pointing "finger of shame." I wanted to load the finger into a truck and take it on a tour to the offending lawmakers' local offices, with television cameras in tow. Several of my coalition allies, especially several church organizations, explained that the tactic was just too theatrical for them to join in. Since unity was key, we put the finger back in its storage closet. As an alternative, we held a news conference featuring the local Methodist bishop, who scolded the lawmakers as "flipfloppers," a tactic that probably worked better anyway.

Coalition partners should be clear with each other about this kind of internal constraints. It is not always easy to reconcile different limitations among diverse coalition members, but when the decision-making process fails to do so, the coalition risks blowing itself apart. Coalition leaders play an important role in helping the coalition address hard questions in a smooth way. In both formal meetings and in informal conversations, effective coalition leaders listen carefully for potential points of conflict and for potential common ground. By proposing potential solutions and listening carefully to members' reactions, coalition leaders can steadily move the members toward closure and consensus on the key issues before them.

Communication

Information sharing and communication are another important part of coalition work. Some of this happens in meetings, which need to be well-organized and not overused. Much of the communication in a coalition happens informally, as the leaders call and visit with coalition members to discuss the coalition's work and keep participants informed. In the coalitions I have led, I have always found it essential to check in with people, informally, by phone on an ongoing basis, especially if there has been any tension within the coalition or if we are facing an especially difficult strategic challenge. People will share things with you one-on-one (complaints, suggestions, advice) that they won't offer in formal meetings, information that is crucial for coalition leaders to hear.

A great deal of coalition communication is also conveyed in writing, through fax alerts, newsletter mailings, and e-mail distribution, for example. Written communication needs to be done thoughtfully, especially when aimed at grassroots organizations. Coalition members often complain about being bombarded with too many faxes and being given advocacy information that doesn't fit their needs. Alerts or other notices to coalition members should be used sparingly and only when updates are most important. If an action is requested, coalition leaders should make that request specific and clear. They should give members a clear sense of how that action (letter writing, calls, turning out for an event) directly serves the coalition's goals. That information should also be appropriate in form and language for the audience involved. "We need information that we can present to members," explained Maggie Bowman of Senior Action Network in San Francisco. "[Sometimes] it almost takes a policy analyst to translate the information."[7]

Organizing the Work

Ultimately, the purpose of a coalition is getting work done—lobbying, media work, public actions, and other strategies. Effective coalitions divide that work up clearly, identifying the tasks to be done and matching each with the coalition members that have the right mix of organizational resources (staff, volunteers, experience, contacts) to carry it out. Ideally, these work assignments give each member group just enough responsibility (neither too little nor too much) and the right kind of responsibility. Accountability is also crucial. When the work is divided, each group should make a specific commitment about what it will do and by when, with their progress checked by the coalition leaders on a regular basis. When important projects start to fall through the cracks, the coalition needs to get the member organization some help or reassign the task to a group that can handle it. Many larger or permanent coalitions hire staff to carry out the coalition's work.

Dealing with Tensions and Conflict

Building and managing effective coalitions is not only about organizing the work involved but also about dealing with the chemistry between the people and organizations involved. Coalitions that gather together a wide variety of organizations, interests, and personalities are fertile ground for tension and conflict. Sometimes conflict arises over strategy, tactics, or message. Tensions erupt between those who favor compromise and those who don't, and between newcomers and old hands. Coalitions get into fights about who is and who is not doing their share of the work and over who is getting credit for that work. Organizations and people alike can bring in old rivalries that don't have anything to do with the coalition or the issue, but get acted out there anyway. Diverse coalitions also bring in issues about race, class, and gender that affect the coalition and its chemistry. All the while, the coalition's opposition may be actively working to take advantage of those tensions, to divide and conquer it.

Tensions such as these are inherent in coalition work. The goal should not be to squelch them (which is usually impossible anyway) but to manage them, by addressing constructively the issues involved and not letting conflict get so out of hand that conflict becomes all that the coalition is about. Having clarity about the coalition's goals and decision-making process, and the rights and responsibilities of the coalition members, helps, by lessening the potential for misunderstandings. It also helps to pay careful attention to the goals of each of the participating individuals and organizations. Are there some specific ways to make sure that each gets the public credit it needs—for example, through media exposure, or recognition by lawmakers? Are there some ways the coalition can also give the participating groups and individuals opportunities to expand their experiences and contacts in ways that will encourage them to deepen their involvement and commitment?

Where tensions exist that need to be worked through, coalitions are wise to make specific room to put those issues on the table. By discussing those tensions or potential tensions early on, coalitions reduce the chance that they will pop up later, in the middle of an advocacy campaign, or in a public hearing or news conference, when they could be far more damaging. A national Citizen Labor Energy Coalition working for an alternative energy policy almost fell apart when, at its founding meeting, several key organizations demanded that the coalition take a position in support of nuclear power, directly contrary to the stance of the environmental groups involved. One coalition member explained, "At the moment when passions were at their highest, we adjourned the meeting, brought the competing forces together in a small room, locked the door, and spent two hours reaching an agreement [for the coalition to take no position, pro or con, on nuclear power]."[8]

Issues that don't get worked out by the coalition but remain major issues for a number of members will get raised over and over again in indirect and usually unconstructive ways until they are finally addressed. Often, addressing such issues directly can help a coalition strategically. No one group or person has a complete perspective on what might work best to advance the issue. The best advocacy strategy usually comes from a synthesis of many ideas. On the other hand, once an issue that is a source of tension has been raised, discussed adequately, and resolved, coalitions need to practice the difficult discipline of not allowing the same coalition members to bring that same issue up over and over again. Sometimes a coalition must make hard choices about how much conflict it can survive.

Again, the coalition's leaders play a crucial part in keeping a positive chemistry in the coalition. They do this by checking in with people after meetings to find out what didn't get said, by giving people praise for their contributions, and by working to make each participant's involvement personal, not just intellectual or institutional. Leaders also play an important role in helping new groups and people who come into the coalition feel as if they are full participants.

Ultimately, the best way to address tension and conflict in a coalition is to build trust by through creating genuine connections between the people involved. Another coalition I helped form while working with Consumers Union took aim at abuses by health insurers against people with chronic illnesses. At one of our earliest meetings we brought together a group that included two well-dressed, upper class women from the Diabetes Association and a gay man, dressed in black leather, from ACT-UP. The discomfort in the room was obvious and continued up until the moment when the man from ACT-UP interrupted a strategy discussion to announce, "Hold on, wait a minute! I think I'm channeling Madonna!" The room broke into laughter, breaking the tension as well. In the end these people and their organizations became solid allies.

Human relations are easier to build than institutional ones, and personal trust, built up over time, is the oil between groups that keeps a coalition running smoothly. These relations between coalition members are built in many ways—by working together over a long period, by celebrating victories together, by laughing together, and by taking the time to listen to one another, one on one, about the organizational or personal issues that people are dealing with in doing the work. Negotiating over power, credit, strategy, compromise, and other issues is a delicate and ongoing process throughout a coalition's life. If those people-to-people relationships are built well at the start, trust is also built, and those negotiations become easier over time.

THE END—AND AFTER

Few coalitions are permanent. Most have a birth, a life, and a time to end. The fact that a coalition has run its course doesn't mean that it or its leaders have failed; more likely it has just served its purpose. Where coalitions have been organized around a specific objective, the time for the coalition to end is often obvious, such as a victory won or a loss that leads participants to decide to move to a different battle. Coalitions that try to linger on past their time usually see their participants drift away to other, more productive activist projects.

Yet, while the formal coalition may fade away, the connections between the people and organizations within the coalition do not necessarily fade. In fact, many continue to grow, and those same coalitions get resurrected in a different configuration on other issues. One of the side effects of coalition work is that people start to enjoy working together and organizations begin to teach one another about related issues. The coalition originally assembled to campaign for alcohol-related-birth-defect warnings in California later converted itself into a new coalition that won new alcohol and drug recovery services for pregnant women. After that, many of the groups in the coalition joined with an entirely new set of health advocates to campaign successfully for legislation to expand public prenatal care. The bonds and connections that are created in one coalition often march on, reappearing in others coalitions and on other issues, for many years after.

CHAPTER TEN

Messages and Media

Democracy's Megaphones

If you don't exist in the media, you don't exist."

—DANIEL SCHORR[1]

How much influence does the media have on what our democracy decides and delivers? As the media wizard Tony Schwartz writes, "God-like, the media can change the course of a war, bring down a President or a King, elevate the lowly and humiliate the proud, by directing the attention of millions on the same event and in the same manner."[2] It is through the media that we form much of our public and political opinion. It is through the media that politicians, power brokers, and movement leaders interpret and influence the political winds. During the Vietnam War, public opinion and policy were shaped by media images of dead soldiers being carried away from far-off jungles. During the historic debate over President Clinton's health care reform proposals, public opinion and policy were shaped by the insurance industry's paid "Harry and Louise" ads against those proposals.

It is precisely because the media does wield so much power in our democracy that we need to understand how television, radio, and print journalism operate and how we can shape and influence the kind of coverage each offers. Taking public action is about being able to communicate with large numbers of people, and the media is our chief instrument for doing so.

DEVELOPING YOUR MEDIA STRATEGY

"Media advocacy," like all aspects of public advocacy, must be strategic. You need a clear sense of your objectives, of whom you need to reach and move, and a plausible plan for how to do that. The development of an effective media strategy revolves around several questions.

What Are You Trying to Accomplish?

We try to get media coverage for many different reasons, and since the strategy for each can be very different, it is important to be clear from the start about what it is you are trying to achieve. In some cases the goal is simply to raise public awareness about an issue. Planned Parenthood sponsored a series of high-profile newspaper ads to promote awareness about teen pregnancy and create a general public climate more sympathetic to its work on the issue. The San Francisco Council on Homelessness had the same goals in mind when it sponsored a series of bus shelter posters featuring photographs and quotes of homeless people. An effort like this is often a precursor to more pointed media work aimed at supporting a specific political agenda.

Other media advocacy efforts aim at moving people to take some specific action: to stop smoking, to vote a certain way on a ballot proposition, to show up at a community hearing, to get a mammogram, to switch to public transit. Using the media like a massive public address system, groups are able to nudge thousands, if not millions, of people to take actions that range from purely personal to very political. Media work is also an essential part of putting pressure on public officials. Journalist Walter Lippmann once described the media as "the beam of a searchlight that moves relentlessly about, bringing one episode and another out of the darkness and into vision."[3] Nothing moves politicians and political institutions more swiftly than when an issue comes into that clear public light. Like moths drawn to a lit bulb, they can't resist it.

In other cases, the main goal of media work is to promote your own organization, to help it become more powerful simply by being more visible. Every time you carry out a successful media event, get covered in an article, get an opinion piece published in your local paper, have your face on television or your voice on radio, political leaders, journalists, and community leaders take notice. Again, it is important to be clear which of these is your goal for media work. It may well be a combination of more than one.

Who Is Your Audience?

Once your goal is clear, whom do you need to reach and move in order to achieve it? Is your audience the general public? Is it women? Is it parents with children? Is it a specific ethnic group? If your target audience is a public official or political institution, then which one? I once waged a media campaign aimed at an audience of just one person. In 1990, California's then-Superintendent of Schools, Bill Honig, who also owned a wine-making business, announced his opposition to a state alcohol-tax initiative. As the health issues advocate for Consumers Union (and a backer of the measure), my goal was to let Mr. Honig know that his opposition would not play well with voters. The next day he awoke to his photo and an article in the *Sacramento Bee*, with the message, "Bill Honig the alcohol maker is using his position as Superintendent of Schools to be a front for the booze lobby."[4] Mr. Honig never publicly mentioned his opposition to the proposal again.

What Message Do They Need to Hear?

Knowing your audiences, what message can you deliver, simply and repeatedly, that will move them? The message might primarily appeal to their sense of right and wrong, "There are too many handguns and too many kids losing their lives to this epidemic." It might appeal instead to their sense of political self-interest, "More than 25,000 people have signed these petitions calling for gun control and we are waiting to hear what our senator has to say." Given the people you are trying to move, what headline will most help you?

Who Do They Need to Hear It From?

Almost as important as your message is who delivers it. Who has the most credibility and persuasive power with your target audience? When activists were fighting the auto insurance industry on a California ballot initiative to lower insurance rates, they enlisted Ralph Nader to be their messenger, which immediately communicated to voters which side was fighting for consumers. Public efforts to draw attention to the tragedy of drunk driving never caught fire until Candy Lightner, the mother of a young girl killed by a drunk driver, started Mothers Against Drunk Driving (MADD) and became its public symbol and spokesperson. The messengers you put up front symbolize the campaign and they need to be individuals or organizations that have pull with the people you are trying to reach.

Which Medium Should You Use to Reach Them?

Each major form of media has its own strengths and weaknesses as a tool for delivering a public message. Which media is the most likely to reach the audiences you need? Which is most likely to cover your story the way you would like it to be covered? In the case of paid advertising, which can you afford?

Television

By far, the most effective way to reach large numbers of people is through television. It is the medium from which most people get their news. It brings powerful images right into our living rooms—grieving parents at Columbine High School, homeless families sleeping on freezing sidewalks—images that connect with people at an emotional level. On the other hand, television is also usually the hardest medium to gain access to. A local thirty-minute newscast, after commercials, sports, and weather, only has about twelve minutes left for hard news, and the stories that get covered are generally the most sensational. If your news conference, protest, event, or announcement can't compete with murder, sex, or scandal, you probably won't make it onto the air. Access to cable television is somewhat easier, though it draws a far smaller audience.

Radio

Although it's not as emotionally powerful as television, radio still reaches huge audiences and is far easier to gain access to. Radio is our daily background music, as we drive to work, make dinner, or wash the dishes. Most cities and towns have dozens of stations, each one with hours of airtime to fill, often with a substantial part of it dedicated to news. Radio also allows you to target your audiences—young people, Latinos, women, and others—based on the type of station. Getting radio attention can often be as simple as picking up the phone and offering an interview.

Newspapers

Much has been written about the declining number of people who read newspapers each year. Even so, good print coverage is remains a mainstay of most advocacy campaigns. While not everyone reads the morning paper, the people who do may include exactly those who you are trying to influence—your city council member, state legislator, local journalists, business and community leaders, and others. Getting covered in the paper, whether as news, in an editorial, or with a guest opinion piece you write yourself, gives you a record, a clipping you can share far and wide with people who may not have read it when it first ran. More important, what is covered by television and radio usually begins with what is in the newspaper. The first thing radio and television producers do each day is look at the morning paper for possible stories. As an advocate in San Francisco, I knew that any time my name appeared in the *Examiner* or the *Chronicle* on an issue, I could expect follow-up calls from television and radio stations wanting to talk about the same story.

The Internet

More recently, the Internet has become an increasingly powerful tool for advocacy. Through e-mail, the Web, list-serves, and other Internet tools, activists are able to leapfrog right over established media to get their messages out to thousands, even millions, of people. These same tools have also given us powerful new ways to take action, applying pressure on public and corporate officials from the comfort of our keyboards. See chapter 13 for the strategies for using these new tools.

What Type of Coverage Will Best Get Your Message Delivered?

Generally, advocates want their issues to be covered as a news story. While news coverage is important, many other types of coverage serve advocacy efforts well. Editorial support builds attention and credibility and helps spin the issue your way. Newspaper columnists, who often have a larger readership than the regular news, are another point of entry for coverage and have greater latitude in what they can cover. The most effective type of coverage for your cause may not be news, editorials, or columnists, but a feature article or broadcast segment spotlighting one person's story. A Stanford Research Institute study tested how people responded when handed an information packet containing a news article, a summary of a government report, a community newsletter, a letter from a lawmaker, and a feature story. Of those surveyed, 93 percent first turned to the feature story.[5] Radio and television talk shows are still another vehicle for attention. Effective media campaigns use a mixture of all these types of coverage.

Finally, an effective media strategy is not set in stone. It should remain fluid, revisited and reworked at different points throughout the campaign. Have your audiences changed? Is your message working, or does it needs to be revised? Are

---

THE STRATEGY BEHIND THE MESSAGE

"I Thought I Was Covered"

In early 1990, the leaders of California's fledgling health advocacy movement came together to see if they could meld their diverse interests and agendas into one unified public message. Coming from AIDS and other disease groups, organized labor, consumer organizations, nurses unions, and many other corners, their health care concerns ranged from long-term care, to the cancellation of benefits for people who became ill, to the screening out of patients with pre-existing conditions.

The advocates had several hard strategy knots to untangle. First, they needed to find a way to interest middle-class consumers in health care reform. While the problems for the poor were more obvious, reform efforts were stalled politically until middle-class consumers also became aware of the dangers they faced. Public opinion research, however, showed clearly that most middle-class consumers assumed (wrongly) that if they ever really needed their health coverage it would be there. Second, advocates also needed to build the case for public intervention in the private health care market, a move opposite the public tide for less government in general.

After a great deal of discussion and planning, the groups settled on a powerfully simple message: "I thought I was covered." Delivered by people like Rose Hughes, who had to fight with her insurance company for her son's cancer care, the message linked together all of the different issues the groups were concerned with and spoke directly to the middle class's stake in health reform. "Anyone could identify with how horrific it would be to experience a family illness and realize that you or your loved ones weren't covered," recalled Lois Salisbury, one of the reform movement's leaders. "The slogan also implicitly made insurance companies the enemy, which was strategically and analytically, the right target."

With a careful media strategy, health care advocates pushed the "I thought I was covered" theme and its variations for two years, helping contribute to the atmosphere that made health care a leading issue in the 1992 presidential race and President Clinton's main agenda item as he took office. Echoes of that same theme continue today, keeping health care reform a top issue across the nation.

---

there some news opportunities or unexpected barriers to coverage you didn't anticipate? These are all questions to ask, re-ask, and re-ask again.

DESIGNING YOUR MESSAGE

Rose Hughes, the mother of a young son diagnosed with cancer, was dealing with every parent's worst nightmare, painful treatments, repeated hospitalizations, and not knowing whether her son would survive or die. She discovered, however, that fighting her son's disease was not her only nightmare. Just when her family needed it most, her health insurer started slapping limits on her health coverage. Later, as an activist for health insurance reform, Rose would deliver the same message over and over again to reporters as she told her story, "Like most people, I thought I was covered."

A powerful, well-told, strategic message is the core of any strong advocacy campaign. It is your story, your sheet music, the words and the theme that you use to create your public argument on the issue. What is the problem? What is the solution? Why should people care? All the media attention in the world will do you little good and have little public impact if it does not deliver the right message. While the most powerful public messages may sound simple, in fact, developing them takes a good deal of time and thought, as well as attention to these basic rules:

Develop a Message that Genuinely Appeals to Your Audience

Effective media messages need to strike what Tony Schwartz called "responsive chords," the values, emotions, and beliefs that people already possess, not just those we might wish people had. This is a challenge for many advocacy campaigns. "What is an emotional hit for the activists doesn't necessarily move other people," warns media consultant Leo McElroy.[6] The way to begin is to find out how your audiences already feel about the issue. Sometimes you pick up this intelligence informally, by talking to people who don't necessarily share your point of view and by listening carefully to what they think and why. Focus groups and polling are more formal tools for gauging public opinion, employing much larger samples and more scientific methods. This does not mean that you should simply pander to people you disagree with, but it is important to understand the views of those you need to convince, and communicate with them accordingly. For example, if you are on television being interviewed about alternatives to jail for nonviolent crimes, you might get more people to listen to you if you begin, "We all agree that violent criminals should be prevented from putting the rest of us at risk, but . . . "

Strong media messages also need to appeal to people's hearts, not just their heads. "Unless you grab the public's emotions, you don't give them a reason to engage intellectually," says McElroy. We connect with and respond to public messages and stories that speak to what we value—fairness, justice, safety, family, community. People respond to the mother battling her son's cancer and her insurance company because they can see in her their own fears and feel the anger they would feel if that were their family.

Frame Your Issue to Your Maximum Advantage

Every teenager is familiar with the concept of "framing" or "spinning" a message. It is the tactic we used to focus our parents on the A we got in English as opposed to the D we brought home in math. In the public arena, the principle of message framing is the same—making your case in a way that puts your position in the best light possible and your opponents' in the worst. When President Reagan first wanted to put missiles in outer space he called the plan the "Strategic Defense Initiative." His opponents ridiculed it as "Star Wars." Community advocates pushing limits on local gun dealers framed their message, "There are 18 times more gun dealers in California than McDonalds restaurants," a description with a lot more public punch than simply saying there are 240,000.[7]

Robert Reich, the former secretary of labor, has written that Americans tend to interpret, or frame, public events through four different "public myths" that resonate powerfully with the fears, hopes and imagery built into our national culture. The first of these he calls "the mob at the gates," which plays to public fears about outsiders threatening our way of life. In ways both subtle and overt, social conservatives use this imagery to speak to issues and fan public fears on issues such as gay rights, youth crime, and immigration. The only way to counter the image of the nameless mob is to replace it with real stories about real people (such as specific immigrant families and their struggles). A second theme, "rot at the top," strikes a strong public chord about the arrogance of power. It is used by conservatives to attack government (Ronald Reagan's "beltway bureaucrats") and by progressives to attack big corporations (Ralph Nader's message of "corporate greed"). A third theme, "the triumphant individual," speaks to deep American values of individualism and liberty, a chord plucked often to make the case for keeping government out of the marketplace and the nation's economic life. In contrast, the final theme, "the benevolent community," speaks to equally powerful values about how Americans work together to provide for the common good, for example, by providing public health coverage to poor children.[8]

These themes reflect ways in which people connect viscerally with certain issues. They can be used by both sides in public discourse . Advocates crusading for new restrictions on tobacco marketing, for example, knew that tobacco giants would talk about "meddling federal bureaucrats." Focus group research told the advocates that the antibureaucrat theme was a powerful one, but not as strong as the countertheme of "protecting our children from the tobacco industry," a message that resonated directly with Reich's theme of "rot at the top." To frame an advocacy message effectively, it is important to look at the debate in the widest terms, talking about issue s in ways that speak to people's deepest values and most common fears and taking into clear account the framing and arguments you will face from your opposition.

Make Effective Use of Symbols and Images

Messages are also made more powerful when they become embodied in people and other symbols that grab attention and support. At the birth of the U.S. civil rights movement, Rosa Parks became such a symbol when she refused to give up her seat on a Montgomery bus. Environmentalists fighting against the destruction of the last ancient redwoods on California's northern coast made lumber baron Charles Hurwitz a negative public symbol, with his name becoming synonymous with corporate greed. During the 1988 California election battle over insurance rates, consumer activists created a visual confrontation to serve as a symbol and draw public attention to the well-financed lies being told by the insurance industry in its campaign advertising. On a sunny preelection morning, consumer leaders drove a truck loaded with cow manure up Los Angeles's famed Wilshire Boulevard, parked it in front of the headquarters of Farmers Insurance, and hand delivered a bucket of the manure to the guard at the front door. Bashing the industry's ads as "just plain bull," the stunt made the evening news all over the state, a powerful public image of the two sides of the campaign.

Symbols and imagery are important even in language. In one of their famous presidential debates in 1960, Richard Nixon and John Kennedy were both asked about the state of the nation's economy. Nixon spoke in statistics, about the growth in gross national product. Kennedy spoke in images, of a little girl he had met in West Virginia who took home part of her school lunch in order to help feed her destitute family. Especially in the television age, people tend to think in pictures, and public language, whether used by presidential candidates or community advocates, is most powerful when it conjures up clear, compelling images in people's minds.

Lead With "Sound Bites" and Add the Facts as Time Allows

Typical media advocacy messages include a lot of different information, not all of which you can or should try to deliver at any one time. There is a discipline to speaking through the media, communicating just as much information as can be absorbed and nothing more, separating out the key themes from the more cumbersome details. The lead of any media message is the "sound bite," a simple and easily repeated quote that captures the essence of your message in a sentence or two. Whether speaking to a reporter on the phone, holding a news conference, or putting out a press release, one or two simple sentences are usually all that will get used. The sounds bites we develop must be simple and pack a punch.

Mary Leigh Blek, a mother who lost her son to gun violence, made the connection between her son's death and the handgun industry, telling reporters, "Why do we tolerate junk guns? The gun used to kill Mathew was probably manufactured in Southern California, Mathew's own backyard."[9] Claudia Garate, a Chilean immigrant testifying at a United Nations hearing on the abuse suffered by immigrant women from their employers, explained her experience this way, "For thirteen months I was not allowed to speak to anyone, I was like a slave. Even if you are legal they take advantage of you."[10]

Effective sound bites not only talk about the problem but also introduce the solution. Teresa Gallegos, a parent advocate from San Francisco, wanted to make the connection between public welfare cuts and the need for more park recreation programs. "Children will need park services more than ever as parents receiving government aid enter the work force."[11] Then, as time and attention allow, add the basic facts that add bring more depth. "Guns kill 37,000 people each year in the U.S. and California leads the nation both in gun deaths and in gun production."[12] "Immigrants pay $90 billion per year in taxes and receive only $5 billion in welfare.[13] Then wrap up with your specific pitch—for a new law restricting handgun sales, for legal protection for immigrant workers, for a 25 percent budget increase in park and recreation programs for children.

The key is simplicity and repetition. In a media world full of so much noise and so many stories competing for public attention, your best chance of getting your message heard is to make it simple and to repeat it over and over and over again. Ultimately, a strong message incorporates all these elements—a sense of your audience, framing that works to your best advantage, powerful symbols, pithy sound bites, and facts pulled together to tell a compelling public story.

ATTRACTING MEDIA ATTENTION

Above all else, there is one basic rule for getting media coverage—do as much of the media's job for them as possible. To attract attention from the media, think like a journalist. Make your story one that journalists will want to cover, and make your story as easy as possible for them to cover. "If you can save newspapers work, they love you," says Daniel Sneider, a veteran editor at the *San Jose Mercury News*.[14] It is love of this kind that wins you media attention.

Make Your Story Newsworthy

Newspapers and television and radio stations are looking for what will attract readers, viewers, and listeners (for each, the key to increased advertising revenue). Your story is in competition with dozens of others happening on the same day, from shootings to political scandals to earthquakes. If you expect to squeeze your issue into the morning paper or onto the evening news, you have to be worth covering. Four "news hooks" are standard for making a story newsworthy—make it new, make it human, create a conflict, or link it to something else big that is already in the news. Even better, do all four at once.

News is new: new numbers about children living in poverty, a new charge against a public official, new revelations about a corporation's pollution practices, a new lawsuit. Reporters and editors ask, "Why is it news today, but not yesterday and not tomorrow?" News is also about people, human stories that take dry facts and bring them to life (the story of one mother losing a child to a drunk driver). Adding a celebrity presence or angle can also bring major attention to a story that would otherwise go unnoticed. Labor rights activists struggled for years to draw media attention to the sweatshop labor practices lurking behind large U.S. clothing labels. The issue finally grabbed the public spotlight when activists, testifying before Congress, revealed that Kathy Lee Gifford's clothing line was produced by abused child labor.

Public conflict is another major media draw. In April 1998, human rights and labor groups made headlines by filing a lawsuit against Nike over its sweatshop factories in Vietnam. The story was covered by ABC, NBC, CBS, CNN, Fox, the *New York Times*, *USA Today,* and many others. Long before the case was ever heard

---

HOOKS THAT MAKE A STORY "NEWSWORTHY"

✓**Newness:** new announcement, new information, new political or public support, new action

✓**Human Interest:** personal stories, celebrities, injustice, irony

✓**Conflict:** taking on a public official or a corporate power, filing a lawsuit, staging a protest

✓**Piggy-Backing on the News:** local angle on a national/state story, linking the story to a holiday, milestone, anniversaries

---

in court, the media attention forced the shoe giant to announce new minimum wages and safety protections in its Asian factories.[15]

The media feeds as well on stories that piggyback on other major stories making news. O. J. Simpson's trial sent reporters scrambling for local stories about domestic violence and potential solutions. The massacre of students at Columbine High School opened up space for advocates to raise issues about guns and youth violence. The anniversaries of major events such as these are also a hook for news stories, as are holidays. The California Council of Churches used Christmas as an opportunity to draw media attention to cuts in food stamp benefits for the poor. Citing large increases in the number of poor people lining up at church soup kitchens, the Council chided legislators in a Christmas Eve opinion article, just as they were returning home for their own family feasts. "Another group of Californians will sit down at a holiday table that is empty—the direct result of the food stamp cuts that lawmakers made before they left the State Capitol last September."

Sometimes your opponents give you the hook you need for media coverage. In 1996, then- California Attorney General Dan Lungren decided to execute a pre-election raid of California organizations dispensing medicinal marijuana, hoping to drum up public opposition to a voter initiative that would have legalized marijuana for medical use. Instead, the news hook of the raids sent journalists scurrying for stories about people using the drug for medical purposes. Many of these stories featured the elderly and frail describing how marijuana was the only option they had for relieving their pain. The result was a huge increase in public support for making such use legal and led to a victory for the ballot measure.

Build Relationships with Reporters

When reporters are assigned to cover a story, the first people they usually call are the people they know. Building relationships with reporters, editors, and other journalists is one of the most important things that citizen advocates can do increase their media access and exposure. "What's important is that I have a contact so that I know who to call when I do write something," said *Los Angeles Times* columnist George Skelton.[16] Effective advocates work hard to be that contact.

Begin with the reporter contacts you already have. Show them that you are a source of swift, reliable information and that you know how to package that information in a compelling, summarized way that journalists can use. Establish yourself also as an invaluable link to other people with personal stories and expertise on the issue. An analysis I once conducted for the advocacy group Health Access showed that more than half the coverage the group received came from returning calls from reporters. The most important thing the group had done, from a media advocacy standpoint, was to establish itself as an indispensable source.

It is also important for advocates to build relationships with journalists even when not dealing with them or pitching them on a specific story. Send reporters a short note if you liked a story they wrote or aired. Find opportunities to have casual conversations with them, over coffee, lunch, or a drink. Informal contacts with journalists give you a chance to plant ideas for potential stories, to find out more about the kinds of stories they are interested in, and to expand your media connections. Too often, we look at newspapers, television, and radio stations as big institutions to be pummeled with news releases. Actually, they are made up of scores of people, each one a potential access point for coverage.

Media Materials—The Tools of the Trade

Successful media advocacy work requires a specific set of tools and materials, each of which needs to be developed thoughtfully and strategically. It is also important to plan and develop these materials as far in advance as possible to avoid last-minute scrambling.

Media Lists

These lists should include all the main contact people (reporters and editors) at local newspapers and television and radio stations, as well as reporters and editors who have covered your issue in the past and those with whom you have developed good relationships. For each, you should have a mailing address, fax number, phone number, and, when possible, an e-mail address. Advocacy groups that carry out extensive media work often keep one larger master list and then smaller lists broken down by issue topics. Media lists also have to be maintained, always adding new names and noting changes at various media outlets.

News Advisory

This is the tool used to give the media advance notice of an event that you want them to cover. It should give reporters and editors enough information to understand what the event is and why it is newsworthy, but not so much information that it delivers the details of the story. The format should be kept simple: who, what, when, where, along with reliable contact phone numbers. The more the advisory can identify participants with credibility and media drawing power (such as celebrities and officials), the better. As a rule, news advisories should be only one page and should go out to the media two to three days before the event, followed up with phone calls.

Consumers Union
Publisher of Consumer Reports

ADVISORY

FOR IMMEDIATE RELEASE:
Monday, September 18, 2000

CONTACT:
Michael McCauley – 415-431-6747

CONSUMERS UNION TO URGE CALIFORNIA ATTORNEY GENERAL TO INVESTIGATE WHETHER CRIMINAL CHARGES SHOULD BE FILED AGAINST BRIDGESTONE/FIRESTONE AND FORD

Company Executives May Have Violated California Law If They Failed to Notify State Officials Once They Learned of Tire Defects

WHAT: News Conference to explain Consumers Union's call for California Attorney General Bill Lockyer to investigate whether company officials at Bridgestone/Firestone and Ford may have violated California law by failing to properly notify state officials about dangerous tire defects. If an investigation determines the companies violated California's unique product defect notification law, company executives could be subject to criminal prosecution.

On August 9, Bridgestone/Firestone announced the recall of its *P235/75R15 Firestone ATX, ATX II*, and *Wilderness AT* tires. The tires have been recalled because of tread separations that have been blamed for dozens of fatal crashes. Officials at both companies have maintained that they were not aware of the scope of the tire defects until shortly before they announced the recall. However, evidence is mounting that officials at Bridgestone/Firestone and Ford may have been aware of these dangerous defects long before the tire recall was announced.

WHEN: Tuesday, September 19, 2000
10:30 am

WHERE: Consumers Union
1535 Mission Street
San Francisco, CA 94103
415-431-6747

###

Consumers Union, publisher of Consumer Reports, is an independent, nonprofit testing and information organization, serving only the consumer. We are a comprehensive source of unbiased advice about products and services, personal finance, health, nutrition, and other consumer concerns. Since 1936, our mission has been to test products, inform the public, and protect consumers.

News Releases

The news release is your story, written just as you'd like to see the article in the next day's paper. The headline and a short first paragraph should quickly frame your basic message, "Consumers Union, the nonprofit publisher of Consumer Reports, called on California Attorney General Bill Lockyer today to investigate whether executives of Bridgestone/Firestone and Ford violated a California law by failing to alert state officials about dangerous tire defects in a timely manner." After adding just enough additional detail to cover the basics, the release should hammer home the message with a quote, "This case reminds us of the need for greater accountability when corporations knowingly sell dangerous, defective products to consumers." The rest of the release should, briefly, lay out other important details and history and, if appropriate, a listing of supporters. The writing should be dynamic, with short crisp sentences and verbs that convey action, "demanded, warned, insisted, rejected, praised, lambasted." The release should be short (two to three pages maximum), and should always list a release date as well as clear contact names and phone numbers at the top of the first page. It should hit the highlights of the story, putting more detailed facts in the background material that you'll distribute along with the release.

Fact Sheets and Other Background Material

Reporters are grateful for summary materials that lay out key facts that they can use to round out a story. To make this material useful, it needs to be simple and accessible, allowing harried journalists to skim it quickly for what they need. Fact sheets are the most basic of these materials, usually no more than one page, and listing in bullet form five to ten key facts about a topic, covering both the problem you are tackling and the solution you are proposing. During the 1998 debate over welfare reform in California, the San Francisco Homeless Prenatal Program prepared a background sheet for reporters called "Esther's Budget," which showed the actual monthly income and expenses of a mother of three trying to survive on $1,023 per month. Most reporters had never seen this real-life information before.

Another useful format for presenting your information is a "questions and answers" sheet or a "myths and facts" sheet. For example, "myth: immigrants take jobs away from American workers," followed by a citation from *Business Week* concluding otherwise. For more complicated issues, you might add reference papers or studies related to the issue but, again, giving journalists only the amount of material they can absorb and no more. To help build your credibility, you should also include a list of organizations supporting you. All the material you hand out to the media should be clearly titled at the top and should always include a contact name and phone number for follow-up.

Story Suggestions and Contacts

Another useful handout for reporters is a listing of specific story ideas along with the background information and contact names they need. Health Access, for

Publisher of Consumer Reports

NEWS

FOR IMMEDIATE RELEASE:
Tuesday, September 19, 2000

CONTACT:
Elisa Odabashian or Harry Snyder
415-431-6747

CONSUMERS UNION CALLS ON CALIFORNIA ATTORNEY GENERAL TO INVESTIGATE WHETHER CRIMINAL CHARGES SHOULD BE FILED AGAINST BRIDGESTONE/FIRESTONE & FORD

Company Executives May Have Violated California's Corporate Criminal Liability Act if They Failed to Notify State Officials Once They Learned About Tire Defects

SAN FRANCISCO – Consumers Union, the non-profit publisher of *Consumer Reports*, called on California Attorney General Bill Lockyer today to investigate whether executives of Bridgestone/Firestone and Ford violated a California law by failing to alert state officials about dangerous tire defects in a timely manner.

Under California's Corporate Criminal Liability Act, managers of businesses, including officers and executives, can face criminal prosecution for concealing dangers in products or workplace settings that could put consumers or workers at risk of death or injury if they fail to notify state officials within fifteen days of learning of the defects.

"This case once again reminds us of the need for greater accountability when corporations knowingly sell dangerous, defective products to consumers," said Harry Snyder, Senior Advocate for Consumers Union's West Coast Regional Office. "If company officials at Bridgestone/Firestone or Ford knew of the serious concealed dangers in these tires and failed to properly notify California officials about them, then they should face criminal prosecution."

On August 9, Bridgestone/Firestone announced the recall of its *P235/75R15 Firestone ATX, ATX II, and Wilderness AT* tires. The tires have been recalled because of tread separations that have been blamed for dozens of fatal crashes. Officials at both companies have maintained that they were not aware of the scope of the tire defects until shortly before they announced the recall. However, evidence is mounting that officials at Bridgestone/Firestone and Ford may have been aware of these dangerous defects long before the tire recall was announced.

For example, news accounts have indicated that Congressional investigators have internal documents obtained from Firestone detailing the company's damage and injury claims showing a high incidence of tire failure as early as 1997. Similarly, it has been reported that congressional investigators believe that Ford may have ignored trends in its own warranty data, which showed that the company had received claims for hundreds of defective tires between 1991 and 2000.

- more -

example, prepared a packet for reporters that offered specific story ideas under the "I Thought I Was Covered" theme, real stories about insurers canceling coverage. The packet included a set of fact sheets and the names and telephone numbers of insurance-company victims, nurses, doctors, consumer lawyers, and others ready to talk about the issue. Materials like these make your organization invaluable to journalists, a gatekeeper to the ideas and people that they need to get their work done.

A Web Site

A reporter friend of mine confessed to me recently, "When I get assigned a story, the first place I go to for information is the Web." The Internet is now a crucial information source for reporters where, with a few mouse clicks, they can get the basic background on an issue, see what other journalists have written about it, and identify organizations and people to contact for additional information and quotes. Having a basic Internet presence with an easy-to-use site is now an important part of media advocacy. Common Cause, for example, has a section on its Web site called "On Deadline? A Reporter's Guide to Money in Politics," which features a brief statement about whatever campaign the organization is currently active in, as well as quick links to press releases, studies, background papers, and other information reporters might be searching for. Smaller organizations don't have to offer something that elaborate, but posting your fact sheets and other background material is an important start.

Some organizations put their media materials into formal "press packets," giving journalists not only the information they need for the story they are working on but reference material they might keep for additional stories down the line. The materials you produce and give to reporters should be well done, easily digestible, proofread to perfection, and above all, always accurate. Even one mistake or wrong statistic that gets repeated up by a reporter can damage your credibility for years. For most advocacy efforts, the aim should be to provide materials that are professional and reliable, but not so slick that you lose the authenticity of being regular people instead of sounding like a fancy public relations firm.

TAKING ACTION TO MAKE NEWS

There are many activities you can use to try to get your message out and make the news. Which ones are right for any given advocacy effort depends on the audiences you are trying to reach, the newsworthiness of what you have to say, and what you have the capacity to pull off. The choice is, again, one of strategy.

Issuing a News Release

The simplest way to try to get covered is to send out a news release. A 1990 study of U.S. newspapers found that almost 40 percent of news reports originated with some kind of news release.[17] However, journalists also are bombarded with many, many more news releases than they can ever use, and whether yours gets used depends on how newsworthy journalists judge it to be. If you are announcing a sexual harassment lawsuit against your local member of Congress, your chances are good. If you are announcing Butterfly Appreciation Week, forget it. Assuming that your story is newsworthy, a faxed or mailed news release should be followed up with a phone call to the reporters and producers you think are most likely to be interested, whether because of previous coverage or a personal relationship. Most media outlets have a specific person whose job it is to assign stories to reporters, usually called the assignment editor, a good person with whom to cultivate a strong working relationship. He or she can be the key to getting your issue covered, especially if you don't already have a reporter you can turn to.

Holding a News Conference

If you are sure that what you have to say is newsworthy and you know you are going to need to deliver the same basic message to a half-dozen or more reporters, the best vehicle for doing so is a news conference. Pay careful attention to the timing, location, participants, and the materials you will hand out. Remember that reporters work on deadlines. Typically, reporters for morning newspapers will have to file their stories by four or five the afternoon before. Television reporters working on the evening news usually have to be in the studio editing their stories by two to three in the afternoon. Radio deadlines are more frequent, depending on how many times a day the station broadcasts news. Mid-morning is the best time for most press events. The day of the week is also important, with the start of the week usually slower for most reporters and a better time for news events. Friday is the worst day of the week to hold an event, with reporters busy producing stories for their Sunday editions.

For your location, think about convenience and visuals. Can reporters get to you easily? Can they find parking? Will they have to carry heavy cameras and equipment up stairs? Are there electrical outlets, space to set up tripods? More important for television, what kind of visuals does the location have? When MADD wanted to announce its "nickel per drink" alcohol tax bill in California, it held the news conference in the bar across the street from the state capitol, where reporters regularly met for drinks after work. The image of Candy Lightner, MADD's founder, sitting at a bar holding up a nickel and asking "Is five cents really too much to pay to protect our children's lives?" made TV news all over the state.

Ideally, at least one of the participants in your news conference should be someone with media drawing power, a well-known public official, activist, or celebrity. Other speakers should include someone who can give an overview of the issue, someone who can speak from personal experience, and someone who can answer any technical or legal questions. There should be no more than three to four speakers in all. Each should speak for no more than two or three minutes. You also should have available a set of informational handouts including a news release, fact sheet, and other background material. The whole news conference should last no more than thirty minutes, should start on time, and should leave ample opportunity for reporters to ask questions. After the news conference, it is important that your key spokespeople be easily available by phone for any reporters who have additional questions as they prepare their stories during the day. If there are reporters you expected to come who didn't, follow up with them by phone and make sure they get your materials.

Offering a Media Briefing

News conferences are aimed at getting coverage that day or the next. However, when you are dealing with an issue that is ongoing and involves a lot of information, it is often useful to offer reporters a background "issue briefing" that isn't tied to a specific news story you are pitching. Briefing sessions are an opportunity to increase reporters' general understanding of the issue, to help frame the issue your way, to plant your ideas for potential stories, and to establish you and your organization as a solid information source. Unlike a news conference, you do not need a specific news hook or story for that day, nor do you need a news release. However, as with news conferences, briefings should be scheduled to make them convenient to attend, and you should have a solid team of presenters and solid background materials to hand out.

Staging a "Media Event"

As advocate Diedre Kent writes, "You get in the news if you do something."[18] News releases and news conferences alone are usually not enough to get the media interested. Sometimes you need a rally, a protest, a march, a public confrontation, civil disobedience, a gimmick, something that makes journalists decide you are worth covering. MADD staged a candlelight vigil of parents on the lawn of the state capitol. ACT-UP, protesting price gouging by the makers of AIDS drugs, organized a protest aimed at shutting down Wall Street. Housing activists in San Francisco, trying to call attention to the lack of heat in low-income apartments, showed up at a county hearing with someone wearing a polar bear costume.

Especially with rallies or other big events, it is worth taking time to contact and work with reporters in advance. When California immigrant rights leaders were preparing an important state capitol rally of more than two thousand immigrants to protest welfare cuts in March 1997, they visited the week before with *Los Angeles Times* reporter Virginia Ellis to explain the event and its goals. "Often the best way to convince us that an event is a legitimate news story is to talk to us about it in advance, either by telephone or in person," says Ellis. "It provides us with a little more background on the event and gives us an opportunity to take the measure of the people who are staging it."[19] The advance work immigrants did with Ellis resulted in a major story and photograph of the event in the *Times* the following day.

In thinking about whether and how to stage some sort of event, confrontation, or gimmick to woo media interest, be strategic. Who is your audience and will your action move them in your direction, or will it cause them to harden their stance against you? Is it worth the work, or would something much simpler (a news conference or release) do the same job? Is what you are planning really newsworthy? As reporter Sabin Russell of the *San Francisco Chronicle* explains, "I think that people organizing demonstrations forget that you have a state of thirty million people, so two hundred people holding signs isn't that big . . . an event."[20] If you do decide to do an event, be sure to do your media homework first, planning carefully your timing, location, participants, and materials.

Releasing a Study or Report

In 1987, University of California at Davis physician Garn Wintemute used some simple state statistics to put a powerful public spotlight on the special risks that guns posed to children. Looking at state data, he reported that in six years more than eighty California children, from infants to fourteen-year-olds, had been accidentally shot and killed either by other children or themselves. His report, "When Children Shoot Children," drew broad newspaper and television coverage and helped contribute to a growing public consciousness about the need for gun laws.[21] Journalists have a fascination with studies that take a topic already deemed newsworthy and package together new information that sheds light on the issue. To make the news, reports don't need to be huge and complicated, just interesting and relevant to what's in the news. In 1996, the Center on Alcohol Advertising made headlines in *USA Today* and other papers across the country with a simple survey of 221 fourth and fifth graders, showing that more of the students could recognize the Budweiser frogs than Bugs Bunny.

"The news media seeks to cover 'what's new' and a report with the latest data or analysis of an issue can serve as a powerful hook for reporters," explains Amy Dominguez-Arms of the national advocacy group Children Now. "While the pitching of a report starts with the facts, we also try to give reporters ways to make the story more human and more local, such as by arranging interviews with local families that are directly affected by the issue."[22] It is helpful to give longer or more complicated reports to reporters several days in advance (with an implied agreement that the recipients will abide by the release date), giving them time to study the information, ask questions, and to plan their stories. Longer reports also need to include a brief executive summary and, as always, a well-crafted news release that frames the issue and gives it punch.

Pitching a Columnist

Newspaper and magazine columnists usually have some of the largest readerships in their publications; they also choose their stories in a different way. Regular beat reporters may have to produce a story every day or two, and their stories have to be news that day. Columnists have more freedom. They can usually write about what they want and express their own opinions. They also normally only need to produce two to three columns each week, and what they write about doesn't have to be breaking news. For all these reasons, columnists are good people to pitch your story to if you have something worthwhile to offer. Begin by tracking what your local columnists are interested in and whether they seem sympathetic to your basic views on issues (for example, a columnist who regularly praises Christian conservatives may be a good target for a pitch about homelessness but may not be your best audience for a gay rights issue). Approach a columnist as you would any reporter, making contact, framing your story briefly and in the most newsworthy way possible, and offering to provide more information.

Requesting a Supporting Editorial

Editorial support boosts your credibility and is one more vehicle for getting out your message. Most newspapers (as well as the relatively few radio and television stations that air editorials) will meet with community groups that want to request editorial support. These visits should be carefully planned in terms of who will participate, the arguments you want to make, and what materials you will bring with you. Three or four participants should be the maximum and, as in a news conference, this should include someone who can make your general case, someone who can speak about the issue in personal terms, and someone who has a mastery of any technical knowledge involved. The more participants who are from the local area, the better. You should research beforehand what the paper or station has written or said in the past about the issue, in both editorials and in the news section.

Writing Op-Ed Articles and Letters to the Editor

Advocates don't have to wait for reporters to cover their news; they also can publish their story themselves in the editorial pages of newspapers that have op-ed pages or publish letters to the editor. Op-ed pages are usually opposite the page on which most newspapers run their own editorials. These can come from well-known public figures and from private citizens who have something important to say. Publishing an op-ed article is an especially effective way to get your message out to policymakers, reporters, and other opinion leaders, who often pay special attention to this section. When ACT-UP staged its 1987 Wall Street protest, it also published an op-ed article the day before in the *New York Times*, explaining the reasons for the protest. Group members handed out copies to people on the street during the march.[23] How can you make your opinion article worthy of publication in the eyes of opinion editors? "What we are looking for is an article that has a real point to make, bite to it, a perspective that has not been made over and over again," explains James Boyd, deputy editorial page editor for the *Minneapolis Star Tribune*. "The better the writing and the more current the topic, the better."[24]

Shorter, but easier to get published, are letters to the editor. Usually a maximum of 250–300 words, these letters, like op-ed articles, give you a chance to communicate your message in public to public officials and others who pay close attention to opinion pages. Sometimes having a number of people and groups all write at once on a topic is a way to ensure that at least some get published. Following the defeat of an alcohol-birth defects warning bill in a California senate committee, the state leadership of MADD, Consumers Union, the PTA, the March of Dimes and others all wrote letters to the *Los Angeles Times*, naming the senators who had voted against them. Almost all of the letters were published.

Writes *San Francisco Chronicle* editorial page editor John Diaz, "Personally, I think the strongest letters are often among the shortest, which is why three years ago we added the frank phrase to our how-to-reach-us box, 'shorter letters have a better chance of publication.'" Like many editors, Diaz also advises letter writers to relate their submissions to what is in the news and to make their letters lively, thoughtful, and provocative, but to keep the tone civil. "Save the screaming for talk radio."[25] Letters should make their points clearly and quickly and should always include the writer's name, address, and telephone number. Most papers publish on their editorial page the rules and contact information for submitting both op-ed articles and letters to the editor.

Appearing on Radio and TV Talk Shows

Interview and phone-in programs on TV and radio are another venue for getting out your message. Even a program that runs at five in the morning may have an audience of five hundred, a thousand, or more. Find out as much as you can ahead of time about what the program's host is likely to ask you, who else will be on, and, for radio, if there will be call-ins from the audience. Be aware, however, that producers may still surprise you with hostile questions to make the show more controversial. To get on interview and phone-in programs, telephone the station and ask to speak to the producer of the show you are interested in. Another tactic is to tune in when a public official you are trying to influence is a guest on a phone-in show. The receipt of a large number of civil but pointed calls from your side is a demonstration of public interest he or she isn't likely to forget.

Paid Advertising

For advocacy campaigns that can afford it, buying paid media is a way of guaranteeing coverage and total control of your message. Paid advertising ranges from inexpensive homemade commercials on local radio stations to full-page ads in major daily newspapers to expensive ads on television. Often the goal of paid advertising is to pressure a small group of public officials or make a statement so controversial that your advertising itself becomes a news story.

The Public Media Center, a public relations firm that specializes in progressive political causes, for example, once ran a full-page ad in the *San Francisco Chronicle* protesting a court settlement in a consumer case against the banking giant Well Fargo. Under the headline "The Lawyers Get Rich, the Banks Get Off, and Consumers Get Zilch", the ad included a mail-in form to send to the judge in the case. After receiving twenty thousands protests in the mail, the judge threw out the settlement and ordered a new round of negotiations.[26] In 1987, opponents of Robert Bork's nomination to the U.S. Supreme Court produced a sixty-second anti-Bork TV ad, narrated by actor Gregory Peck. The ad, which highlighted

Bork's controversial judicial record on civil rights, only ran on a few cable and local stations in Washington, D.C., and in a handful of states represented by undecided senators. Nevertheless, the ad itself became a news story with a huge national effect. As one analysis put it, "The television campaign cost only $160,000. But the ad generated additional coverage that was worth millions."[27]

As with all media, paid advertising should be carefully guided by the audience you are trying to move and the messages you know offer the best chance of doing that. On a small scale (local newspapers, radio or cable TV), you may be able to produce and place the ads yourself. But for more ambitious and expensive advertising campaigns it may make more sense to enlist the involvement of a paid public relations or advertising firm that knows what it's doing.

Regardless of what mix of media actions you pick, keep these tips in mind. First, save clippings of your print coverage and audio/video tapes of all your radio and television coverage. These are worth their weight in gold to give to policymakers and journalists, and to share with your supporters to build enthusiasm and momentum. Second, try to build an echo to your story, keeping it in the news. If you are going to release a report, arrange in advance for a public official to respond to your findings a day or so later. If you've drawn some solid news coverage, follow it up with letters to the editor or an op-ed article. Finally, never forget that every media contact you make is one more opportunity to establish a relationship with a reporter or editor who later might be just the contact you need.

TALKING TO JOURNALISTS

Ultimately, the work of delivering your message and drawing media attention comes down to the conversations you have with reporters, editors, and producers. Much of the time you may be pitching a story to them. At other times, they'll be asking you for information. In either case, the task is, as always, to stick to your message and make it as newsworthy as possible.

Pitching Your Story

The first step is to think very carefully about whom you ought to be pitching your story to. At newspapers the best choice is a reporter who has covered the issue before or with whom you've had some good prior contact. If you don't have a clear idea, then a good starting point at newspapers is the "city editor," whose job is to look at potential stories and assign them to reporters. At television and radio stations, again, the best contact is a producer who you know personally or who has covered the issue in the past. Absent that kind of connection you can contact the assignment editor, the person who decides which stories to cover and assigns them to producers or reporters. You also can pitch your story to the photo editor of the local paper. A good picture with a caption may be worth more than a long article. Finally,

A TALE OF TWO PITCHES

"The Gruff Reporter"

Advocate: Hi, my name is Shandra Miller from People for Better Health Care. Do you have a minute?

Reporter: Barely.

Advocate: We're sponsoring a demonstration tomorrow morning at the headquarters of Integrity Insurance to protest their practice of canceling people's health coverage when they get seriously ill. We also have some new numbers on that to release.

Reporter: Fine, well send me something, I'll take a look.

Advocate: Great, I'll fax it off to you right now, I have the number. Thank you for your time [faxes news advisory].

"The Interested Reporter"

Advocate: Hi, my name is Shandra Miller from People for Better Health Care. Do you have a minute?

Reporter: Sure, Shandra, what do you have?

Advocate: We're sponsoring a demonstration tomorrow morning at the headquarters of Integrity Insurance to protest their practice of canceling people's health coverage when they get seriously ill. We'll also be releasing a new report detailing how many times Integrity has done this in the past year.

Reporter: Sounds interesting. Do you have some specific Integrity victims I can talk to?

Advocate: Absolutely. We have a couple of families who are very happy to share their stories with the press. Margaret Sandler, for example, had her coverage cancelled the day her son, who has cancer, went in the hospital for a bone marrow transplant. She's very articulate.

Reporter: I'd like to talk to her, this afternoon if possible, to give me more time to write it up. Can we do that?

Advocate: I'd be happy to. Let me give you her phone number and I'll also fax over a copy of our news advisory and the report to give you some time to go through the numbers [wraps-up the call, faxes the information and calls back later that day to be sure the reporter has everything she needs].

most large cities also have a local "news calendar" service that provides journalists with a listing of the main news events (new conferences and so forth) happening that day. Send your information also to them to get your event on the list.

The art of pitching a story is as much about listening as it is talking. If you are making a cold call to someone you don't know, your opening pitch should be no more than a sentence or two, then judge your listener's interest and proceed accordingly. If their interest seems weak or they sound annoyed, arrange to fax them some information and get off the line gracefully. If they seem interested and open to talking, figure out which angle on the story seems to interest them most. Time your calls to avoid catching journalists on deadline, and if you do, ask when would be a good time to call back.

While it is important not to be a pest or to oversell your story, persistence is important. *San Francisco Examiner* reporter Eric Brazil tells the story about being approached by environmental activists about a woman who climbed to the top of an ancient redwood in Northern California to protest logging. "When they came to talk to me after she'd been there a month, I said 'no.' When they came back after she'd been there three months, we sent a photographer." Eventually the story was covered by the *Examiner*, the *Los Angeles Times*, the *New York Times,* and by media in Japan, Italy and elsewhere around the world.[28]

If what you have is especially newsworthy, some journalists may ask for an exclusive, an agreement to give them the story before anyone else has it. If granting the exclusive means that you will get much more prominent coverage, it may be worth it. On the other hand, the papers or stations you don't give the story to may be less inclined later to do you any favors. How to respond is a question of tradeoffs.

Responding to a Call from a Reporter

When you receive a call from reporters working on a story, first try to get a sense of exactly how they are putting the story together. Ask what angle they are working on, who else they'll be talking to, what aspect of the issue they hope you will comment on, and so on. This allows you to focus on what the reporter will actually use from you and help you figure out what points you'll want to emphasize. It is also perfectly appropriate to tell reporters you'll call them back, which gives you some time to think about what you want to say and to consult with other people about facts or for guidance. Be sure to find out when the deadline is and call back well in advance of that.

On an issue where you have strong opponents, it is good strategy to tell reporters who that opposition is and how to contact them. Give reporters the strongest arguments your opposition will raise against you and your refutation of those arguments. Reporters will talk to your opposition and hear those arguments anyway, so better to signal that you think the arguments are weak and get your refutation in the story. Sometimes when reporters call they will be looking for help finding "real people," those effected personally by the issue, or others with technical expertise. Well-planned advocacy campaigns make it easy for reporters to connect with these people and train them in how to deal well with reporters when they call.

Sometimes, the calls you get from the media won't be friendly. Reporters may be working on a story critical of you or your organization or may already have decided how to write the story. The story may even be written and you are being called just for a response or comment. Again, it is perfectly appropriate, and usually just plain smart, to take a reporter's number and deadline and call back, buying some time to think and consult. The reporter is obliged by custom to give you at least one quote, so stick to a simple, clear, short message to make sure that it is the one that gets used. Avoid sounding defensive or angry, stay factual, and don't try to cover up mistakes or other unflattering facts that will come out anyway. However you respond, it has to have integrity, for your own sake and for the sake of your press relations over the long term. Do your best not to be caught by surprise. Anticipate the hard questions that might come to you and plan thoughtfully about who should respond and how.

The Art of Being Interviewed

When I think of news interviews, I think of a scene in the movie *Annie Hall*. Woody Allen and Diane Keaton are out on a first date. Allen suddenly says to her, "Kiss me." He then explains that since they have never kissed before, they are nervous about it, but if they kiss at that moment and get it out of the way, they won't be nervous and "we can go digest our food." Most reporters are looking for two things from you in an interview—quotes and background information. As in the movie, get the kiss of the quotable sound bite out of the way first so you and the reporter can relax and move on to a larger background discussion about the issue; always remember. though, that anything you say can be quoted.

Again, think strategically ahead of time. What is the main message you want to communicate? What language can you use to make that message interesting, colorful, and irresistible to the reporter? What questions are likely to come up and how will you handle them? Also think about the tone you want to use and the impression you want to create—how sober or wild? If you are on the attack against corporate polluters you can either talk about them as "greedy scumbags" or as "corporate leaders willing to put profit ahead of public health." Which approach works most to your advantage? Often, extreme rhetoric ends up just making those who use it look more extreme.

Television and radio, because they capture your voice and your image directly, require some special rules for interviewing. On television, you need to pay attention not just to what you say but how you look, what clothes you wear, your hand gestures, and any nervous habits you don't want to commit on the air, like biting your nails. Radio is a medium in which listeners are eavesdropping on someone else's conversation. Speaking to your interviewer ("and I think one thing people might want to remember is . . .") creates a warmer and more engaging impression than trying to speak directly to the audience ("and I'd like to say this to those of you listening . . .").

In all your dealings with reporters, stay clear about your message and don't wander too far afield. Sometimes writing it down in advance, just for yourself, is a way to stay focused. Respect the journalist's objectivity. It is his job to ask hard questions and to give equal access to the other side. When reporters make errors in their stories, point it out to them but not in a way that is confrontational or burns that bridge. If the error is serious or damaging and the reporter won't correct it, take it the next step to his editor or boss, asking for a correction or an agreement to run a letter to the editor or an op-ed article.

Patience is also a virtue in media work. Throughout the 1980s, religious community activists struggled, often with little success, to get media attention for their efforts to cut off U.S. aid for the bloody war in El Salvador. After years of hard work and little attention to show for it, El Salvador finally burst into the news in November 1989 following the military's massacre of six Jesuit priests, their house-keeper, and her daughter. Because of all the work done over many years, reporters knew just who to contact and activists knew just what to say. The resulting public attention and outrage undermined support for the war in Congress and in the Bush administration, leading to the negotiations that brought the war to an end.

THE NEED FOR MEDIA REFORM

All the strategies, tactics, and techniques discussed here can help democratic activists gain more and better access to the media. At the same time, however, we need to recognize that public access to the media is under threat from larger forces. The media in the United States are falling under more and more concentrated corporate control and influence each year. Even respected newspapers like the *Los Angeles Times* have blurred the separation between news and advertising. ABC and Disney have merged and are breaking down the wall between news and entertainment. PBS now fills its airwaves with long corporate promotions it says aren't ads.

The media space for hard news and the illumination of public issues is being eroded by fluff and sensationalism aimed at selling advertising. As Eduardo Galeano writes, "The mass media does not reveal reality, it masks it. It doesn't help bring about change, it helps avoid change. It doesn't encourage democratic participation, it induces passivity, resignation and selfishness. It doesn't generate creativity; it creates consumers."[29]

In addition to becoming skilled media advocates, pay attention as well to issues concerning reform of the media itself. Valuable organizations such as Fairness and Accuracy in Reporting (FAIR) monitor the media for biases in coverage and hold the media accountable by pointing them out. Groups such as the Media Access Project are fighting for government rules against increasing corporate monopolization within the media and for the protection of media access for diverse communities and points of view. Organizations such as the Pacific News Service are creating new media outlets to give a direct voice to those most excluded, including pioneering media work by young people of color and by juveniles in jail.[30]

As citizens and activists, using the media well and working to assure its openness and journalistic integrity is as urgent a challenge as we will find. The media is the central nervous system that connects us together, that allows us to see, listen and read about the issues that shape our lives. It is how we develop our understanding of those issues and it is the forum in which we debate the solutions to them. The media is too important to have its ways left solely in the hands of those who own it. Working to make the media more open and learning how to use it smartly are cornerstones of a thriving democracy.

CHAPTER ELEVEN

Lobbying

The Art of Influencing Public Officials

Behold, I send you out as sheep in the midst of wolves, so be ye therefore as wise as serpents and as innocent as doves.

—MATTHEW 10:16

The term "lobby" comes from an old practice in the British Parliament: those who wished to speak with a member would wait in the lobby outside the parliamentary chamber. Today, lobbying means much more than that. Effective citizen lobbying involves not only talking with public officials but also building broad coalitions, working with the media, mobilizing grassroots pressure, changing public opinion, undermining your opposition, and much, much more. We have a right not just to speak to our government but to pressure it to act in ways we believe are in the public interest. Lobbying is how we do that.

Public officials, even the many who are good-hearted public servants, live in a house of mirrors. Each year they may be called on to make hundreds of public decisions, and as they do they are always looking to see how their image appears to their constituents, the media, campaign contributors, their colleagues, and the other audiences they play to. The job of a citizen lobbyist is to make the issues you care about visible, to use the tactics of public activism to influence how officials see themselves in those mirrors, so that to look good they need to do what you want them to do.

Most successful lobbying efforts have two sides. One is inside lobbying—all those actions that take place inside the corridors of government—suggesting ideas for legislation, proposing amendments, formally registering your support or opposition to proposed laws, testifying in committees. The other is outside lobbying, all those activities carried out beyond the halls of power—letter writing, visiting lawmakers in their districts, media work, protests, and other tactics. Both of these are important; the key is to meld them together into an effective, winning lobbying campaign.

Lobbying is also where you enter "the land of wolves." Your city council, state legislature, and Congress are all institutions governed by political games and hidden agendas. On the one hand, it is important to learn the rules of the political game and play it well. On the other hand, you must be "as innocent as doves," careful to play that game for a just cause and not get so caught up in it that you lose the ability to hear legitimate criticism. It is a balancing act that a friend of mine once called half Machiavelli, half Dudley Do Right. Lobbying is power, and power must be used wisely.

    Whether you are new to the game of lobbying or an old hand, the most important rules and steps are these: know the legislative process; get your allies together; know your opposition; prepare for the battle; pick your lobbying targets; deliver the message; lobby the executive branch; and deal strategically with the win or loss you end up with.

KNOW THE LEGISLATIVE PROCESS

In the words of one Massachusetts activist, "My son's 'Dungeons and Dragons' game isn't as full of intrigue and complex alliances as our legislature, but then his game hasn't been going on as long as the legislature's."[1] Lawmaking bodies operate under specific and complicated procedures that you need to understand and deal with. Each city or state legislative body has its own specific rules, but some parts of the lawmaking process are fairly universal.

How Bills Get Started

Lawmakers get their ideas for the bills or ordinances they want to sponsor from all kinds of sources—including constituents, lobby groups, articles in the newspaper, personal experience, and requests from the executive branch. An assemblywoman I worked for introduced a bill requiring clearer disclosure of the charge limits on credit cards after she tried to make a purchase at a local department store and was denied for having reached her limit. Anyone is free to suggest an idea for a bill, and many bills start exactly this way. The ideas then get drafted into legal language (usually by legislative counsel) and are formally introduced, printed up in bill form, and made available to the public.

The Committee Process

The first stop for all proposed legislation is a policy committee, lawmakers who specialize in a given subject (such as health care, housing, or taxes). In legislative bodies that have staff, aides will usually write an analysis of the proposal and the committee will hold a public hearing to listen to witnesses who support and oppose it. This is the point in the process where legislation is most closely examined, and, if a proposal moves forward, it is often amended in order to correct problems or mollify some of the opposition. In some larger legislative bodies such as Congress, the bill may be taken up first by an even more specialized subcommittee that must approve the bill before it can move to a full committee. If the bill involves spending any significant sum of public money it may also need to go through a fiscal or finance committee, which looks specifically at how the bill fits in with other competing demands on the budget. One important strategy for committee work is to try

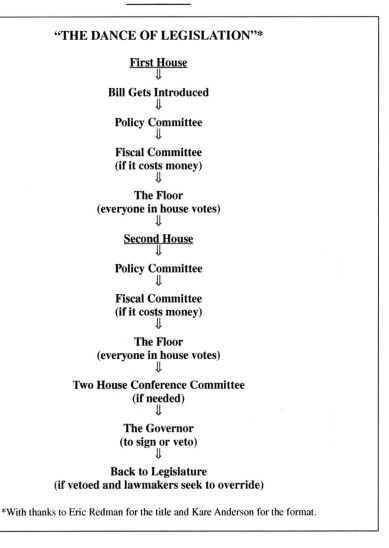

"THE DANCE OF LEGISLATION"*

<u>First House</u>
⇓
Bill Gets Introduced
⇓
Policy Committee
⇓
**Fiscal Committee
(if it costs money)**
⇓
**The Floor
(everyone in house votes)**
⇓
<u>Second House</u>
⇓
Policy Committee
⇓
**Fiscal Committee
(if it costs money)**
⇓
**The Floor
(everyone in house votes)**
⇓
**Two House Conference Committee
(if needed)**
⇓
**The Governor
(to sign or veto)**
⇓
**Back to Legislature
(if vetoed and lawmakers seek to override)**

*With thanks to Eric Redman for the title and Kare Anderson for the format.

to steer your proposal to the most sympathetic panel possible. You might do this by writing the bill in a way that changes which laws are covered by that committee and by lobbying the legislative leadership who decide which committee will take up the measure.

Floor Debates

After a bill has cleared all the necessary committees, it proceeds to the full floor (in a legislature) or the full council (at the city level), where it is again debated and voted on. In legislatures, generally, the only people who can speak at this point are the lawmakers. Hearings before city councils or county boards usually include an opportunity for members of the public to testify directly. Some bills and ordinances get very little attention, others can be debated for hours. Advocates can influence floor debates in a variety of ways, by meeting with lawmakers beforehand, providing them with written statements, and a whole variety of other actions. Most proposals will just require a majority vote for passage, but in some cases procedure may require a "super majority," such as a two-thirds vote.

The Second House

Like Congress, state legislatures (in all states but Nebraska) have two houses. Even if a measure wins approval in one house it must move to the second house, where the process is virtually the same—consideration by subcommittee, committee, fiscal committee, and then a debate on the floor. Along the way bills are often amended and re-amended over and over again. If a bill wins approval in the second house it must be returned to the "house of origin" for approval of any added amendments. The first house can either approve the amendments without changes or the two houses can convene a joint "conference committee" whose members try to reach a compromise acceptable to majorities in each chamber. In Congress the process is slightly different, with parallel bills are often introduced in the House and Senate at the same time, but with the differences still reconciled in a conference committee.

The Executive Branch

After a bill or ordinance is approved by the legislative branch, it proceeds to the executive (such as the governor or mayor), who can either sign it into law or veto it, preventing it from becoming law. Generally, the executive's staff will prepare an analysis of the measure explaining what it does and who supports and opposes it. Advocates can lobby these staff people and, in some cases, the executive directly. If the measure is vetoed, the legislative branch can override that veto, usually by a two-thirds vote in each house, allowing it to become law. After a bill becomes a law, the executive branch is in charge of its implementation, including writing regulations, rules that spell out in more detail how the law is to be implemented by the designated agencies or departments. Here as well is a process that the public can and should influence.

The Budget Process

Legislative consideration and approval of the budget follows basically the same process as for any other bill, with a few key differences. Unlike regular bills, the budget originates from the executive branch rather than from the legislative. All the various city, state, or federal departments begin working nearly a year in advance to develop budget proposals, what they would like to spend in the coming fiscal year. These proposals are usually then funneled into one central department of finance, which makes changes and crunches the numbers into one whole budget for

---

KEY LEGISLATIVE TERMS

Amendments: Changes made to a bill on its way through the legislative process.

Bills Or Ordinances: The actual legislative proposal voted on.

Budget Proposals: Funding requests made by departments for inclusion in the budget.

Conference Committee: A special committee made up of an equal number of members from both houses to reconcile the two different versions of a bill that each has approved.

Control Language: Language that legislators insert into a budget to specify a certain action that a department may or may not take with the money approved.

Fiscal Committee: The committee that reviews all bills that have a substantial cost.

Fiscal Year: The time period that applies to a specific budget (for example, July 1 to June 30).

Floor: The full house, where all members vote.

House Of Origin: The house where the bill was introduced.

Introduced: When an idea is formally presented as a bill for consideration.

Legislative Counsel: Government lawyers who translate general ideas into legal language.

Line Item Veto: When a chief executive (such as governor or mayor) vetoes specific expenditures in a budget.

Line Items: Specific expenditures or programs (such as for a particular park or road).

On-Call: When a bill has been voted on initially, but the voting process remains open in committee or on the floor for members to add or change their votes.

Override: When lawmakers, by a two-thirds vote, enact a law over the executive's veto.

Policy Committee: A subgroup of lawmakers who specialize in a certain policy issue.

Regulations: Rules made by administrative agencies to implement laws.

Super Majority: A vote requirement greater than a simple majority (50 percent plus one).

Veto: When the executive disapproves a bill, blocking it from becoming law.

---

the executive to modify and submit to the legislative branch. This difference from regular bills is important because it is often at the department level, early in the game, that advocates can have the most impact on the budget.

After the budget is submitted to the Congress, legislature, or council, staff members carefully analyzes it, and it begins to move through special budget sub-committees and committees, often simultaneously in each house. These committees hear public testimony and can either add or subtract funds from various programs or line items in the budget. In some cases, the committees can also add control language, specifying certain restrictions on how the money can be spent (for example, telling an agriculture department that it can't spend the funds to promote the use of certain pesticides). After each house approves a common version of the budget it is sent on to the executive, who can either sign the budget or veto it, again subject to override. In most states, governors have the authority to line-item veto specific items in the budget while approving it as a whole. At the federal level the budget process is more complicated, passed in different pieces rather than one overall spending measure.

For budgets and regular lawmaking, citizens can participate in each phase, lobby, and make their opinions heard. It is important to keep in mind, to be enacted, a proposal must survive each one of these hurdles in the legislative process, making it easier to stop a proposed piece of legislation than to promote it. In fact, some of the most important legislative action isn't about promoting or killing bills but about amending them along the way. One of the best things new advocates can do is watch the process in action, get a feel for how it works, and develop a strategy that will work for their issue.

GET YOUR ALLIES TOGETHER

Effective lobbying is a team effort, and at the start of any lobbying campaign it is important to put together the coalition of support that you will need to win. Most lobbying campaigns are started by a small group of advocates or organizations who have a general idea of what they want to push for and then recruit new allies among groups with similar objectives. This original base of support for a lobbying campaign is critical and must be put together at the very start.

One important strength that coalitions bring to a lobbying campaign is diversity, the kind of broad appeal that can help win support from lawmakers across the political map. When I worked with a coalition of consumer, health, and children's groups on legislation to require birth-defect warnings on alcohol, the coalition sent me in (then a young, bearded consumer advocate) when it was time to approach liberal lawmakers. When we needed to lobby conservative lawmakers, we sent in the Reverend Harvey Chinn, a conservative, gray-haired, baritone-voiced Methodist minister. That kind of diversity is critical in a lobbying coalition, as is diversity of race, class and gender.

Strong lobbying coalitions also include groups with an array of different skills and resources—a large membership base that can be mobilized on the issue, a glowing public reputation, media skills and access, strong relationships with lawmakers, lobbying experience, and more. Your coalition should also include people who can speak from experience (as nurses did on the alcohol-warning-label bill) and recognized experts who can go toe to toe with your adversaries (the labeling coalition included medical professors). No one group will have all of these. Coalitions are a way to patch these resources together into a dynamic force. Building and expanding your lobbying coalition is a nonstop function. You never know who might have some information, contact, or skill that will prove useful to the cause.

KNOW YOUR OPPOSITION

Almost as important as bringing together your allies is having a clear sense of your opposition. Who are they? How powerful are they? How adamant are they about the issue? What are their arguments and how can you refute them? How will your opponents lobby the issue, openly or behind the scenes? Who are their key allies? What kind of relationships do they have with the officials whose votes you'll need? Is there any way to divide and conquer them? Know your opposition well so that you can devise a lobbying strategy to weaken, block, and undermine them.

It is usually worth meeting your opposition face to face. Don't expect such a meeting to convince them to back down (more likely they will try to persuade you and your allies to back off). But meeting with your opponents may give you some valuable intelligence, including a preview of the case they will make to lawmakers and how the opposition is likely to handle itself. As a rule, you have two options for how to deal with lobbying opponents, compromise with them or work to undermine them.

The Soft Path—Compromise

In some cases what drives your opponents are concerns that are peripheral to your main goal and worth compromising on. As a young legislative assistant in California, I worked on legislation to guarantee high school students confidentiality in their conversations with school counselors. Our main opponent was the state attorney general, not the kind of opposition one likes to have. In meeting with his staff, we discovered that they were concerned the bill would prohibit counselors from reporting serious crimes (such as rape or arson). Our goal was to give students confidentiality while talking to counselors about issues such as romantic breakups, family problems, and conflicts with teachers. Keeping information about serious crimes under wraps was never our intention, and by amending the bill specifically to allow counselors to report such crimes we neutralized our toughest opponent and kept our main objectives intact. Decisions about compromise involve weighing how much is given away against what is gained.

The Hard Road—Undermine Them

In most cases, the challenge is to undermine your opponents, especially ones with a far bigger arsenal of money and inside connections than you have. The key is to find your opposition's weak spot and do all you can to highlight it, attack it, and make it as public as possible. That weak spot might be taking their strongest argument and proving it false. Advocates for an increased federal minimum wage knocked down their opposition's claim that it would cost jobs by presenting credible studies showing that an increase would boost the economy by increasing the spending power of low-wage workers. It might be finding the opposition's most nervous ally and peeling them off. Antitobacco advocates did this when a leading cigarette manufacturer broke from the united industry line that smoking isn't addictive. That weak spot may even be the fact that your opposition is so powerful. During the lobbying effort on behalf of birth defect warnings we spoke constantly about "the liquor industry versus healthy babies," a veritable David versus Goliath image that the media loved and for which the alcohol industry suffered dearly.

In some cases powerful opponents will use their lobbying clout as clandestinely as possible, a strategy that the Advocacy Institute has labeled "stealth lobbying." Lobbying interests such as the chemical and tobacco industries are able to convert dollars into false science, fake facts, the illusion of legitimacy and grassroots support, as well as friends in high places and silence from those who might otherwise speak out. These lobbying groups hire contract firms to crank out constituent communications to lawmakers at a rate of $500 per letter and $150 per fax. As the vice president of one firm boasted regarding a paid lobbying effort aimed at Congress, "We know what message went because we wrote the message. We know how many were delivered because we ordered them."[2]

Corporate lobbies engineer false images of legitimacy with industry-financed research and neutral-sounding front groups (the National Agricultural Chemicals Association, for example, changed its name to the American Crop Protection Association). The best strategy for undermining these "stealth" tactics, writes the Advocacy Institute, is to highlight the specific deceptions that have the best media appeal. Antismoking advocates in Utica, New York, for example, learned that a tobacco industry–sponsored "smokers' rights" group was holding a meeting at a local hotel. They rented the meeting room next door and staged their own event at the same time, inviting children to participate in an antismoking art contest, with the media invited.

GET PREPARED FOR THE BATTLE

Lobbying campaigns must be carefully prepared in advance. Before any actual lobbying begins, legislation needs to be crafted, arguments and messages need to be developed, and your grassroots support must be organized.

Research and Drafting

Regardless of whether your lobbying campaign is about pushing a bill or trying to stop one, an important part of being prepared is research, both policy and political. On the policy side, you want to find out as much as you can about the issue. Who is affected by it and how? What solutions have been tried and with what result? Are there success stories you can use? Can you quantify the problem (how many people effected, at what cost)? Advocates supporting a California motorcycle helmet law uncovered research showing that over 80 percent of orthopedic costs for injured motorcyclists were being paid for by taxpayers, giving them a powerful argument that the state had a right to require riders to wear helmets.[3] On the political side, what reforms have been proposed in the past and how have they fared? Who voted which way? What arguments have been used before on the issue and with what effect?

When drafting a bill, there are several important considerations to keep in mind. First, make sure it actually accomplishes what you want it to. If the language is unclear (sometimes purposely in order to calm opposition), this leaves a lot of room for your goal to be lost during the law's implementation. Consider who will be given that implementation authority. Is it a department or official who will be friendly to your aims, or hostile to them? Keep your proposal as simple as possible. The more complicated you make it the bigger target it becomes for opponents who, if they are smart, will take aim at your weakest provisions. Finally, leave yourself some wiggle room for compromise and amendments. Legislators love nothing so much as amending proposals to try to make everyone happy.

Arguments and Messages

Among your most important lobbying weapons are the messages and arguments you will aim at lawmakers, staff, the media, and the general public. In lobbying, strong arguments always have two parts. First, make the case that you are right on the issue, that your position (whether in support or opposition) is genuinely in the public interest. Second, appeal to the political self-interest of whoever it is you are lobbying, convincing them that it is also to their political benefit to be on your side (because, for example, you have thousands of supporters, or are getting favorable press attention). Any parent will recognize this two-fisted approach from the way we are lobbied by our own children, "Daddy, *Titanic* is a really good movie, and also if we go see it I'll sweep the sidewalk for you."

It is also critical to acknowledge the strongest argument on the other side and then refute it. As one lawmaker I knew used to advise advocates, "I'm sure going to hear it from them so I'd better hear it from you first and hear what you have to say about it." A good lobbying message also keeps its roots in real stories about real people affected by the issue. While motorcycle-helmet-advocate Mary Price always took time to talk about the statistics on the issue, she also never stopped telling the story of the crash that killed her helmetless son.

On the political side, the objective is always to demonstrate your broad and powerful support. Sometimes this is done by engaging large coalitions, other times by just enlisting one key supporter close to the lawmaker. When heath care advocates in California were trying to spark lawmakers' interest in HMO reform, they used polling as a lobbying tool. "Democratic leaders were looking for a hot issue," recalled consumer lobbyist Beth Capell, "and I was able to show them that HMO reform polled beautifully [that it drew strong public support]."[4] As advocacy author Kare Anderson writes, "Every official carries an invisible scale in her hand which weights all decisions; is it more to her advantage to vote with you or against you? Interpret your cause in terms of the legislator's needs and beliefs— not yours."[5]

LOBBYING TOOLS CHECKLIST

About the Issue

✓ Action alerts
✓ Fact sheets
✓ Questions and answers
✓ Responses to opponents' arguments
✓ Sample letters to officials
✓ Web sites for more information
✓ Visuals, pictures, posters etc.
✓ More extensive research or data

About Lawmakers

✓ Lists by district
✓ Staff names
✓ Contact info. (mail, phone, fax, e-mail)
✓ Committee assignments
✓ Committee staff names
✓ Names to contact within the administration

Other

✓ Coalition list
✓ News clippings
✓ Editorials
✓ Contact information for capitol lobbyists
  working on the campaign

Lobbying Tools

Especially for lobbying campaigns that aim to mobilize large numbers of people, the campaign needs to put together a set of specific materials and tools to equip the people involved. Some of these tools deal with the policy topic involved—fact sheets, questions and answers, responses to opponents' arguments, sample letters, and Web sites where people can get more information—all of which help your supporters educate themselves about the issue. Other tools give people the information they need about the lawmakers they will need to lobby and how they should go about doing that—such as action alerts, lists of legislators with their contact information.

It is also helpful to give activists copies of news clippings, editorials, a complete coalition list, and contact information for the lobbyists leading the campaign. These can either be mailed to supporters in a combined action packet or posted on the Web, alerting people to it via e-mail. If you have the time and the resources, it is extremely useful to provide a lobbying training session for the activists who will be participating in the campaign to walk them through the process, explaining what to expect and giving them a chance to meet and interact with law-makers or staff.

PICK YOUR LOBBYING TARGETS

The public officials you might wish to influence fall into very different categories. Some will already be with you, some you will never win over, and most will likely be somewhere in the middle. Correctly targeting your lobbying efforts is essential. Too often, advocates just aim their lobbying the easiest target (for progressive causes, urban liberals). "We get lots of calls from people who are preaching to the converted," explains one state Democratic aide. "We tell people that if they really want to be effective they should sit down and make a list of everyone they know who lives in Republican districts, and tell them to call their legislator."[6]

Effective lobbying campaigns begin with strong intelligence gathering, through meetings with members, staff, and lobbyists, to find out where lawmakers might stand on the issue. Lawmakers, as a rule, fall into one of these categories, each requiring its own strategy:[7]

Champions

One of the most important choices made in a lobbying campaign is which law-maker you will pick to serve as the campaign's champion. This is the person who will officially sponsor your bill, anchor your news conferences, give you inside in-telligence on where his or her colleagues stand, lead your committee presentations, speak for you on the floor, get you your last and most hard-fought votes, negotiate on your behalf with colleagues, and give you solid political counsel along the way about what is winnable and what is not.

The right choice of a champion can propel you to victory, the wrong choice can torpedo your whole campaign. There are a variety of criteria to look for in choosing champions. Are they committed? Do they know the issue and are they committed to it deeply? Are they tenacious and willing to really twist their col-league's arms when the going gets tough? How are their relations with other law-makers, with the governor or mayor? Do they win you support or lose it? The author of your bill, as Judith Bell of the national advocacy group PolicyLink, ex-plains, "puts a legislative face on your issue and this is a key part of the public and legislative shaping of the debate. It is important to take into account gender, race, as well as their political and geographic base."[8] Sometimes it is helpful to have a champion who is part of the legislative leadership, giving your campaign extra ac-cess and clout. However, legislative leaders also may have conflicting agendas, and twisting an arm on your issue may end up taking a backseat to the need to twist that same arm on a different issue that your champion decides is more important.

In the end, the main question may be who can get you the critical support you will need to win. In 1986, when California children's advocates were gearing up for a lobbying campaign on expanding state prenatal services to the poor, they knew that their toughest hurdle would be getting the bill signed into law by then-Governor George Deukmejian, a Republican conservative with little sympathy for their cause. For their champion and author, the advocates targeted another GOP conservative, Senator Marion Bergeson of Orange County, a former kindergarten teacher and close ally of the governor. "We invited the senator to join us for a visit to the neonatal intensive care unit at the UC Irvine hospital, in her district," explained campaign leader, Wendy Lazarus. "Senator Bergeson was noticeably moved by the tiny premature babies and told us her concerns about the continuing educational difficulties many of them would face later."[9] The senator agreed to author their bill and fought tenaciously for it, ultimately winning Governor Deukmejian's signature on legislation extending prenatal care to thirty thousand additional low-income women.

It is important that the champions you pick are willing to work closely with you, especially when it comes time to negotiate a compromise. "We've gotten burned sometimes when our champions didn't know when to walk away from negotiations with the administration or the opposition," said Angie Wei, a California immigrant rights lobbyist. "It is critical to have early discussions with them about what the bottom line is and when to walk away from a deal."[9] Advocates need to support their champions by getting them the information they need when they need it, by backing them up with good lobbying and press work, and by making sure that they get public credit (the currency of political life) and personal thanks for their hard work. Long-term lobbying campaigns also need to steadily recruit new champions, making sure that there is someone to pick up the torch when other lawmakers retire or move on to other offices.

Soft Supporters

Other lawmakers will say they are with you, vote right when the time comes, but do very little else on your behalf. The challenge is to get them to do more. "Staff always tell us, 'ask for something specific,'" notes Angie Wei. They can be asked to be co-authors, lending their name to a bill. They can be given questions or statements to raise or read in committee hearings or in floor debates. They can be asked to participate in media events or to approach one specific colleague with whom they have a close relationship. Sometimes drumming up a little support from their districts (though not at the expense of lobbying the lawmakers you need to win over) will sharpen their interest in helping more actively.

Fence Sitters

In any lobbying campaign the real targets are the fence sitters, the lawmakers who could end up voting either way. They are really your main targets for almost all of your lobbying activities. First comes some intelligence gathering. How have they voted on the issue in the past? What aspects of the issue seem to concern them most? What arguments are likely to be the most persuasive? What organizations are they close to that might be able to influence them? Who can you get to lobby them from their district? The strategy is about knowing what buttons you need to push to move them in your direction and then pushing those buttons skillfully and relentlessly from every angle possible—lobbying, media, letter writing, visits, and more.

Soft Opponents

There are other lawmakers who will vote against you no matter what you do, but whose vehemence you can diminish. It is one thing, for example, for a legislator to vote against you, but quite another for that same legislator to attack your witnesses in committee or to speak or twist arms during a floor vote. Through meetings, district visits, letter writing, and local press work, it is possible to give these members pause about sticking their neck out too far against you. Again, this should not distract you from the effort to woo the fence sitters, but where there are organizational or constituent connections available with these lawmakers, it is worth using them.

Hard Opponents

Then there are the lawmakers and officials who not only oppose you but also are leading the charge against you. Your goal with these legislators is to isolate them and to highlight the most extreme, most unsympathetic aspects of their opinions and actions. Immigrant advocates in California uncovered an overtly racist poem distributed to colleagues by a champion of state anti-immigrant legislation, and made sure it was widely released to the media. Putting the public spotlight on your opponents most extreme statements or positions discredits them and makes other officials afraid to associate with them and with their political positions. As Angie Wei explains, anti-immigrant leaders often hung themselves, "Their harsh, reactive statements actually made our supporters more incensed and our opposition more embarrassed."[10]

Legislative Leaders

Finally, whether they are for you, against you, or neutral, legislative leaders will always have some effect on your political fortunes. Leaders include the speaker or the president of each house, chair of the city council, committee chairs, and others. It is important to make your case to them and their staffs early and throughout the process. Often these leaders are most concerned with how the legislation will hurt or help their political party, their campaign contributors, or the future of politically vulnerable members. Being able to show that your position is in alliance with those interests is extremely important.

DELIVER THE MESSAGE

With a clear sense of your targets and of what messages they need to hear, the main task of all lobbying campaigns is the delivery of that message. The goal, as the

Advocacy Institute's David Cohen has describes, is to "create a buzz" around an issue, to let officials hear your message and see your activity from all corners—from professional lobbyists, constituents, friends, fellow lawmakers, contributors, the media, even their clergy and family. These lobbying efforts need to begin early enough so that you beat your opponents to the punch of educating officials first, but not so early that your message is forgotten before it is time to vote. The methods for this contact come in many varieties, all of which need to be woven together into a coherent lobbying strategy that creates a sense of forward momentum around your campaign.

Letter Writing

The mainstay of constituent communication with lawmakers is letter writing, and it remains one of the most important gauges that public officials use to measure constituent opinion on an issue. The assemblywoman I worked for would take every letter she received on a bill with her to committee and to the floor on the day of a vote, to read as she listened to the arguments. I have seen lawmakers read aloud from particularly moving constituent letters they have received.

Effective letter writing boils down to four rules. First, be clear and to the point. Second, make your letters personal. Third, make sure the official receives as many letters as possible. Fourth, make sure that letters are from that legislator's constituents. Strong letters cite the specific bill number you are writing about, your position on the bill, the specific action you are asking for (for example, vote yes), and a request that he or she write back explaining his or her position on the matter. Effective letters also put the issue in personal terms, explaining how you, your family, your school, or your community will be affected. Most lawmakers are far more likely to remember and be moved by personal stories than they are by abstract arguments. Lawmakers also look for numbers. Most bills draw virtually no constituent mail, so when a lawmaker receives ten, twenty, thirty, or more letters on an issue it moves quickly to the center of his or her political attention. Finally, the letters that count are from constituents, who represent votes. Letters from other districts matter very little.

Public officials also know the difference between letters that took time to write versus form letters, preprinted post cards, or petitions that constituents simply sign and send with little thought. These mass forms of constituent mail are worthwhile, if they are delivered in huge numbers, but they are still no substitute for real letter writing. When groups do organize letter-writing campaigns, adding a slight gimmick can sometimes get lawmakers to take special notice. Activists in Illinois, promoting state legislation on childhood hunger, wrote their letters to lawmakers on paper plates, gaining notice both by officials and by the media.

Organized letter-writing campaigns are most successful when organizers set up tables at events (PTA meetings, church gatherings, rallies) where large numbers of supporters are gathered. Participants are asked on the spot to write a letter to their legislator, with organizers providing the paper, pens, and sample messages, then taking responsibility to address, stamp, and mail the letter for people (although to be effective each letter has to be sent individually). Supporters should also be asked to send back to the campaign a copy of the responses they receive from lawmakers, an important source of political intelligence, and on occasion a promise of support that a waffling legislator can be reminded of later.

E-Mail

Sending e-mail to lawmakers is still relatively new, and its effectiveness is still difficult to gauge. On the one hand, officials know that, like form letters and postcards, e-mail is far easier to send then a regular letter and not as much of an indication of public intensity. However, because of that ease, it is also possible to flood an official's office with electronic messages far faster than with regular mail. When I was trying to persuade the U.S. ambassador to Bolivia to investigate a human rights case there, I sent a request for support to an e-mail list of friends. My request was forwarded and reforwarded to many others, generating more than one hundred messages to the ambassador in less than two weeks, enough pressure to prompt an embassy investigation of the case. Even more promising is the development of Web sites where activists can electronically send, free, a fax to their representatives or other public officials. This was used to send tens of thousands of faxes to senators in the unsuccessful 2001 campaign opposing John Ashcroft's nomination for U.S. attorney general.

Telephone Calls

Contacting officials' offices by phone, while not as effective as letter writing, can have an enormous impact if done in large numbers in a concentrated way. In the late 1980s, California lawmakers approved a bill to prohibit the sale of certain automatic weapons, and Governor Deukmejian, a known opponent of gun control, was expected to veto it. By coincidence, while the bill was sitting on his desk, the state PTA, a strong supporter of the bill, was also holding its annual five-thousand-person state convention in San Diego. From the podium, PTA leaders explained the situation to the assembled delegates and implored them to go to the pay phones outside to call the governor's office and demand his support. To the phones they went, in lines a dozen deep for two days straight, until the governor finally sent an official communication to PTA leaders that he would sign the bill and a request that people stop calling. Not everyone is in a position to generate thousands of calls in a few days' time, but the principle is the same for all phone lobbying campaigns—concentrate your effort. Send out notices to supporters, with a complete list of local and capitol phone numbers for targeted members, suggesting a quick one-sentence message and one designated day for all the calls to be made. What you want are legislative offices with their phones ringing off the hook and worried staff communicating that to their lawmaker bosses. As with letter writing, the calls should be made by people who are actual district constituents of that member.

Lobbying Visits

Meeting directly with officials provides advocates with the chance to deliver their message face to face, to interact with and build relationships with those lawmakers. With legislators, it is far more effective to meet with them in their home districts than in the Capitol, where they are much busier and where you will be just one among many groups competing for their time and attention. Even better, you should try to set up the meeting not in their office at all, but on your turf, in some location that makes the issue real for them. John Carr of the U.S. Catholic Conference says, "If we want to talk about housing we ought to do it in a shelter back home not in a member's office up here [in Washington]."[11] A nurse who wanted to lobby her local assemblyman on a the bill expanding prenatal care persuaded him to visit her in the neonatal intensive care unit where she worked, to see the tiny and fragile babies confined to incubators. Later he surprised his colleagues by sharing the experience during the floor debate, concluding, "I don't know if this bill is the right thing, but I do know we need to do something."

Visiting lawmakers is still valuable, however, especially if it's close to the time when they'll be voting. Sometimes these appointments can be arranged in advance and kept. Many times, however, you may have to track down the legislator, in committee or on the floor, having your meeting in a hallway in a stolen moment. Once I even lobbied California's then-U.S. Senator Pete Wilson on cutting off U.S. aid to the war in Nicaragua when I ran into him in a hotel swimming pool.

Regardless of where your meeting with the official takes place, there are a handful of important considerations to keep in mind. First, think carefully and strategically about the group you put together to meet with the lawmaker. Ideally, it should consist of no more than four to five people (most of whom should be district constituents). The group should include: someone well versed on the legislation, someone representing a key constituency (labor union, business group) that the lawmaker considers important; someone who already knows the official personally to help break the ice; and someone directly affected who can speak personally about the issue. Also, pay attention to having some diversity in the group, in terms of race, sex, and age. Explain how many people you represent and your plans (such as meetings, newsletters) for sharing the results of your meeting.

In all cases, be sure to do your homework in advance. First, know the lawmaker's record on the issue, the concerns he or she might raise, and have a premeeting to plan what everyone will say, including an opener to get going and a clear request for action. Second, practice in advance what each person will say. You might even role-play the visit beforehand. Third, stay focused, don't try to cover more than one issue, and if the legislator wanders off to another topic have a plan to get back on the subject. Fourth, listen as much as you speak. The meeting is a chance to pick up clues that are critical to winning the legislator's vote—what concerns does he or she raise, who else has he or she heard from, what arguments seem most persuasive to him or her? Never threaten the lawmaker and avoid getting into direct arguments. Fifth, have some written material to leave behind (though not too much), such as a fact sheet, some news clippings, or editorials.

Finally, have a plan for ending the meeting. Ask legislators if they know how they will vote, and have a specific plan for follow-up. Who should you contact on the legislative staff, and when? What additional information should you send? Afterward, send a note thanking legislators for taking time to meet with you. It is important to see these visits as an opportunity to build a relationship with officials that will be useful over time on other issues as well, not just on a single bill.

Sometimes you may have trouble getting a meeting with lawmakers, perhaps because they are busy or perhaps because they know they aren't likely to vote your way and don't want to tell you so directly. Be persistent and use whatever leverage you've got. In the 1980s, during the lobbying campaign aimed at getting Congress to block the MX missile, one East Coast congressman refused to meet with local church activists, even after being asked to do so by the local bishop. Local religious leaders then told the congressman's scheduler that, sadly, they would have to publish in the local Catholic paper that the representative was too busy to meet with the bishop. Miraculously, the congressman agreed to meet, and after persistent lobbying became the key vote on the House floor to defeat deployment of the missile.[12]

Working with Staff

In many cases it isn't possible to meet directly with the legislator and the next best thing (and in some cases better) is to meet with staff. Typically, legislators have three different types of staff assistants: personal staff at the Capitol who work directly for that member on legislation; district staff who work on constituent problems and district issues; and for committee chairs, committee staff who specialize in a given issue area. All of these staff people are in a position to pass your information along to the legislator and influence how he or she will vote.

Use staff members as sounding boards; they usually have a good sense of how their boss will react to an issue and what concerns you need to address. Staff can also pass on to members suggested amendments to bills you oppose, as well as comments or questions to raise in committee hearings and on the floor. Member's personal secretaries are also important contacts to cultivate. In a pinch, they can usually tell you where to find legislator and are usually the gatekeepers who decide if you will get to see them. It is also important to figure out which lawmakers don't listen to their staff, and in those cases to devise a strategy to get to the lawmaker directly.

Media

Thoughtful media work is also a critical part of almost every lobbying campaign. Public officials are extremely conscious of their public image, especially in front of their constituents, and the media is the mirror they look in to see that image. News conferences, press events, news stories, feature articles, letters to the editors, editorials, and appearances on talk shows are all ways to deliver your message to your target lawmakers, and are all the more powerful because those messages are public. Media coverage at the start of a lobbying campaign can help frame the issue your way. Media attention during the process puts added pressure on lawmakers to vote with you. Media reaction after a vote can put the heat on lawmakers who voted against you and send a powerful message to others who might do the same.

Committee Hearings and Floor Votes

Committee hearings and floor votes on a bill give both sides the chance to present their case in a formal and public way. They are also the legislative version of theater. Nothing should be left to chance. Learn how to manage the choreography before, during, and after all these proceedings.

Beforehand, that involves lobbying contacts and making the best count you can of how many votes you have and who the key undecideds are you'll need to sway. That advance work also includes careful attention to the analysis for each bill that legislative staff prepare, for both committee hearings and floor debate. In general, these analyses will describe what the bill does and present the basic arguments of both sides; it may list the organizations that support and oppose it. Because these analyses can have such an important effect on legislators' views, your side will want to influence what the staff writes and get your allies to submit letters in order to get listed either as support or opposition in that analysis.

The choreography for committee hearings is about witnesses, testimony, exhibits, and building an audience. An effective lineup of witnesses is much the same as for legislative visits—someone who can describe the issue in general and deliver your spin effectively, an expert who can match the best of the other side, and someone directly affected. Their testimony should be clear, brief (two to three minutes may be all each person gets), and pack some emotional punch. For our committee hearing on the student-counselor confidentiality bill, our most powerful witness was a seventeen year-old named Heidi, who was eight months pregnant and told legislators, "There are some things that are just hard to talk about with your parents at first." For a committee hearing on restoring cuts made in public assistance to immigrants, advocates presented testimony from a elderly Laotian man who spoke about fighting alongside U.S. soldiers in Vietnam, only to be rewarded in his old age by having Congress eliminate his food stamp benefits. Your testimony should also provide powerful and direct refutation of your opponents' strongest points.

Building an audience of supporters and media is also important. When legislators see a hearing room packed with supporters wearing buttons, T-shirts, or other identifying items to make it clear who they are, it makes a difference, and even more so if there are television cameras broadcasting the hearing and the vote back home. One of my favorite stories is about an advocacy group that invested in an old TV news camera that they brought into hearings to make legislators think their comments and votes were being filmed for the news.

During the hearing, committee members can make statements, question witnesses, and offer amendments to the bill being heard. All this should be choreographed as well. You should equip your allies on the committee beforehand with supporting statements, hard questions for your opponents, and your responses to potential amendments that opponents might offer. For floor votes, the advance work is much the same (though in most cases bills aren't significantly amended on the floor) and because only the legislators themselves can speak, it is all the more important to equip your lawmaker allies on the floor with effective statements and questions.

In many legislatures, even when the vote is taken, the voting isn't over. A number of legislators won't be in committee or on the floor when the first vote is taken and it is possible for them to add or change their votes until the committee or floor wraps up its business for the day (this is known as putting a bill on-call). That gives you and your allies, as well as your opposition, the task of finding the additional votes you need, tracking lawmakers down wherever they might be—sitting in other committees, working in their office, or even getting their shoes shined—and getting them to come and vote while there is still time. Be well prepared for this tracking down of lawmakers (this is where having good relations with their secretaries comes in especially handy) by having enough people on hand to do it. Also, keep a watchful eye on those who have voted with you but are wobbly and vulnerable to the lobbying of your opposition.

Remember always that working a vote is about arithmetic. How many votes do you need to win? You don't need every vote, so focus your attention on the ones you do need and have the best chance at getting. It makes no sense to waste time and energy trying to track down and woo a lawmaker who will never be on your side at the expense of working on someone who is genuinely on the fence and persuadable.

After a vote the choreography continues. Your side will want to put the best public spin possible on either a win or a loss. Thank the legislators who supported you, and send an appropriate message as well to those who opposed you. One way to do this is with follow-up constituent mail, "Dear Assemblywoman, the five hundred members of our organization are deeply disappointed to hear about your vote against . . . " That disappointment can also be communicated through the media, with press statements, opinion articles, letters to the editor, and so on.

Public Actions

Some lobbying campaigns also use public actions to draw public attention and turn up the political heat on their issue. When cosmetology students around the country were fighting in Congress to protect their access to student aid, they descended on Washington bearing mannequin heads with professionally done hairdos, to make the case that their training was just as serious as that of other students. Sometimes actions like this can have an influence on lawmakers, but most officials are used to seeing rallies and protests, and over the years the effectiveness of these methods has diminished. The key to making such events useful is to have large numbers and a skillful manipulation of the symbols so that the media will take note and your issue gets framed to your best advantage.

LOBBYING AND NONPROFIT ORGANIZATIONS

A Note About the IRS Rules

For many nonprofit organizations, the term "lobbying" (the "L" word) strikes terror, the fear that any advocacy communication with an elected official will put in jeopardy their nonprofit tax status. While groups should be careful, in fact nonprofits are allowed to be involved in far more lobbying-type activity than most organizations think.

Nonprofits registered as 501©3 organizations (nonprofits to which contributions may be deducted as a donation to charity) are specifically restricted from endorsing candidates for political office. 501©3 also need to be cautious about election season activities that could be construed as candidate endorsements (such as election season scorecards that rate lawmakers). However, a whole range of lobbying activities are specifically allowed: endorsing bills, meeting with lawmakers to ask for their vote, promoting legislation in the media, sending out alerts and information to members, endorsing and campaigning for ballot measures, and more. There are, however, legal limits on how much of this lobbying activity a nonprofit can engage in and knowing those limits is what is important.

Under IRS rules for 501©3 nonprofits, "no substantial part" of the group's activities may involve, "carrying on propaganda or otherwise attempting to influence legislation." This standard is extremely vague and while not a problem for groups that do very little lobbying, it can be for groups which do more. For that reason IRS rules also give nonprofits another option, filing what is known as a "501(h) election," which provides the organization with a much clearer limit, spending no more than twenty percent (of its first $500,000 of total spending) on lobbying activities. Not restricted as "lobbying" are activities such as litigation, involvement and advocacy with regulatory or administrative agencies, and general public education about an issue.

For a much more detailed description groups should obtain a copy of the report, "Being a Player, A Guide to IRS Lobbying Regulations for Advocacy Charities," published by Alliance for Justice in Washington, DC. Cost: $15. Tel: (202) 822-6070. Information is also available online from the organization Independent Sector at: "http://www.indepsec.org/clpi."

Using Elections as a Lobbying Tool

Election seasons offer advocates a special political window in which politicians are far more accessible and accountable to citizen lobbying efforts. Mary Price, the mother behind California's motorcycle helmet law, couldn't even get in to see Governor George Deukmejian, who vetoed the bill. However, during the election of 1990 she easily got meetings with both the Democratic and Republican candidates to replace Deukmejian, and commitments from both to sign the bill if elected, which the winner, Republican Pete Wilson, eventually did.[13]

There are many ways to take advantage of that extra access and accountability. One is to take advantage of candidates' own town meetings or debates to ask them publicly about an issue. Nothing made the legislators I worked for take more notice of an issue than to be asked about it publicly during their election campaigns in front of a roomful of voters. Your lobbying coalition can also host its own town meetings, focused on your specific issues and invite the candidates to come. Election season is also a good time to get candidates to go on the record on an issue, with a candidate survey asking them where they stand on your issues. Since candidates are always aiming to please, they are more likely than ever to agree with you.

LOBBYING THE EXECUTIVE BRANCH

While most lobbying is aimed at the legislative branch of government , the executive branch—the president, governors, mayors, and the people who work for them—are also a critical target. Some executive branch lobbying is about getting your bill or ordinance signed into law, or getting one you oppose vetoed. The lobbying strategies for delivering your message to executive branch officials are basically the same as for legislators—meetings, letter writing, constituent pressure, and media attention. Also, as with legislative lobbying campaigns, it is important to find champions and allies within the administrative bureaucracy, people who can let you know what is going on and help press your case within agencies and departments.

The executive branch of government also holds the enormous power of implementing laws once they are passed. Federal, state, and local departments, boards, agencies and commissions hold sway over everything from allowable pollution levels to what families can be charged for funerals. They do this by issuing regulations, executive branch rules that take approved legislation and make its requirements more specific. Participating in the development of these regulations is important. It is a way of following up to make sure a law that you supported is fully implemented and is also a way to minimize the damage done by laws enacted over your objections. In some cases it is possible to win changes, through administrative regulation, that were not possible to win in the legislature.

One of the most effective strategies through which citizen lobbyists can influence executive branch rulemaking is through administrative petitions. A majority of states have laws guaranteeing the right of any citizen to petition any state department or agency to make a formal regulation and requiring those departments and agencies to either take action or explain in writing why they won't. Petitions like these aren't large collections of signatures; they are detailed requests for actions which lay out the case for doing so.[14] Administrative petitions can galvanize public attention on an issue, serve as catalysts for coalition building, and force officials to take concrete action they wouldn't otherwise. They have been used to lower milk prices, extend rights to disabled children, establish emergency food projects for the hungry, and challenge the practice by insurers of canceling policies when patients become sick.

You don't need to be a lawyer to draft one and while there is no set format required, most include the following.

- An introduction that summarizes the whole petition
- A description of the facts and the problem that needs to be addressed (such as the numbers of sick patients who have their coverage cancelled)
- The specific action you want the department to take (such as a regulation prohibiting cancellation of coverage when a person becomes ill)
- The legal authority of the department to take that action (what state laws give them the power to act)
- A list and short description of each of the petitioning organizations;
- Exhibits—news articles, studies, testimonies and other evidence that supports you

The petition can be prepared with a cover sheet that lists all the petitioning groups and the department being petitioned, formatted to look like a lawsuit filing. This gives the petition an added air of authority when you hold your news conference to announce it. If the department agrees to hold the hearing, your coalition should prepare for it just as for a legislative hearing, with strong witnesses, testimony, press attention, and an audience of supporters. If the department declines to act, you can make that a press story, adding more attention to the issue, more pressure on the department or agency to act, and opening up the door for new legislative action on the issue as well.

DEALING WITH A WIN OR A LOSS

The great New York Yankees' catcher Yogi Berra is often quoted as having said, "It ain't over 'til it's over." Lobbying campaigns are almost never over. When you lose an important vote, in committee or on the floor, or suffer an executive veto, the campaign is not over. There is almost always some opportunity to resurrect your issue. If you lost in one house, can you try again in the other? If you lost in the legislative branch, can you try to get some of what you're after through rule making in the executive branch? If you've been defeated at the state level can you make progress on the issue locally? If you can't win this year, can you organize a base of support even stronger and come back the next?

Citizen advocates need to be opportunistic, in the best sense of the term, to be looking for any new opening to advance the issue, especially ones that come by surprise. In the end, the supporters of alcohol-birth-defect warnings lost over and over again in the California legislature, only to come up victorious through two developments they had never predicted. The first was the passage of a voter initiative requiring that the state create a formal list of chemicals known to cause birth defects and that manufacturers using those chemicals provide consumers with clear warning. Because of the organizing and media work done by labeling advocates, alcohol ended up being one of the first chemicals named to the list. Then, in part because the long fight in California had cost them such bad publicity, the alcohol industry decided to acquiesce to warning-label legislation drafted by Congress. You never know how and where you might win if you just keep fighting.

Even a legislative victory is not an occasion to drop the campaign. Legislation enacted into law must be monitored, to make sure it is fully funded and implemented and to identify problems you didn't anticipate that might require follow-up legislation later. Advocates need to do some of that monitoring themselves and to recruit their allies in the legislature to do the same. It is also true that no victory is permanent. In the same way that your side wouldn't quit the issue because of a temporary loss, neither will your opponents. Whether in the legislature, the executive branch, or the courts, your opposition will be looking for the opportunity to undo the victory you have won. Five years after mothers and health professionals won enactment of California's motorcycle helmet law, they found themselves back in the halls of the state capitol working to stave off an aggressive campaign to repeal it. It is important, even after winning, to keep your eyes on the issue and your support base intact, in case you need to fight the battle again.

For all these different parts of citizen lobbying, the keys are the same. Have a clear strategy—know what you want and who can give it to you, understand what arguments and messages will persuade them, and communicate those messages in a forceful, effective way. Have strong messengers, do aggressive media work, and use every opportunity for contact and communication you can find. Always know what the other side is up to and stay one step ahead of it. Remember also that intensity is important. Lobbying must always be a campaign, which gives all those who participate the sense that their one letter or their one call makes a difference and is a part of something larger.

CHAPTER TWELVE

Initiatives

The Power of the Ballot

I believe in the initiative and referendum, which should be used not to destroy representative government, but to correct it whenever it becomes misrepresentative.

—THEODORE ROOSEVELT

As any half-awake high school government student will tell you, the United States is not a democracy, it is a republic. It isn't the people who make thousands of public choices each year, about how high taxes will be or what color fire hydrants should be painted. We elect representatives to make those choices. And for as long as we have been a republic we have had problems with our representatives not always exercising that power in our best interests. The initiative process gives the people the power to make laws directly, and its twin, the referendum, gives the people the direct power to repeal laws they don't like.

This is direct democracy, which some people love and others hate. Its supporters view it as the ultimate guarantee of democratic rule and the ultimate protection against wealthy interests taking control of government. It critics see direct democracy as rule by the mob, a process in which half-interested voters are too easily manipulated and minority groups are made victims of majority prejudice. Regardless of which general view you take, initiatives are a democratic tool that you need to understand well, whether you are promoting a ballot measure or trying to stop one.

A BRIEF HISTORY OF INITIATIVE POLITICS

This idea of letting the people take lawmaking directly into their own hands dates back more than two centuries; Thomas Jefferson proposed in 1775 that it be a part of Virginia's state constitution.[1] The real birth of the initiative process in the United States came at the turn of the twentieth century, however. Railroads, power utilities. and other interests born during industrialization, especially in the West, converted their economic wealth into enormous influence if not outright control over state and local governments. In response to this corruption, a series of populist and progressive citizen movements arose, making the establishment of the initiative and referendum among their first objectives. South Dakota became the first state to adopt the initiative, in 1898, followed in short order by Oregon, Montana, Oklahoma, Maine, Michigan, and California.[2] Today twenty-seven states and hundreds of cities across the nation provide citizens with that same power.

The power of direct democracy has brought to a public vote a dizzying array of public issues—tax reform, establishing an official day of Sabbath, legislative term limits, gay rights, greyhound racing, gun control, the death penalty, discrimination in housing, environmental protection, and many more. If you can think of an issue, it has probably been voted on somewhere. San Francisco voters were once presented with a local ballot initiative allowing police officers to carry puppets on patrol.

In general, ballot measures fall into three categories. Many deal with social issues, such as gay rights, immigration, and affirmative action. On these questions the initiative process has been used with increasing success by social conservatives to target the civil rights of minority groups, tapping into the fears and resentments of the political majority. These initiative fights rarely involve huge expenditures of money on either side, yet they are usually the most emotional and visible initiative votes.

A second category of ballot measures deals with economic questions, cutting or raising taxes, or making public rules for businesses and the marketplace, such as health reform, and environmental protections. Because initiatives like these often hit some wealthy interest directly in their wallet, these battles often feature enormous spending by the affected industry on the one side and low-budget citizen campaigns on the other. Initiative battles such as these go to the heart of why the initiative process was originally established, to give people the power to take on economic powerhouses that can buy what they want in the regular legislative process. A California tobacco tax proposal that won on the ballot there couldn't even get out of committee in the state legislature. However, big money is often able to win initiative fights as well, using big spending on television advertising to take over the very process that was created to control those interests.

Finally, a number of ballot measures are about the political process itself—campaign finance reform, term limits, reapportionment—the rules of the political game. Outwardly, the debates over these issues are about competing visions of "good government," and many are sponsored by groups dedicated to that purpose. However, any attempt to change the rules of the game also ends up working to the advantage or disadvantage of some political interest or party. How campaign money is regulated, for example, can have a huge effect on the fortunes of both big donors and the politicians they give to.

THE BASIC RULES OF INITIATIVE POLITICS

The idealistic promise of the initiative process is the image of a small band of ordinary people taking on and beating powerful political interests. Yet fewer than half of the measures that even reach the ballot win, and most initiatives never make it to the ballot at all. Winning an initiative campaign, whether you are fighting for a yes vote or a no, requires a difficult combination of skill, determination, organizing, luck, and good timing. Before deciding to go forward, prospective initiative leaders need to ask themselves some hard questions. Does the public support what you're proposing? Do you have a political base able to raise the funds and do the hard work involved? Is the effort worth the huge resources of time and money (which could also be invested in something else) that it will take to win? If the answers to each of these questions is yes and you do decide to move forward, there are six basic rules of initiative politics that you should carefully consider as you develop your campaign strategy.

Winning Elections Is About Moving Swing Voters

Winning an election campaign is ultimately about getting 51 percent of the people who show up to the polls to vote your way. This begins with having a very clear sense of which voters you need to reach. Some people will be with you automatically, others against you no matter what. The real group of voters you need to focus on are the undecideds, the swing vote. For most progressive causes—environmental issues, tax justice, civil rights, consumer protection—that swing vote is often white, middle-class voters, especially women, who live in the suburbs.

There is another important block of voters to target, the people who agree with you on the issue but who, without a hard nudge, may not vote at all. This is especially the case with African Americans, Latinos, and younger voters. On both economic issues (such as health reform) and social issues (such as affirmative action and immigration), polling shows that these voters usually back the progressive side, but they vote in far smaller numbers than their proportion of the population. A hard challenge for progressive initiative campaigns is to find a way to campaign to both swing voters (white suburbanites) and nonvoters (ethnic minorities and young people) at the same time, as each is moved by a different set of campaign messages and a different group of public spokespeople.

Initiatives Are Fueled by Public Discontent

The most potent force in initiative politics, more potent than money, is the power of public discontent. The most dramatic initiative victories have been fueled by voter anger, traditionally against something: antitax; anticrime; antipollution; anti-insurance companies; antipolitician; anti-immigrant. "Public anger exists," observes Harvey Rosenfield, author of California's landmark anti-insurance industry measure, Proposition 103. "Initiatives are choices about where it gets directed."[3] In some cases that anger is spontaneous (as it has been on taxes and insurance) and the challenge is to direct it in your political favor. In other cases that public discontent is created slowly over time through the work of advocates, as in the case of the anti-tobacco movement. If that public fury is on your side, even big money may not be able to defeat you. If that discontent runs against you, your chances are winning are very, very slim.

Initiative Campaigns Are About Harvesting Public Opinion, Not Changing It

Another false notion in initiative politics is that initiative campaigns are grand opportunities to shift public opinion to your side, even in the face of powerful special interests opposing you. In fact, initiative campaigns are a poor time to educate the public, especially while you are being outspent ten to one or more. Initiative campaigns are often big-money battles of quick sound bytes and images aimed at manipulating voters, not educating them. Most experienced initiative campaigners will tell you that if an initiative doesn't start out with support (as measured by serious polling) in the range of at least 65 to 70 percent, it has very little chance of maintaining 51 percent by Election Day. In almost every case, the "yes" vote for a measure only falls as the election approaches.

Some advocates learn this lesson the hard way. In 1994, California health care advocates qualified an initiative to establish a state-run health care system, despite many polls showing the public's strong skepticism about such a move. Instead of the grand public education effort that proponents hoped would sway voters to their side, they were crushed three to one following a multimillion-dollar ad blitz by health insurers that set the cause backward, not forward.

Initiatives Are Defeated by Their Weakest Provision

A basic strategy in almost all campaigns opposing an initiative is to target the measure's most controversial provision and attack it relentlessly. In many cases, that provision is really peripheral to the central question the initiative addresses. For no campaigns the task is to find that one weak spot and fix voters attention on it. For yes campaigns the task is to try to find that weak spot and weed it out during the drafting process, or, if that can't be done, to design a capable defense. Alcohol industry opponents of a 1990 California "nickel per drink" initiative targeted an obscure provision that they claimed would force increases in other taxes. Highlighted with millions of dollars of industry-sponsored advertising, that one provision became an Achilles heel that took down the whole proposition.

When Voters Are Confused, They Tend to Vote No

Often, the most effective strategy for the no side of an initiative campaign is simply to raise voters' doubts. "When voters are uncertain or confused by a measure they typically vote no," notes M. Dane Waters, executive director of the Initiative and Referendum Institute. "This is why only 40 percent of all initiatives pass."[4] In Missouri, for example, polls showed in 1995 that at least 70 percent of the state's voters supported term limits for legislators. However, opponents were able to defeat a term-limits initiative on the ballot that year, not by challenging the idea of term limits but by charging that the initiative was poorly drafted and that no one could say clearly who would be affected by the term limits and who wouldn't.

First Make It Controversial, Then Define the Sides to Your Advantage

Another basic strategy is to make the initiative controversial so that the public is paying attention, then define the two sides so that you are the good guys and the other side is evil incarnate. During a 1994 California campaign on a tobacco industry–sponsored smoking initiative, the Public Media Center ran advertisements that simply listed the top five contributors to each side. With $12 million from Philip Morris on one side versus $500,000 from the American Cancer Society on the other, most voters knew easily which side they wanted to support.

In other campaigns, defining the sides is done with the subtlety of a sledgehammer. The backers of California's initiative to cut auto insurance rates drove a truckload of cow manure to the corporate headquarters of Farmers Insurance, with more than a dozen news cameras along for the ride. When issues are complicated, voters look for shortcuts to understanding the politics involved. Lifting up powerful symbols of good and bad— the American Cancer Society versus the tobacco lobby—gives voters the shortcut they are looking for.

Which Election You Pick Matters—A Lot

Initiative campaigns are not waged in a political vacuum. Events in the world and other issues on the ballot will have a major effect on an initiative's political fortunes. In many states an early consideration is whether to aim for the primary election or the general election ballot. The conventional wisdom is that general elections are more favorable for progressive initiatives because greater numbers of younger and minority voters are likely to turnout for a final vote for governor or president. However, general-election ballots are usually much more crowded, with large numbers of both initiatives and candidates competing for voter attention and making it even harder for low-budget campaigns to get a share of public attention. It is also hard to predict the larger political winds that will shape a given election. When initiative sponsors made their decisions to go to the ballot a year beforehand, few campaigns foresaw that the November 1994 election would turn out to be a conservative juggernaut across the entire country. That election not only delivered a Republican takeover of Congress but doomed a number of progressive ballot measures as well.

THE TEN INGREDIENTS OF A SUCCESSFUL INITIATIVE CAMPAIGN

Successful initiative campaigns are put together with a mix of critical ingredients. In some larger states, where campaigns have larger budgets, all of them might be used. In smaller states or at the local level, initiative campaigning is often simpler and may use just a few. In either case, all campaigns need to consider which elements are the most important and how to use them strategically and effectively.

Polling and Focus Groups

Winning initiative campaigns is about speaking to voters based on where they already stand on an issue, not where you wish they stood. Finding out how voters think and how best to engage and persuade them is done through careful public-opinion research based on the use of two main tools, focus groups and polling. Research about public opinion is important to initiative campaigns in several different ways. First, it is a way to test an initiative's political viability—does it have a chance of winning? Second, polling results that show viability are an extremely helpful tool for early fund-raising, showing potential donors that the initiative can win or, for a no campaign, that it can be defeated. Third, focus groups and polls give campaigns important information about how to draft the initiative—which provisions will win voter support and which will lose it. Finally and critically, focus group and polling research helps a campaign identify the key swing voters it will need to reach and the messages and spokespeople that will be most persuasive to them.

Focus groups bring together a dozen or so randomly selected voters to spend a couple of hours talking about an issue with a professional facilitator. "You're looking for how people on the street are really going to talk about it," explains Karen Kapler, a consultant with the national campaign firm Woodward/McDowell. "What you really want to know is what arguments will specifically cause people to change their vote."[5] Campaigns that can afford it will typically do two focus groups, at a cost of four to five thousand dollars each.

Polling takes the language, opinions, and arguments raised by the focus groups and tests them with a representative sampling of voters. "Polls test to see if these [focus group] results are real and to what degree," notes veteran initiative pollster David Binder.[6] Typically, an initiative poll will test a voter's first impression of a measure, then recite a list of arguments, pro and con, and then test the voter's opinion again, in an effort to simulate the debate that the voter will likely hear during the campaign. Initiative polls also test voter reaction to potential provisions, as well as the messages and messengers that the campaign might use. Poll research, for example, moved opponents of a 1992 antiwelfare initiative in California to focus (winningly) on an unpopular provision to give then-Governor Pete Wilson new authority over the state budget.

A well-done initiative poll will survey between eight hundred and twelve hundred voters. Such a survey might take up to twenty-five minutes and include up to one hundred questions. A full-scale poll such as this could cost up to twenty-five thousand dollars. Often campaigns will run at least two polls, the first to guide the drafting process and the second to help shape the campaign. At a more local level and for campaigns that can't afford polling like this, it is possible to create a homegrown version at very little cost. To create a random sample of voters to survey you can use the phone book, plucking out the first name listed on every tenth page. To develop appropriate, unslanted polling questions, you might consult with a local political science professor trained in polling techniques. You can then train your campaign volunteers to make the calls and tally the results.

It is important, however, to note some important cautions about the use of polls. A lot can happen between the time a poll is taken and the day voters actually go to the polls. Initiatives that have started out with public support of more than 60 percent have plummeted to below 20 percent by Election Day. Polling is also unreliable if a campaign doesn't include the harshest, ugliest arguments that it will face in the campaign. "You need to know the worst case," says Kapler. In an election campaign, public opinion is everything. Without good polling, the campaign is flying blind.

Fund Raising

Money will not guarantee victory for an initiative campaign, nor does the lack of money necessarily mean a campaign will lose. However, when it comes to initiatives, money does make a huge difference and you need a plan for raising it. The cost of running an initiative campaign varies immensely from state to state and community to community. Some local initiatives can be won on budgets of just a few thousand dollars. For large statewide campaigns, where television is the medium of choice, those costs may easily run into the millions (and for corporate-led campaigns, into the tens of millions).

There is no one formula for how to raise funds for initiative campaigns. The approach you take will depend on the issue, who supports it, and what resources you have to work with. Most progressive initiatives are funded through a mix of sources, with the major one being cash from organizations that have either a strong philosophical stake or a direct self-interest in the initiative. Labor unions and professional associations, which have a built-in ability to raise money, are a typical source for progressive initiative campaigns. Teachers unions, for example, are usually the leading funders of campaigns dealing with education issues. The key to raising organizational financial support is to appeal to a group's self-interest, to demonstrate that the campaign is winnable, and to involve the group's leaders early on.

Some progressive initiative campaigns have been able to tap into the deep pockets of well-heeled liberals, known in the trade as big donors. Other campaigns have had success in getting sympathetic politicians to transfer some of their own campaign funds to the initiative effort, especially when those politicians see that support as a way to link themselves to a popular issue. Whether from individuals or politicians, big donor fund raising requires a long and deliberate courting ritual of identifying potential givers and selling them on your cause.

For issues that have a strong base of supporters who might be willing to become small contributors, direct mail and telephone solicitation are useful fundraising strategies. To work, however, campaigns must have a base of support that is genuinely excited, and lists of those supporters must be available from which to make contact. Lists like these are not invented in the heat of a campaign but developed over several years. A 1990 mountain lion protection initiative in California netted more than $400,000 from a mailing to 20,000 existing members of the Mountain Lion Foundation. A volunteer telephone bank in support of the 1994 California health care initiative raised more than $150,000 in just six weeks to help pay for campaign radio ads.

In all cases, successful campaign fund-raising requires that you start early, get some seed money up front to get things moving, convince potential donors that you can win, establish realistic fund-raising goals, and develop a careful system of accountability to ensure that the people and organizations involved actually raise what they say they can raise.

Drafting

Up to a full year before voters go to the ballot, a small group of people make the most significant decisions of the campaign: what to put in the initiative. Initiative campaigns are often won or lost in the drafting process. For initiative drafters, there are two basic, often competing challenges—making the initiative good law and making it a winning political campaign. Getting both those tasks right is what good initiative drafting is all about.

"Drafting an initiative is carving words into legal stone," explains David Roe, author of a successful California antitoxics initiative. "Be sure you're carving the right words."[7] Will the initiative really do what you want it to do? Does it go far enough, or has it been compromised down to something less than what is worth the effort? Does it have any glaring gaps? If it wins, will it survive assault via amendment by the legislature? Is it written in a way that can survive the sort of full-scale legal challenges that have become commonplace in many states? Finally, will it be fully implemented? Does some department or agency have a specific mandate to carry out the law, and is that entity sympathetic to your initiative or hostile to it?

Some state initiative proponents seek to protect themselves against a post-passage assault either in the legislature or the courts by writing their measures as amendments to the state constitution, a drastic step that also makes mistakes extremely difficult to correct. Others write their initiatives as simple statutes but protect them by requiring that any amendments by the legislature be approved by a supermajority of two-thirds or more. One more consideration that initiative proponents need to keep in mind is to include a provision guaranteeing their legal standing to defend the measure in court if it is challenged, rather than leaving that defense to public officials who might have opposed the original measure. Some initiatives create new agencies to carry out their provisions, such as California's Coastal Protection Act, which established a new state commission to implement its environmental protections.

Drafting a measure to get the politics right means looking at it through the eyes of three different audiences—your allies, your opposition, and the public. You will want to draft the initiative in a way that encourages your allies to support it. Will it make them enthusiastic and willing to commit time, energy, and resources to the campaign? Can you draft it in a way that keeps your opposition from becoming more intense and better funded? Ultimately, however, the main audience for your initiative is the voters. The questions to ask in relation to them are: Is the initiative simple and understandable? Does it have an "Achilles heel," some provision like the clause that sank the California alcohol tax initiative that will undermine it? You should also give the measure an official title that wins visceral support from voters when they hear it—Coastal Protection Act, Taxpayer Protection Act—since that title will be repeated to voters by the news media repeatedly throughout the campaign.

Preparing a solid initiative requires time. There is research to be conducted about policy and public opinion, drafting to be done, and consultations to be carried out with prospective allies. When this process is too rushed, mistakes are made that can undo a whole campaign. Allow ample time to draft and redraft your proposal until you get it right. Avoid drafting the measure by a complicated committee and actively seek outside advice and criticism before you set your proposal in stone. In most cases it is a significant advantage to introduce potential initiatives first in the legislature. In addition to giving you the ability to say publicly, "We tried the legislative route but our opposition was too strong," it also forces your opponents to identify your initiative's weaknesses for you when there is still time to fix them.

Coalition Building

As in most advocacy work, in initiative campaigning it is very useful to have a large and broad coalition on your side. Strong coalitions are a way to equip your campaign with the diversity of resources it needs to win. For initiative campaigning the mix of resources needed is very specific, and the core group of people who start the campaign should have a plan for how to recruit partners that bring these resources on board.

A crucial resource to look for in coalition allies, sadly, is money. Usually, this comes from of membership groups, such as labor unions. Another resource that an ally can bring to the campaign is the capacity to deliver signatures for the qualification drive. The best groups for this are large volunteer organizations that already have a strong track record of signature gathering. It is also important to have groups on your side that have direct appeal and credibility with the electorate; this is one of the things good polling tests for. When voters see organizations such as MADD, the PTA, the League of Women Voters, or AARP on your side, it gives you legitimacy and wins votes.

Coalition partners can also bring staff and volunteer time as well as expertise and experience with initiative campaigning. The latter is essential. Ballot politics is not the same as other advocacy politics. Facing the voters is very different than lobbying, organizing, or protesting. You need someone on your side who has been there and understands the game.

Building this kind of initiative coalition is tricky work, involving the difficult management of both organizational and individual egos, often while under political fire. The most important phase of coalition building happens at the very start, during the drafting process. If organizations don't get what they care about included at the start it becomes much harder to get them involved with any real enthusiasm and commitment later. The leaders of the campaign need to understand what groups want and also the internal rules and procedures by which they make their decisions. Often selling an organization on an initiative requires reaching out not only to its leadership but to its larger membership base as well. "It's like selling straw hats or refrigerators," says veteran initiative manager Gerald Meral of California's Planning and Conservation League, "You go out and meet and meet and meet."[8]

Finally, initiative leaders will have to deal with the inevitable clash of both personalities and organizations that occur in every campaign. Some are disagreements over strategy or message. What will the ads say? Will scarce resources get spent on television or voter organizing? There are also tensions over blame and credit. Who speaks to the media? Who gets to be the recognized leader? There are several ways to resolve tensions in initiative coalitions. One is to anticipate loaded issues early and get them on the table for discussion before they explode, and preferably before the campaign is in full gear. Another way is to work early on developing a strong level of trust among the individuals and organizations involved. In the end there also needs to be one individual or group that is clearly in charge of the campaign, respected enough by all the players so that they can make tough decisions on the campaign's behalf.

Gathering Signatures

The first concrete test of any initiative campaign is whether it can collect the signatures needed to qualify the measure for the ballot. How many signatures are required varies from state to state. Typically, the requirement is 5 to 8 percent of the number of voters in the state's or city's most recent full election. In some small cities that requirement may translate into just a few thousand signers. In large states it can mean close to one million. In addition, initiative promoters not only need to gather the number of signatures legally required, but also need to gather as many as 30 to 40 percent more, since many of the signatures will be from people disqualified because they aren't registered to vote or who write the wrong address.

Qualification drives come in all stripes, from all-volunteer efforts run on a shoestring to lavish operations with armies of paid signature gatherers. For campaigns with a strong base of dedicated supporters, a volunteer petition drive can be quite powerful. A volunteer effort can help build a base that can be tapped later for fund-raising, voter registration and voter outreach. A volunteer drive also sends a message to the media, potential donors, and other key audiences that the measure has strong support. On the other hand, volunteer drives are very labor intensive and require a high level of coordination and organization to ensure that people are in the places they need to be, when they need to be, with the materials they need to have, doing what they need to do. Even if the signature gatherers themselves aren't paid, in most cases it takes a paid staff of organizers to make the drive work. Volunteer drives can also be unpredictable. Organizations or people who haven't been involved in signature gathering before often wildly overestimate how many signatures they can collect.

The more common route to the ballot in the bigger states is to contract with a professional signature-gathering firm. There are a growing number of these firms, each with an extensive network of circulators for hire who move from initiative to initiative. The firms charge on a per signature basis and the rates vary from election to election depending on how many different initiatives are competing for circulators. Typical rates can range from forty cents to seventy cents per signature, with some campaigns paying much more. Philip Morris paid two dollars per signature in 1994 to qualify its California smoking initiative. The advantage of contracting for paid signatures is simplicity—you write the check and you get the signatures. The disadvantage is the lost opportunity to involve large numbers of volunteers. Many campaigns use a mix, having volunteers collect the signatures they can and using paid firms to get the rest.

The "Cadillac" method of qualifying initiatives, used only by corporate interests with deep, deep pockets, is signature gathering by direct mail. Two dollars or more per signature is standard for the firms that offer this service. One advertised, "We will qualify a constitutional amendment, even to 110% [of the required signature amount], in 45 days. And we guarantee specific numbers of valid signatures on a money back basis."

Citizen initiative efforts need to pick the mix of methods that works best for their set of circumstances. Along the way, campaigns should keep a careful count of how many signatures they have in hand, including spot checks for the proportion of valid to invalid signatures. When the drive is complete, campaigns can use the turning in of signatures as an important hook for media coverage, signaling legitimacy and momentum and launching the messages that proponents will carry forward into the campaign.

Campaign Messages and Messengers

An initiative campaign is mostly about the message it uses to woo voters to its side. The first step in defining that message is defining the key groups of voters that the campaign most needs to reach and move. In order to get noticed, the campaign's message must not only speak to people's minds but also to their emotions. Anger, fear, nostalgia, and humor are all emotions that campaigns use in their messages. Backers of a successful Maine initiative to restrict moose hunting used humor, with a commercial featuring the cartoon character Bullwinkle. Sponsors of a winning

California park bonds measure used nostalgia to appeal to the elderly, with an ad that included lush scenes of the California landscape as the backdrop and the message, "California, the way it was, the way it still can be."

Having the right messengers is also crucial. In most cases, effectiveness is about credibility. It is also powerful when a campaign can put together a combination of odd allies. Other initiatives seek celebrities to be their messengers in order to attract the public's attention. In many cases the campaign's actual leaders are not the most credible spokespeople with voters.

Voters face many distractions in the midst of a campaign, and the only real chance a message has of getting through is if it is simple, compelling, and repeated at every opportunity. The message should, in one clear sentence, define the problem and promote the initiative as the solution (or, for a no vote, define the initiative as the problem). "Auto insurance rates are much too high, Proposition 103 lowers them." "Vote for Proposition 65 to protect our drinking water." These are the kinds of messages that cut through political noise and reach persuadable voters.

Media

The most important way in which initiative campaigns communicate their message is through the media—through news coverage and also through paid campaign ads. An effective strategy for using the media is absolutely vital. The expression "free media" refers to coverage that isn't paid advertising, but that doesn't necessarily mean it is free. Initiative campaigns spend a great deal of time and resources trying to attract media coverage to their cause and spinning the way that coverage comes out. Some campaigners call these efforts "earned media." Initiative media efforts need to begin with a clear sense of what the media considers to be news and what it doesn't. Reporters are looking for what will draw an audience, stories that, as *San Francisco Chronicle* reporter Sabin Russell describes, "will get the blood pumping of my editors and my readers."[9] Against that standard, initiative campaigns are often a pretty tough sell.

Unless the measure provokes deep emotions or public conflict (such as immigration, gay rights, abortion, assisted-suicide), your best strategy is to focus on the campaign events that will reliably draw coverage. These include the announcement of the initiative, the turning in of signatures, the release of poll results by local newspapers, the filing of campaign financial reports, or the release of a new ad by either side. These are each potential "hooks" for news coverage and opportunities for either side to get out its message and try to demonstrate that political momentum is with them. For example, a new financial report showing $1 million in contributions flowing in from special interest groups is an opportunity, once again, to charge opponents with trying to buy the election. A new voter poll showing you standing strong is an opportunity to claim public support.

It is also possible for campaigns to create their own hooks for news coverage. These might include the release of studies, the announcement of new endorsements, and events that are carefully designed to stimulate media interest.

However, to draw press attention these media events have to be more than just the typical news conference or protest. Having celebrities or public figures is a big plus. California Governor Pete Wilson, campaigning for reelection in 1994, drew constant media attention for his anti-immigrant measure, Proposition 187, with events such as visits to the California-Mexico border. A 1986 antitoxics initiative in California received huge media attention when Jane Fonda and a bus full of Hollywood stars set out on a statewide tour to promote the initiative. A flock of movie stars packing into the local McDonald's for lunch drew media attention everywhere it went. Campaigns can also get their message out through visits with editorial boards and with appearances on radio and television talk shows.

It is also crucial to establish, early on, solid relationships with the handful of reporters who will cover the campaign the most. In almost all cases, these are the reporters at major daily newspapers who are assigned to cover the campaign. What they write will create the early impressions, influencing other reporters, editorial writers, opinion leaders, potential contributors, and the public. What these reporters want and need from campaigns is solid, reliable information. They also need help with ideas for stories and contacts with people who can help put a human face on the issue involved. Campaigns that get a reputation for loose facts or an overreliance on rhetoric can end up turning these reporters against them.

Unfortunately, however, the real battleground in most initiative campaigns is paid advertising. The growing use and increasing costs of paid ads are driving up the cost of campaigning and increasing the hold of wealthy special interests over the initiative process. The cost of these ads varies widely from community to community and medium to medium. In some rural areas a radio ad might cost a few hundred dollars. In Los Angeles, a thirty-second prime-time television ad can cost upwards of twenty thousand dollars.

Like all initiative campaign strategy, paid media is about targeting swing voters. Television is the medium of choice for campaigns that have the resources required because it can reach a high volume of voters quickly and also packs an emotional, visual punch that sticks with them. For campaigns without that kind of money, radio ads are much cheaper to produce and also much cheaper to air. They can also be targeted very directly at specific audiences—from Rush Limbaugh to rap.

High-profile ads in major newspapers are aimed more at impressing opinion leaders and policymakers than at reaching the general public. Full-page ads in major dailies can be hugely expensive and not worth the cost. Advertising in smaller local papers may be a more practical option for most campaigns. One approach is the "names" ad. Working with a predesigned ad created by the campaign, local supporters contact lists of local backers and ask for permission to list their name in the ad and for a small contribution to help place it in the local paper. The other common paid advertising tool is direct mail. Again, it can be expensive, but it allows for very specific targeting of certain blocks of voters—for example, women registered to vote as "Ms." and therefore assumed to be more feminist in their political outlook.

The bottom line is that each campaign needs to come up with a media strategy that works for its specific circumstances. Who do you need to reach and how much money will it take to reach them? Influencing and encouraging favorable news coverage is the foundation for citizen initiative efforts, augmented by as much well-targeted, paid media as the campaign can afford.

The Ballot Pamphlet

Many states and localities mail out to all registered voters an official ballot pamphlet in which the two sides of an initiative can publish an official "argument" and, in some cases, some form of paid advertising. How influential these official mailings are with voters, in comparison with television and radio advertising, is debatable, but because it is the one piece of campaign information that every voter will receive, campaigns should use it with a keen sense of strategy.

The format of voter pamphlets varies, but in general they include the official title and summary of each measure, the actual text, and arguments and rebuttals submitted by proponents and opponents. Campaigns can and should seek to influence the summaries of measures to their advantage, but their real control is over their own published arguments. Campaigns need to keep in mind that many voters will only skim these ballot statements, so the most important consideration is who signs them. Use names that voters will recognize and that boost your side's credibility. Campaigns should also try to play to their weak side. Progressives, for example, often try to include signers with some type of business affiliation. It may also be possible to list not only a few signers but also a longer list of endorsing organizations. As a rule, campaigns will want to use the ballot pamphlet to make the same basic arguments they want to use for the whole election. Rebuttal space should be used to refute, simply and clearly, the arguments raised by the other side, but then go right back to reinforcing the same campaign message once again.

Mobilizing Activists

The promise of the initiative process is supposed to be the opportunity for common citizens to directly change the laws of the land. In the big-money arena of ballot measures, it would be easy to believe that volunteer politics is a relic of the past, but it is still possible for ordinary citizens to make a difference, through smart campaign organizing.

Organizing in initiative campaigns does not mean the same thing as long-term community organizing. For initiatives, that organizing is about mobilizing volunteers to take on the time-limited tasks of trying to win an election. It could lead to longer-term movement building, or it could just be about that one campaign. Volunteers can play a variety of significant roles in ballot campaigns. They can help gather the signatures to qualify an initiative. They can participate in phone banks to reach voters, contributors and other volunteers. They can help the campaign win endorsements from the organizations they belong to or sponsor house parties to recruit financial and volunteer support from their friends. With training, volunteers can be public speakers on the campaign's behalf and they can participate in media work (such as making press calls). Volunteers can also help in the campaign office or out in the field with leafleting, voter registration, and get-out-the-vote drives.

Volunteers give a campaign their time and enthusiasm. Campaigns that want to recruit and keep volunteers need to make sure that the volunteer experience is a good one. Campaigns do this by giving volunteers an ongoing sense of how their small contributions are part of the larger effort. Some campaigns do this by plastering the campaign office with visual charts that track a campaign's progress (with signature gathering, phoning, fund-raising, and so on). Volunteers also need to be assigned work that matches their skills and the time they have available. Campaigns should support them with training and clearly defined tasks and responsibilities. Many long-term political activists begin their involvement as campaign volunteers. Initiative campaigns, if they chose to, can play an important role in helping people discover their own talents as leaders.

Campaign Leadership

Every initiative campaign has to put together a decision-making and management structure that fits its constituency and political needs. Most campaigns begin with a catalyst, some person or organization that brings together the initial policy ideas, supporters, and resources that makes people feel the campaign is real and gets it off the ground. The person or organization who takes on this role needs credibility on the issue and as the leader of a political campaign.

Next, campaigns need to put together a strong decision-making structure that can make good choices quickly and win buy-in from the broad constituencies involved. A typical campaign structure will involve, at the top, an executive committee of three to five people to supervise the implementation of the campaign plan and make judgment calls on issues like the hiring of staff, the types of ads to run, and how to respond to developments in the media. Usually, this group is made up of the advocates and organizations which have the closest association with the issue and those who are putting the most resources into the campaign.

Most campaigns then also have a larger "campaign committee," which includes the larger group of organizations with a stake in the initiative, up to two dozen people who meet periodically to coordinate their activities and to give input into key campaign decisions. Statewide campaigns may also have parallel local committees that carry out activities such as signature gathering, local media work, voter registration and outreach, phone banks, and fund-raising.

Larger campaigns usually hire staff and consultants who manage the day-to-day work. This might include: a campaign director who runs things overall and reports to the executive committee; a communications director in charge of day-to-day relations with reporters; an organizing director who develops and manages the various field operations of the campaign; and a finance director/treasurer who develops and oversees all the fund-raising work. Some or all of these positions might also be filled by volunteers or by staff from supporting organizations.

A NOTE ABOUT THE RULES FOR NONPROFITS

As with lobbying, nonprofit groups are often able to have much more involvement in initiative campaigns than they might otherwise suspect, but at the same time they need to be extraordinarily careful about IRS rules. For an excellent guide on the dos and don'ts for nonprofits involved in initiative campaigning see, Seize the Initiative, published by Alliance for Justice of Washington, DC Tell. (202) 822-6070 ($20).

The value of outside campaign consultants is hotly debated among initiative activists. Some see consultants as skilled political professionals whose expertise is crucial and who bring to the campaign a valuable outside perspective. Others see consultants as a waste of funds, since most have little background on the issue and even less commitment to it. Most initiatives that do hire consultants hire them to take on specific parts of a campaign—polling, advertising, media, or voter outreach. Campaigns that rely substantially on professional consultants need to be sure that the campaign's leaders retain control over the basic strategy and messages.

The work of an initiative campaign is seldom over after the votes are counted. If you win, you have to start focusing on implementation and protecting your victory from assault in other arenas (in the courts and in the legislature). Winners need to start analyzing what implementation and political defense work will be needed and assembling the team of people who will carry it out. If you lose, the campaign leaders need to think about a strategy for keeping the issue alive and staging a comeback, by spinning the message you want supporters and the public to remember and, perhaps, preparing a legal challenge.

THE NEED FOR REFORM

Finally, the initiative process itself is in serious need for reform. A process that was launched to give power to the people over wealthy special interests is more and more being taken over by those same special interests. While big money still rarely wins a yes vote on its own initiatives, the ability of huge sums to secure a no vote against populist measures is quite clear. Unfortunately, the United States Supreme Court has been insistent in its rulings that unlimited initiative contributions and spending are "free speech" protected by the First Amendment, so that money continues to flow without restriction. The Federal Communications Commission has made this situation worse by striking down, in 1992, the federal Fairness Doctrine, which formerly guaranteed low-budget campaigns at least some form of free access to the airwaves.

To return the initiative process to its original "people power" roots, states must adopt some new rules. First, where possible, Limits need to be placed on how much money can be spent on and contributed to an initiative campaign (challenging the Court's decision along the way). Second, campaigns should be required to clearly disclose their largest contributors in all paid ads. Third, we need to create some new public tools for voter education, such as more engaging ballot pamphlets or free access to the airwaves. Only these will allow campaigns to get their message out, even if they can't afford twenty thousand dollars for a television ad.

CHAPTER THIRTEEN

The Internet

Democracy's Newest Tool

I think there is a world market for maybe five computers.

—THOMAS WATSON, CHAIRMAN OF IBM, 1943

When I first moved to Bolivia from California in 1991, I had never seen an e-mail message or a Web page. My correspondence with people was carried out through long handwritten letters that often took up to eight weeks to reach their destination. My access to world news was so limited that I first heard about the dismantling of the Soviet Union almost two weeks after it happened. A decade later, living in Bolivia once again, I often exchange e-mail back and forth with two dozen people in a day, communications that fly from one hemisphere to the other in a few seconds. I check the fresh headlines almost every morning in the electronic edition of the *New York Times*. With a few clicks of a mouse I send alerts and information to a list of nearly two thousand people all over the world.

Such is the reach and power of the Internet. To be sure, I often miss the long, slow communication of letters and often wish I knew much less about the goings-on outside the Andean valley where I live. However, the Internet does connect us, on a global scale, in a way that was virtually undreamed of a decade ago, and those connections are also powerful new tools for public activism and advocacy.

While some of the Internet's potential has been overhyped, in theory anyone with a computer and a modem has potential access to a worldwide audience, at an extraordinarily low cost. The Internet allows us to publish and read important news, uncensored and unfiltered by formal news organizations. It provides access to an unfathomable volume of research and information and serves as an unprecedented forum for discussion and the exchange of ideas. Through our keyboards we are able to knit together communities from people and organizations spread to the far winds. Clearly, activism by Internet can never completely replace the traditional methods of civic action—grassroots organizing, media work, lobbying, coalition building. However, understanding the new tools and integrating them thoughtfully with the old is now a crucial part of developing an effective advocacy campaign.

HOW PEOPLE USE THE INTERNET FOR ACTIVISM

The Internet—e-mail, the World Wide Web, list serves, discussion groups, and forums—is being used as an important advocacy tool in many different ways. We need to employ each of these in a manner that is strategic and clear:

Research

It is hard to imagine a piece of information that is not posted somewhere on the Web—statistics about child health, the arguments for and against affirmative action, documentation of human rights abuses in a faraway land—almost anything a group might need to educate itself about the issue at hand. Gone are the days when research meant going to the local library to struggle through the periodical guide. The sheer volume of information posted on the Web also creates two problems, however. First, with so much material available, how do you sort through it all quickly to find what you need? Second, how do you assess the reliability and accuracy of what you find?

There are a few tips worth keeping in mind. One, don't waste your time hopping around from page to page within a Web site that doesn't have what you need. Web sites can suck you in for an hour and end up yielding nothing you can actually use. Look at a site and judge quickly whether it is likely to have what you need. If not, move on quickly to more fertile territory. Established policy organizations such as the Urban Institute, Brookings, or the Heritage Foundation or respected publications with searchable data bases such as the *New York Times* and the *Nation* are usually much more fruitful places to spend your time than an organization you only discovered through a Web search.

Also very important, use an Internet search engine that fits what you are looking for. Yahoo, for example, one of the Internet's most popular search tools, is fine if you are looking for commercial sites where you can buy something, but it is not especially useful if you are trying to do serious research. In my own work I have found www.google.com to be a quick and efficient pathway to more research-oriented sites. When you do find a site with strong information, bookmark it so you can find it again, and also take a close look at whatever links the site might include. A well-crafted links page means that someone has already done a lot of your research work for you, so take advantage of it.

Finally and most critically, do not assume, just because something is posted on the Internet, that it is credible or true. Before you rely on that information check it out. Who posted it? Are they known and credible? Are the sources of the information cited, and can you check those citations? How close is the information to its original source? Information on the Internet is plentiful and easy to find, but it is also subject to far less scrutiny than the information used by traditional research sources such as newspapers, journals, and magazines. With the Internet you need to take responsibility for that scrutiny yourself.

Public and Voter Education

Organizations use the Internet as a powerful forum for providing educational information to members of the public. Through electronic newsletters and alerts, groups provide information targeted directly to their members and supporters, bringing them up to date on current issues and often inviting them to take action. Through their Web sites, organizations make available to their members and the public reams of information—reports, articles, audio and video material, searchable databases, and more.

Some of the most advanced of these public education sites are aimed at providing voters with analysis and information about candidates and issues on the ballot. The "Women's Voting Guide" (www.womenvote.org) lets users complete a survey of how they would vote on various legislation and then compares those choices to the actual votes of the user's representative in Congress. A site sponsored by the Markle Foundation (www.webwhiteblue.org), with state-by-state links, leads voters directly to official state election sites, online voter guides, campaign finance data, and election returns.

Public Discussion and Exchange

The Internet has also become a worldwide backyard fence over which people share information and discussion about everything from cookie recipes to economic globalization. While much of this is done ad hoc through individual e-mail, a lot of it is more organized. The Internet is host to thousands of discussion groups, forums, chat rooms, and other vehicles for forming communities, ongoing or temporary, in which public issues can be discussed and debated. Some of these are built into Web sites, some stand on their own. Some are freewheeling, others are controlled or organized by a moderator. These online discussions are also an important tool for building an activist network and helping that network develop its ideas about policy and strategy.

Political Action on the Internet

One of the most promising opportunities raised by the Internet is its potential as a direct tool for inspiring and organizing political action. Across the globe, thousands of organizations are using Internet-based campaigns to bring public pressure to bear on both government and corporate officials. Some of these are based on the simple use of e-mail. For example. the U.S. Public Interest Research Group (www.uspirg.org) mobilized university students to e-mail British Petroleum and other oil companies to protest oil drilling in an Alaska wildlife refuge. Following the e-mail protest, organizers received a call from British Petroleum, setting up a series of high-level meetings they would not have gotten in any other way. "We got their attention and held it," said Athan Manuel, director of the campaign.[1] A similar campaign, which I organized from Bolivia, organized an e-mail bombardment of the U.S. ambassador on a human rights case, forcing the embassy to open an official investigation.

PORTRAIT OF AN INTERNET ADVOCACY CAMPAIGN

"Bechtel out of Bolivia!"

In 1999, under pressure from the World Bank, the government of Bolivia privatized the public water system of its third-largest city, Cochabamba, granting a 40 year lease to a mysterious new company, Aguas Del Tunari. Within just months of taking over, the company hit local water users with rate increases of as much as 300%, forcing some of South America's poorest families to pay up to a third of their income just for water. By April 2000 Cochabamba's residents had declared that the contract must be broken and started what would become a week-long general strike and protest. The government refused to reverse the contract, declared a "state of emergency," arrested the protest's leadership, and sent soldiers in to occupy the town's center, killing a 17 year old boy and wounding scores of others.

In the midst of all this I decided to track down a local rumor that the San Francisco-based Bechtel Corporation was actually the main owner behind the new water company. Searching Bechtel's own library of news releases posted on the company's site I was able to find the evidence. I then sent out an action alert to The Democracy Center's list of nearly 2,000 advocacy organizations and journalists, highlighting Bechtel's role and urging people to contact the company through an e-mail address provided on its Web site. Soon after, a reader furnished us with the personal e-mail address of Bechtel CEO, Riley Bechtel. As the protests and repression in Cochabamba raged on, hundreds of people from all over the world began pummeling the corporation's leaders with a simple message, "Bechtel out of Bolivia!" My Internet reporting was also picked up by newspapers across the United States and Canada, including Bechtel's hometown of San Francisco.

Days later, under pressure both in the streets and in cyberspace, the company fled Bolivia, and the water system was returned to public hands. Shortly afterwards Bechtel, which had remained publicly mute throughout the crisis, made its first public statement, not to any press but to the hundreds of people who had written them by e-mail. The company's statement made headlines in Bolivia. By using the Internet as a research tool we were able to force into the public eye a corporate connection kept quiet. By giving people an easy and clear way to act, using e-mail, we held the company accountable for the injustice and violence being carried out on it's behalf. People all over the world contributed to a historic victory in the fight for globalization with justice.

For those interested, the Center's complete dispatches and reports are posted at "www.democracyctr.org.

Other campaigns use their Web site as their staging area for action. In September 1998, a handful of progressive, Internet-savvy activists launched a Web site (www.moveon.org) dedicated to pressuring Congress to drop the impeachment charges against President Clinton for his role in the Monica Lewinsky scandal. Within a week more than 100,000 people had used the site to send messages to members of Congress, within the first month, 250,000 had done so. By the end of the campaign, MoveOn was credited with generating more than 1,000,000 e-mails and 250,000 telephone calls to members of the Senate and House.[2] While the campaign did not succeed in its goal of stopping the impeachment, it did organize a huge volume of public action, drew enormous media and Congressional attention and created a model for Internet campaigns to come.

Not all groups and causes have the benefit of a powerful, media-driven issue like the Clinton impeachment, but the same techniques are being used, with solid effect, on other issues as well. An environmentalist campaign site (www. greencar.org) gives people an opportunity to send e-mail to the heads of GM, Ford, and Chrysler, pressuring them to make cars that burn fewer fuel emissions. The AFL-CIO has a site that lets union members send e-mail to specific federal officials on issues ranging from workplace safety to limiting carry-on bags aboard airliners.[3]

It is important to recognize that there are also limits to the effectiveness of high-tech activism. For government and corporate officials who aren't accustomed to hearing from the public, carefully orchestrated e-mail bombardment can have a huge effect. However, for members of Congress, state legislators, and others who are used to being targeted by letters, petitions, phone calls, and faxes, e-mail may not really have that much impact. Lawmakers judge constituent correspondence by the amount of effort that people put into it. Pages of names signed to a petition don't require much effort or carry much weight (unless they come in huge volume); such is also the case with scores of e-mails, many of which are not even from a law-maker's district or state. The most promising new tools for Internet activism are Web sites from which activists can send, free, faxes to their own representatives or to corporate officials. Even in the electronic age there is no substitute for filling someone's office with real pieces of paper.

Using the Internet to Organize and Coordinate
Traditional Political Action

Some of the most important political organizing taking place via the Internet is the old-fashioned kind, in which people leave their keyboards to lobby, protest, or gather signatures but use the Internet as a tool to help coordinate all that activity. The MoveOn campaign, in addition to generating a flood of communication to Congress, also used its Web site to organize thousands of volunteers to visit con-gressional offices in person.[4] The Children's Defense Fund used the Internet to or-ganize its 1997 Stand for Children march on Washington, to recruit participants, coordinate travel, and other tasks.[5] Activists in Toledo, Ohio, organized a recall movement against their mayor in which the recall petitions could be downloaded and printed directly off the Web.[6]

For organizing efforts like these and others, the Internet provides an im-portant mechanism for identifying and recruiting volunteers and coordinating the information and activities needed to make advocacy or protest action happen. In-ternet organizing still requires attention to the same basic principles as regular or-ganizing: volunteers need to be found and motivated; they need to be given work that fits their talents and interests; and their progress on that work needs to be mon-itored. Follow-up by those carrying out the organizing remains essential.

Fund Raising

Most recently, some organizations have broken new ground using the Internet as a fund-raising tool. Most notably, MoveOn raised more than $400,000 for selected congressional candidates, more than 90 percent of which came in contributions of $50 or less. The MoveOn site includes a page listing the candidates they support, along with photos, biographies, descriptions of their election contest, links to the candidates' Web sites, and a feature that allows visitors to contribute directly on the spot using their credit cards. Because these contributions are given in small amounts from different people, they fall within federal campaign contribution limits. Many other organizations now help support their lobbying and activist campaigns by including a similar contribution feature on their Web sites. The ability to reach large numbers of small contributors at very low cost through the Internet could eventually have a dramatic effect on both election and advocacy politics.

Election Campaigning

Finally, it is not just causes that are using the Internet to mobilize support and get out their messages, Internet campaigning is becoming a staple for candidates as well. The era of net campaigning came of age in 1998 with the election of independent Jesse Ventura as governor of Minnesota. As *Newsweek* wrote, "For months Ventura had no physical 'headquarters,' just an ever-growing e-mail list. Two thirds his fundraising pledges arrived via the Internet. His final, three-day, get-out-the-vote bus trip was organized by e-mail."[7] In 2000 all the major presidential candidates used elaborate Web sites to promote their campaigns, raise funds, and push the limits of the Internet as a campaign tool, an approach mirrored by state and local candidates across the United States. Especially following the presidential election debacle in Florida, more attention is being paid as well to how the Internet might be used to cast votes.

THE INTERNET'S MAIN TOOLS AND HOW TO USE THEM

At the start of the 1980s, few advocacy groups even had fax machines. By the end of the decade almost every group had one. At the start of the 1990s, few groups had e-mail and virtually none had anything remotely resembling a Web site. A decade later these and other Internet tools have become standard for virtually every advocacy group, but few use them to their full potential.

The Internet's basic tools—e-mail, Web sites, list serves, and discussion groups and forums—each serve a different function in advocacy efforts. E-mail is active, reaching out to people without their having to ask for it. Web sites are passive, requiring that people come to you to see what's there but providing people with much more information. List serves and discussion groups facilitate conversation and dialogue among large networks of people. The trick is to use them together in the most effective way possible.

E-Mail

E-mail is the daily workhorse of electronic activism, available cheaply to almost everyone; even those without computers can get free e-mail and access through local libraries. There are four main methods for using e-mail in a strategic way for activism:

Communication with Networks of People

The first step beyond using e-mail for one-on-one exchanges is using it for ongoing communication with networks of people involved. Traditionally, many organizations have done this with mail or faxes, both of which are far more expensive, wasteful of paper, and slower than e-mail. More importantly, when communication is done via e-mail, people can easily forward it to hundreds of others in just a few seconds and can also cut and paste information for use elsewhere. All this gives e-mail a much broader reach.

Organizations begin this shift to electronic communication by collecting the e-mail addresses of everyone involved in their work, for example requesting it on sign-up sheets at meetings. These addresses are then used to assemble an ever-growing e-mail list, often divided into sublists, by interest. E-mail communication is by no means a complete substitute for printed information, phone conversations, or face-to-face interaction, but it can be much more efficient in many circumstances—such as for sending out meeting announcements, meeting summaries, and action alerts. At the same time, it is also important not to bombard people with too many e-mails, which are more likely to be ignored by the people who receive them.

Newsletters

Some organizations use regular e-mail newsletters as a way to disseminate information and stay in touch with their extended network of friends and allies. In 1997 the Democracy Center began a simple monthly e-mail newsletter distributed to about 200 colleagues and supporters. The newsletter is short (750 words or so) and covers a broad array of topics in which the Center is involved, from political reform in California to human rights in Latin America. As each issue has been passed on by readers to others, more people have asked to be added to the subscription list. After three years the list ballooned to nearly two thousand advocacy groups and journalists worldwide. In addition, nearly every issue is now picked up and published in some U.S. newspaper or magazine. Equally as important, the newsletter has provided a vehicle through which the Center has been able to stay in regular contact with its growing network. Each issue prompts a flurry of e-mail from people who were reminded that they had some reason to be in touch. All issues of the Democracy Center's newsletter and the link to request a free subscription are available at www.democracyctr.org.

To gain readership, the material in such a newsletter must be well written and of genuine interest to the people who receive it. It should include a clear and simple title and a brief introduction to the topic covered so people can gauge their interest. At the bottom, for those who receive the newsletter indirectly, forwarded on from a friend or colleague, each issue should include clear notice about how readers can add themselves to the subscription list. This is the best way to keep the list growing.

Any mass e-mail communication of this sort should also abide by a few other basic points of electronic etiquette. Always list the recipient names in the "bcc" line of the e-mail, never as the recipient or "cc" (you can list yourself in the recipient line). To do otherwise results in your e-mail including the addresses of every person who receives it, making your list public and many of the people on it angry. Again, avoid overload. Too frequent a newsletter will result in people asking to be dropped from the list. In addition, do not add people to your list who have not asked to be added, and quickly and politely delete from your lists anyone who asks to be removed.

Action Alerts

E-mail action alerts allow organizations to notify their networks of supporters quickly, easily, and cheaply when a specific, urgent action needs to be taken, such as calls, letters, faxes, or e-mails to a corporate or public official. Many groups actively recruit a network of supporters who are committed to acting on their alerts. The Action Network (www.actionnetwork.org) recruits activists to its e-mail alert list with the slogan "Save the Environment with a Click of Your Mouse." When a targeted issue requires action, the group sends out a notice via e-mail, which includes a draft letter that recipients can personalize and simply e-mail back. Action Network then sends that e-mail on to the targeted officials.[8]

To make action alerts as effective as possible, establish your credibility as an organization, including a sentence of background and a link to your Web site. If the alert is recirculated (as the best alerts are), not everyone who receives it will know who you are. Date the alert and be clear about how long action still has value—a week, a month, longer? Alerts can keep moving around the Internet well past their window for action. Make the alert self-contained, including all the basic information people need and a Web link where they can get more. Make the action requested clear, compelling, and simple to do. "Send an e-mail note today to CEO Riley Bechtel [list e-mail address], telling him that Bechtel should leave Bolivia immediately as the people there have so clearly demanded." Finally, ask people to let you know if they have acted on the alert by sending you a copy and to share immediately any response they receive.

These alerts can be made far easier to respond to with a few simple additions. If the goal is to encourage people to send e-mail, include the appropriate address using the "mail-to" function. By entering the address in the body of the message as "mailto:info@democracyctr.org," that address will appear as a highlighted link that people can just click to automatically set up the outgoing message. Similarly, Web sites listed should be written out in full, such as "http://www. democracyctr.org." This also turns these site listings into a highlighted link that requires just a mouse click to go to.

In addition to sending out alerts to their own lists, some organizations draw even more attention to their announcements by posting them to relevant discussion groups . Another creative method of spreading the word is to provide a few lines and a Web link that supporters can cut and paste into their e-mail "signature," thus becoming part of all their outgoing e-mail. Greenpeace and Adbusters used this technique in a campaign targeting the Coca-Cola company, urging supporters to add to their e-mail signature, "Coca-Cola's use of HFCs to cool its drinks contributes to climate change. That's not cool. Tell the Real Thing to do the Right Thing—Join the Coke Challenge Campaign! http://www.cokespotlight.org."

Petitions

Almost everyone who has e-mail has, at one time or another, received an e-mail chain letter petition. Like the chain letters of regular mail, recipients are supposed to add their name to the list and send these petitions on to everyone they can think of. In the e-mail variety, every twenty-fifth, fiftieth, or hundredth person is supposed to send the petition and all the names on to the corporation or public official targeted. In theory, such petitions should be great tools, spreading like a wild advocacy virus through the Internet. In reality, however, the tool is a weak one, and there are much better alternatives that serve the same purpose more effectively.

One problem is that most of these petitions include no cut-off date, so they live forever, floating along in cyberspace like some lost NASA capsule in the stars. Often, they have no link where recipients can get more background information, and, usually, it isn't even clear who started the petition. As a result, a lot of people just consider such petitions to be more unwelcome spam (mass e-mails to people who don't want them) and don't respond. A much better approach is to send out specific e-mail action alerts or to give people a chance to participate in a campaign based at a Web site (such as the MoveOn campaign). These provide people with much more information and direction and are also likely to be much more effective. As Phil Agre, of the UCLA department of information studies, writes, "Many fewer people may actually take these actions, but they will have a much greater impact than simply forwarding a lot of e-mail down the rabbit holes of the Internet."[9]

Web Sites

Every year, more organizations use their Web sites as one of their most important advocacy tools. An effective Web site can be a combination of many things— library, calling card, meeting room, a platform for taking action, a portal to other groups and resources, and, with the most modern features, even a radio and television station.

BASIC ELEMENTS OF AN ADVOCACY-ORIENTED WEB SITE

✓ *Home Page:* Provides a simple overview and links to the site.

✓ *Publications Page:* With links to articles and reports, organized by subject.

✓ *E-mail Address Request:* To enable you to send visitors newsletters or alerts.

✓ *About Us:* Includes background of the group and its leaders.

✓ *Contact Us:* Address, phone, and fax, as well as direct e-mail links.

✓ *Links:* Lead visitors to other groups and useful, related Web sites.

✓ *What's Hot:* Features the group's top current priority.

✓ *Search Engine:* To search the site by key words.

Basic Design

It doesn't necessarily take the fanciest technology to make a Web site effective; often it just takes clear and creative use of the simplest ones. A strong advocacy-oriented Web site gives people the information they need to know, with links to more for those who want it, and the basic tools they need to take action. Typically, such a site will include a home page, a publications section, a request for visitors' e-mail addresses, some information about the organization, and a variety of other basic features. Sites with more elaborate features might include searchable libraries and databases, discussion forums, and an on-line mechanism for contributing money to the group.

When designing a Web site, always keep your users first in mind. Complicated graphics may look good, but they take a long time to load and often frustrate visitors, sometimes enough so that they leave altogether. The best sites are quick to load and simple to grasp at a glance. They focus people on what you want them to most pay attention to—the key issue of the moment, a new report, your big campaign, how to get involved. It is also important to remember that many people who access some part of your site will not do so from your homepage but via some link from another site or Internet search engine. It is important, for this reason, to include on every page in your site a clear identification of your group by name and links back to your home page and the other main sections of your site. Without these you may attract a good number of visitors and then lose them because they don't know where they are.

Attracting Visitors to Your Site

Even the best Web site is worth very little if no one visits it. There are several good ways to draw people to your site. The most basic is your e-mail. Every e-mail message an organization sends should include in its "signature" a direct link to its Web site and perhaps a short line ("See the Democracy Center's new report on tools for civic action!") to attract attention. Other organizations use their e-mail lists to send out mass promotions announcing a new feature on their Web site. The California

Voter Foundation, for example, does this regularly when it unveils its latest on-line voter guides. Announcements such as these can also be posted with user groups or forums.

Another source of attention is links from other, related sites. Many organizations have pages specifically dedicated to links to other organizations doing similar work. It is worth making a methodic effort to identify these potential Web allies and request a link back to your site. This is especially possible if your group is willing to reciprocate by making a link on your site to that organization. Note, however, that too many links on a page make it look confusing and invite people too easily to leave your site. Often the best solution is to list links on a separate links page. Some Web sites purchase paid banner links on Web sites that draw heavy traffic. These banners are actually small graphic ads that, when clicked, take visitors directly to your site. The Democracy Center used such an ad on a site dedicated to California political news (www.rtumble.com) to draw visitors to a site promoting its *Initiative Cookbook*. On a larger scale, the MoveOn campaign purchased a banner ad on Yahoo.com that drew 500,000 visits to its Web site.

There are also key opportunities off the Internet to promote your Web site. Anytime the Democracy Center publishes an article in a newspaper or magazine, it includes the address of its site (www.democracyctr.org) in the author identification. At meetings. groups can distribute a simple flyer promoting their site. They can post a banner promoting their site at any event that might draw TV coverage or a newspaper photo. When appearing live on TV or radio, groups can mention their site. Any opportunity to let people know how to find you on the Web is another opportunity to draw people to you.

Once you do attract people to your site it is important to draw them in further. The Human Rights Campaign (www.hrc.org) used a celebrity to draw visitors in, featuring the smiling face of Ellen DeGeneres as the link to a feature allowing people to write to TV executives in support of gay-friendly programming. Other sites draw people in with material designed to be personally useful. UCAN, a San Diego–area consumer group (www.ucan.org), posted weekly updates about which gas stations were offering the cheapest gas. Mothers and Others, an environmental group (www.mothers.org), mixed its action alerts on dairy hormones with advice about how to get ants out of your kitchen without using poisonous chemicals. The National Wildlife Foundation (www.nwf.org), in addition to providing a tool kits for activists, also provides downloadable environmental educational materials for teachers.[10]

Making Your Site a Solid Information Source

The main thing that people come to Web sites to get is information, and many organizations do an excellent job of making their site a one-stop shop for all the information visitors might need. This begins with posting all the relevant information and material your organization produces anyway—reports, articles, press releases, newsletters, scorecards that rate legislators or their votes. If you have already gone to the trouble of writing it, take the extra time to post it on the Web and make it available to the world. The more material you post, the more important it is that you organize and present that material in a user-friendly format, by subject matter, type of material, or both.

More elaborate sites build in even more features. Net Action, for example, (www.netaction.org) provides visitors with a comprehensive (and excellent) on-line training course called "The Virtual Activist," which includes both information and links to examples and other resources. A number of sites now offer on-line events calendars including links to the organizations sponsoring events where more information can be gotten. Groups that produce huge amounts of information—the Center on Budget and Policy Priorities (www.cpb.org) and The Cato Institute (www.cato.org) are two good, diverse examples—create on-line libraries and bookstores on their site. These are extensive listings of reports, articles, and books, all available on-line either for purchase or downloading. When posting longer material, groups have a choice. That material can be posted in HTML in which it is presented as a Web page that can be printed out or copied and pasted by users into their own documents. It can also be posted in PDF format, an efficient way to print out large documents (but which can't be easily copied as text and reused). Posting material as a Word document allows visitors to use and edit your material. Most useful is to offer a variety of formats.

Some sites now include extensive, searchable databases. The Environmental Defense Fund (www.edf.org) provides on-line access to toxics information from the U.S. Environmental Protection Agency, allowing visitors to enter their zip code and research, by neighborhood, what kinds of pollutants they are being exposed to and from what sources (www.scorecard.org). The site also lets users send a direct fax to the polluters involved. The League of Conservation Voters Web site (www.lcv.org) lets visitors click on a map of the United States and find their local representatives and how they voted on environmental issues. Groups that just want to add a simple search engine to their own site can do so easily and free of charge by using services such as atomz.com.

An additional feature used by groups that maintain extensive relations with the media is a special section designed for reporters, many of whom now use the Internet as a prime information source. Common Cause (www.commoncause.org), for example, offers a feature called "On Deadline? A Reporter's Guide to Money in Politics," which offers an overview of the current issues, the group's latest press releases, and a selection of background information designed especially for journalists. Not all groups need to provide something so elaborate, but designing a Web site with reporters in mind is a good strategy for most organizations.

One other thing to remember in all this is that you don't need to post every piece of relevant information available. Information that is most essential or that your group produced probably should be built into your site. Throughout the Web, however, there will be a great deal of other material and resources directly relevant to the issues you cover. By identifying these resources and creating a well-organized set of links to them, you are making your site a portal to all that material and will attract even more people to you.

Making Your Web Site a Forum for Discussion

Organizations also use their Web sites as a forum to give people an opportunity to communicate with one another on issues. Typically, these forums will be organized by topic, with some introduction by the group followed by posted comments from others with reactions and thoughts of their own. The Environmental Defense Fund, for example, maintains a collage of on-line forums on environmental issues ranging from "Business and the Environment" to "Teacher Talk," in which classroom teachers can share questions, opinions, and even lesson plans related to environmental issues.

Some forums are wide open, and anyone with access to the Internet can join in and post any comment they want. Others are moderated, meaning that comments are screened before posting. Some organizations maintain forums that require a password for entry, where organizational leaders and members can have private conversations, post minutes of meetings, or carry out organizational business on-line.

Making Your Web Site a Tool for Civic Action

One of the most important developments in Web site design is making sites direct tools for taking political or civic action. The key to making an action site effective is to make it as simple as possible to use, with built-in tools to send e-mail and faxes to policymakers, corporate officials, and the media. The technology involved is fairly simple, and in many cases it is possible to link to and piggyback on comprehensive sites already developed by others.

Many sites now let users quickly identify their members of Congress and the links needed to e-mail them; among these are the sites of the ACLU (www.aclu.org), and the Electronic Activist (www.eactivist.org). The Christian Coalition Web site (www.christian-coalition.org) not only offers links to members of Congress but to state lawmakers as well, searchable by zip code or by map. Other organizations, such as the National Abortion Rights Action League (www.naral.org), have designed their sites to allow activists to send faxes to members of Congress. Corporate Watch's Web site (www.corpwatch.org) is set up to let users send faxes at no charge to targeted corporate officials.

Other sites are set up to allow quick e-mail contact with the media. The Democracy Center Web site has a feature called "Write Right Now," which allows users to send letters to the editors of major newspapers easily. Yet another new action tool is the corporate "complaint site," usually targeted against one specific business, where people can share stories about consumer fraud or abuse and often send a direct communication to corporate leaders. A site called he Squeaky Wheel (www.thesqueakywheel.com) allows consumers to post complaints against anyone from a local car dealer to ATT, looking for others who have had similar experiences. Other sites make it possible for people to download material for off-the-net advocacy work, everything from bumper stickers to recall petitions to voter registration and absentee ballot forms.

The Use of Audio and Video

The cutting edge of Web technology is the availability of audio and video on sites. Web users can hear the actual recordings of U.S. Supreme Court arguments on the ACLU Web site (www.ACLU.org). Interested citizens in Washington State can use the Web (www.tvw.org) to tune into live proceedings of their state legislature. ACT-UP New York produced and posted a civil disobedience training video on its Web site (www.actupny.org).

With faster Internet connections and computers, audio and video material are becoming more easily accessible to more people every year. The future of Internet activism will include the ability of any group to hold a live video news conference from any location in the world (a jail where a human rights prisoner is held, a corporate headquarters, the steps of Congress). Announcement of that video conference will be made to tens of thousands via e-mail, inviting them to tune in live via their computer screens to a page that includes not only the live image but all the links necessary to learn more and take direct and immediate action. For those who can't watch live, the same video and information will be available around the clock.

List Serves and Discussion Groups

List serves are e-mail lists that, in many cases, not only allow the person managing the list to send out mail to everyone on it but also allow everyone on the list to send e-mail to everyone else. Discussion groups and forums are more like a bulletin board where people can post comments on some Web site or another, readable as a running conversation. The main question in putting together these tools is how open or controlled you want them to be, both in terms of who can participate and how they will do so. The most accessible of these are open subscription lists and open forums that anyone who finds can join. The more open a forum or list, the more opportunity there is for wide discussion and dissemination. There is also more risk that the list or forum will be clogged with points that aren't relevant or that it will be abused with mass mailings of unsolicited communication.

At the other extreme are forums and lists that are totally closed, essentially one-way communications from the people managing them to the people specifically invited to join. In the middle are moderated lists and forums. Here, participation is still subject to the approval of the manager but participants can post comments or send e-mail to the list, passing first through a screening process. This method provides a check to ensure that communications are relevant, but it also creates a great deal of work for the moderator and the risk that alternative points of view could be screened out.

How open or closed should a list or forum be? The answer depends on each group and its objectives. One list that I participate in uses the open approach, which allows the entire group to communicate with each other and has led to some good information sharing and communication. On the other hand, a good many of the messages are really more appropriate as one-on-one communication between specific people and clutter up the mailboxes of all the others. When an organization decides that its lists or forums should be open, it should also spell out clear guidelines for what communication it considers appropriate. Forums and lists are also both useful ways to disseminate action alerts and other information, linking back to Web sites for more details. There are many Web sites where people can search for potential lists and forums in which they might like to participate. Onelist (www.onelist.com) has a comprehensive portal to a range of "activism lists." Another directory of lists can be found at Liszt www.liszt.com.[11]

Whether advocacy communication takes place via e-mail, a Web page, or an open discussion forum, some important general rules apply. What you write should be designed for wide consumption, as you can't be sure how far and wide it will go. This means including enough background and overview so that newcomers can understand what is going on and using a tone that appeals to a wide swath of public opinion. Even more important, always assume that anything you send out or post will ultimately end up in your opponents' hands. If you don't want something to become public or don't want it used against you, don't send it out.

For groups that invite people to sign on to an e-mail list on their Web site or in alerts, it is important to have a clear privacy policy. Some groups freely share their e-mail lists with others, some never do, some only share the names of people who have specifically authorized them to do so. In any case, it is important for groups to have a privacy policy, to disclose it, and stick to it. The other consideration important for groups that actively use the Internet for outreach is whether they are prepared to deal with the e-mail they are likely to receive in response. Web sites, e-mail action alerts, and newsletters can generate a mountain of e-mail back to the group, communication that is important and must be attended to.

THE LIMITS OF THE INTERNET

While electronic advocacy is a valuable tool, it is important not to overrate what it can accomplish and not to neglect the everlasting importance of old-fashioned lobbying, media work, protest, and grassroots organizing. On huge issues, when strong public motivation is a given, as with the Clinton impeachment episode, the Internet can convert that high interest quickly into massive action. Most issues and campaigns, however, begin with a small group of people and gain steam slowly through careful public education and organizing. Once you have people involved, the Internet can be an incredibly useful tool for communicating with them and coordinating their activities, but the personal touch remains essential.

**A NOTE ABOUT NET ADVOCACY AND THE
IRS RULES FOR NONPROFITS**

Nonprofit advocates using the Internet must pay attention to the same IRS rules that apply to standard advocacy activities, especially when related to elections. To get a clearer understanding about how these rules apply see: <u>E-Advocacy for Nonprofits: The Law of Lobbying and Election Related Activity on the Net</u>, available from Alliance for Justice in Washington, DC (www.afj.org).

There are also criticisms of Internet activism that mirror criticisms of the overall impact of computerization on our culture. Computers and the Internet speed up our lives and work enormously. We find ourselves inundated with information and feel forced into split-second reactions. As technology critic Jerry Mander writes, "It's as if we are all caught at a socially approved video game, where the information on the screen comes faster and faster and we try earnestly to keep up."[12] The risk is not just that we can become lost in our screens and might leave aside other responsibilities and joys in life. The acceleration of advocacy comes at the expense of thinking clearly, strategically, and wisely. With a box full of e-mail and Internet news cycles that change by the hour, we feel compelled to act before we have time to reflect. In the end it is not how much action you take or how quickly you take it that determines your success, it is the wisdom that guides your actions.

When advocacy is conducted at a slower pace, it is possible to ask more clearly, "If we do this, what will be the results? What reaction might we provoke in those we seek to move? Will it help us or hurt us? What other choices do we have?" When we carry out advocacy in one another's direct company, we have a conversation that is more interactive, more reflective, and wiser than what we can do connected only by our modems. Like any new tool, the Internet should be embraced for what it can do for us, but with a clear eye to both its limits and to what it cannot replace.

Conclusion

What is the effect of democracy on those who practice it?

The public issues that confront us can seem so big. How can one person challenge the power of a corporation or the arrogance of a government? Too many of us respond to this sense of powerlessness against might by doing nothing. We focus on being good people with our families and the others immediately around us and treat the political world as we do the weather, something beyond our control that we need to adapt to rather than change. One does not argue with a rainstorm, one gets an umbrella or stays inside.

Democratic activism is not just a different set of actions, it is a different attitude. We try to make a difference in the public sphere, not because we are assured we'll win but because we feel called to make the effort. What calls us? For some that call to democratic activism comes from the soul. My friend, Sister Sheila Walsh, a nun who lobbies for the poor at the California state capitol, described it this way, "There's something that each of us is called to do and if we don't do it, it won't get done." Why did Candy Lightner start Mothers Against Drunk Driving (MADD) after her daughter was run down in the road? She would always tell me, "I wanted to make something positive come out of something horrible."

On issue after issue, in town after town, all over the world, people feel called by soul or circumstance to try to make a difference. And very often, what they find is that precious new sense we call empowerment. It is an awareness that, even though we may not walk with the official trappings of power—money, influence, public office—we can be powerful, we can make change. And, very often, once we have had even an inkling of that in our lives, we are never the same again. Public issues stop looking like an uncontrolled storm and start looking like injustices that need to be challenged. Another friend of mine, Oscar Olivera, the leader of the Cochabamba, Bolivia, uprising that took back the public water system from the Bechtel Corporation, describes the effect of that victory this way, "People lost their fear. People lost their fear about speaking up, their fear to take action."

The most powerful effect that democracy has when we practice it is not the specific changes we make along the way, but the changes we find in ourselves. When we get that sense, in mind and heart, that we can make a difference and when we spread that sense and spirit to others, the world we live in becomes that much more democratic, the people that much more empowered to know what they want and to fight for it.

There is a flip side to this empowerment about which we must always be vigilant—and that is the curse of self-righteousness. To be involved in a public fight is to believe that you are right, that your opponents are wrong, and that you must move forward, in what you say and do, with total confidence and without doubt. While we must believe in ourselves, both our arguments and our actions, our confidence must also have limits. We can not allow our confidence to march that extra step into cockiness and superiority. We may well be right in our analysis and our tactics, but not always completely right. At the same time that we are advocating we must also listen and make room for views other than ours. Our commitment to our position must be superseded by our dedication to truth and fairness. Democracy, by its nature, gives some measure of power to any among us willing to demand it and work for it. However, along with that power comes the responsibility that we listen for and honor truth, even when it requires us to change positions we have previously held or to challenge allies who may not take challenge gracefully.

Finally, in a life of activism there is one other hazard against we must guard—"burn out." The work of citizen democracy is hard on the spirit, the mind, the body, and on families and friendships. To rest and recharge is not abandonment of the cause, it is how we assure that we can remain true to it for the long haul, often for life. There are all kinds of ways that activists can avoid burning out—celebrating victories, taking time to laugh, sharing stories, coming together to deal with a loss, staying close to the people directly affected by the issues involved, and taking time utterly away from that work. The South African civil rights leader the Reverend Desmond Tutu maintains a practice of taking days off from his work each month to sit in reflective prayer. When my children were in elementary school, I worked every Wednesday morning in their classrooms, in an atmosphere utterly different from the adult world of advocacy and political action.

The purpose of democratic activism, in the end, is to make all our lives better, not to make your own life worse. Always, the challenge is to find that right balance between tending our own souls and remaining committed to the struggles that lie beyond our own perimeters. The environmental firebrand Edward Abbey wrote of that challenge this way:

> Do not burn yourselves out. Be as I am—a reluctant enthusiast, and part-time crusader, a half-hearted fanatic. Save the other half of yourselves for pleasure and adventure. It is not enough to fight for the west. It is even more important to enjoy it while you can, while it is still there. So get out there, hunt, fish, mess around with your friends, ramble out yonder and explore the forests, encounter the griz, climb a mountain, bag the peaks, run the rivers, breathe deep of that yet sweet and elusive air. Sit quietly for a while and

contemplate the lovely, mysterious, and awesome space. Enjoy yourselves. Keep your brain in your head and your head firmly attached to the body, the body active and alive. And I promise you this one sweet victory over our enemies, over those desk-bound people with their hearts in safe deposit boxes and their eyes hypnotized by their desk calculators. I promise you this:

You will outlive the bastards.

✳ ✳ ✳ *Resources* ✳ ✳ ✳

There are thousands of publications and organizations dedicated to public issues and public activism. Here are a few favorite resources for readers interested in additional information. Most of the organization listings are for each group's national office, but many also have state and local affiliates which can be reached through their Web sites.

On Democracy in General

Democracy in America by Alexis de Tocqueville

Radical Democracy by C. Douglas Lummis

The Prince by Niccolò Machiavelli

The Rules of Politics

Center for Responsive Politics
1101 14th Street N.W., Suite 1030
Washington, D.C. 20005
Tel: 202-857-0044 / Fax 202-857-7809
info@crp.org / www.opensecrets.org

Center for Voting and Democracy
6930 Carroll Avenue, Suite 901
Takoma Park, Md. 20912
Tel: 301-270-4616 / Fax: 301-270-4133
cvdusa@aol.com / www.fairvote.org

Common Cause
1250 Connecticut Avenue N.W., #600
Washington, D.C. 20036
Tel: 202-833-1200
www.commoncause.org

League of Women Voters
1730 M Street N.W., Suite 1000
Washington, D.C. 20036
Tel: 202-429-1965 / Fax: 202-429-0854
www.lwv.org

Public Campaign
1320 19th Street N.W., Suite M-1
Washington, D.C. 20036

Tel: 202-293-0222 / Fax: 202-293-0202
info@publicampaign.org / www.
publicampaign.org

United States Public Interest Research Group (USPIRG)
218 D Street S.E.
Washington, D.C. 20003
Tel: 202-546-9707 / Fax: 202-546-2461
uspirg@pirg.org / www.uspirg.org

Economic Issues: Taxes and Budgets and Rules for the Economy

Everything for Sale, by Robert Kuttner (Alfred A. Knopf)

Free to Choose, by Milton and Rose Friedman (Harcourt Brace Jovanovich)

Global Village or Global Pillage, by Jeremy Brecher and Tim Costello (South End Press)

Globalization from Below: The Power of Solidarity, by Jeremy Brecher, Tim Costello and Brendan Smith (South End Press)

The Case Against the Global Economy, by Jerry Mander and Edward Goldsmith (Sierra Club Books)

The Lexus and the Olive Tree, by Thomas L. Friedman (Anchor Books/Random House)

The Public Use of Private Interest, by Charles L. Schultze (Brookings)

AFL-CIO
815 16th Street N.W.
Washington, D.C. 20006

Tel: 202-637-5000 / Fax: 202-637-5058
feedback@aflcio.org / www.aflcio.org

American Enterprise Institute
1150 Seventeenth Street N.W.
Washington, D.C. 20036
Tel: 202-862-5800 / Fax: 202-862-7178
info@aei.org / www.aei.org

Cato Institute
1000 Massachusetts Avenue N.W.
Washington D.C. 20001
Tel: 202-842-0200 / Fax: 202-842-3490
librarian@cato.org / www.cato.org

Center on Budget and Policy Priorities
820 First Street N.E., Suite 510
Washington, D.C., 20002
Tel: 202-408-1080 / Fax: 202-408-1056
bazie@cbpp.org / www.cbpp.org

Citizens for Tax Justice
1311 L Street N.W.
Washington, D.C. 20005
Tel: (202) 626-3780 / Fax: (202) 638-3486
mattg@ctj.org / www.ctj.org

Consumers Union
101 Truman Avenue
Yonkers, N.Y. 10703-1057
Tel: 914-378-2000
www.consumersunion.org

Global Exchange
2017 Mission Street #303
San Francisco, Calif. 94110
Tel: 415-255-7296 / Fax: 415-255-7498
info@globalexchange.org / www.
globalexchange.org

National Priorities Project
17 New South Street, Suite 302
Northampton, Mass. 01060
Tel: 413-584-9556 / Fax 413-586-9647
info@natprior.org / www.natprior.org

Public Citizen
1600 20th Street N.W.
Washington, D.C.. 20009

Tel: 202-588-1000
pcmail@citizen.org / www. citizen.org

Social Issues: Rights and Rules for Individuals

The Real War on Crime: The Report of the National Criminal Justice Commission, edited by Steven R. Donziger (Harper Perennial)

Amnesty International
322 8th Avenue
New York, N.Y. 10001
Tel: 212-807-8400
admin-us@aiusa.org / www.
amnesty.org

Children Now
1212 Broadway, 5th Floor
Oakland, Calif. 94612
Tel: 510-763-2444 / Fax: 510-763-1974
children@childrennow.org / www.
childrennow.org

Children's Defense Fund
25 E Street N.W.
Washington, D.C. 20001
Tel: 202-628-8787
cdfinfo@childrensdefense.org / www.
childrensdefense.org

Family Research Council
801 G. Street N.W.
Washington, D.C. 20001
Tel: 800-225-4008
corrdept@frc.org / www.frc.org

Human Rights Campaign (gay rights)
919 18th Street N.W.
Washington, D.C. 20006
Tel: 202-628-4160 / Fax: 202-347-5323
hrc@hrc.org / www.hrc.org

Justice Policy Institute/Center on Juvenile and Criminal Justice
1234 Massachusetts Avenue N.W., Suite C1009
Washington, D.C. 20005

Tel: 202-737-7270 / Fax: 202-737-7271
info@cjcj.org / http://www.cjcj.org

NAACP
4805 Mt. Hope Drive
Baltimore, Md. 21215
Tel: 410-521-4939
www.naacp.org

National Council of La Raza
1111 19th Street N.W., Suite 1000
Washington, D.C. 20036
Tel: 202-785-1670
www.nclr.org

National Organization for Women
733 15th Street NW, Second Floor
Washington, D.C. 20005
Tel: 202-628-8669 / Fax: 202-785-8576
now@now.org / www.now.org

People for the American Way
2000 M Street N.W., Suite 400
Washington, D.C. 20036
Tel: 800-326-7329
pfaw@pfaw.org / www.pfaw.org

Advocacy in General

"Letter from the Birmingham Jail," by Martin
Luther King Jr.
(http://www.msstate.edu/Archives/History/
USA/Afro-Amer/birmingham.king)

Moral Politics, by George Lakoff (University
of Chicago Press)

The Activist's Handbook, by Randy Shaw
(University of California Press)

Advocacy Institute
1629 K Street N.W., #200
Washington, D.C. 20006-1629
Tel: 202-777-7575 / Fax: 202-777-7577
info@advocacy.org / www.advocacy.org

Applied Research Center
3781 Broadway
Oakland, Calif. 94611
Tel: 510-653-3415 / Fax: 510-653-3427
arc@arc.org / www.arc.org

The Democracy Center
P.O. Box 22157
San Francisco, Calif. 94122
Tel: 415-564-4767 / Fax: 978-383-1269
info@democracyctr.org / www.
democracyctr.org

Research and Analysis

The Eight-Step Path of Policy Analysis,
by Eugene Bardach (Berkeley Academic
Press)

The Brookings Institution
1775 Massachusetts Ave N.W.
Washington D.C. 20036
Tel: 202-797-6000 / Fax: 202-797-6004
brookinfo@brook.edu / www.brookings.org

RAND
1700 Main Street
Santa Monica, Calif. 90407
Tel: 310-393-0411 / Fax: 310-393-4818
www.rand.org

Urban Institute
2100 M Street, N.W.
Washington, D.C. 20037
Tel: 202-833-7200
paffairs@ui.urban.org / www.urban.org

U.S. Office of Management and Budget
http://www.whitehouse.gov/omb

Organizing and Coalition Building

Axioms for Organizers, by Fred Ross Sr.
(Neighbor to Neighbor Education Fund, San
Francisco)

Colorlines (magazine produced by the
Center for Third World Organizing,
Oakland, Calif.)

Fundraising for Social Change, by Kim
Klein (Chardon Press)

Grassroots Fundraising Journal, by Kim
Klein (Chardon Press)

Organizing for Social Change, by Kim Bobo,
Jackie Kendall, and Steve Max (Seven Locks
Press)

Rules for Radicals: A Practical Primer for Realistic Radicals, by Saul Alinsky (Random House)
Center for Third World Organizing
1218 E. 21st Street
Oakland, Calif. 94606
Tel: 510-533-7583 / Fax: 510-533-0923
ctwo@ctwo.org / www.ctwo.org

Midwest Academy
28 E. Jackson Street #605
Chicago, Ill. 60604
Tel: 312-427-2304 / Fax: 312-427-2307
mwacademy1@aol.com /
www.mindspring.com/~midwestacademy

Center for Community Change
1000 Wisconsin Avenue, N.W.
Washington, D.C. 20007
Tel: 202-342-0567 / Fax: 202-333-5462
info@communitychange.org / www.communitychange.org

Association of Community Organizations for Reform Now (ACORN)
88 3rd Avenue, 3rd Floor
Brooklyn, N.Y. 11217
Tel: 718-246-7900 / Fax: 718-246-7939
www.acorn.org

Media Advocacy

Media Advocacy, by Michael Pertschuk and Phil Wilbur

Media, The Second God, by Tony Schwartz (Anchor Press/Doubleday)

News For A Change, by Lawrence Wallack, Katie Woodruff, Lori Dorfman, Iris Diaz (Sage Publications)

The Responsive Chord, by Tony Schwartz (Anchor Press/Doubleday)

We the Media, by Don Hazen and Julie Winokur (The New Press)

Berkeley Media Studies Group
2140 Shattuck Avenue Suite 804
Berkeley, Calif. 94704
Tel: 510-204-9700 / Fax: 510-204-9710
woodruff@bmsg.org

Communication Works
Pier 9 Embarcadero, Suite 116
San Francisco, CA 94111
Tel: 415-255-1946 / Fax: 415-255-1947
info@communicationworks.org / www.communicationworks.org

Fairness and Accuracy in Reporting (FAIR)
130 W. 25th Street
New York, N.Y. 10001
Tel: 212-633-6700 / Fax: 212-727-7668
fair@fair.org / www.fair.org

Media Access Project
950 18th Street N.W., Suite 220
Washington, D.C. 20006
Tel: 202-232-4300 / Fax: 202-466-7656
webmaster@mediaaccess.org / www.mediaaccess.org

Public Media Center
466 Green Street
San Francisco, Calif. 94133
Tel: 415-434-1403 / Fax: 415-986-6779
info@publicmediacenter.org / www.publicmediacenter.org

We Interrupt This Message
965 Mission Street, Suite 220
San Francisco, Calif. 94103
Tel: 415-537-9437
www.interrupt.org

Lobbying

Being a Player, A Guide to IRS Lobbying Regulations for Advocacy Charities, by Gail Harmon, Jessica Ladd, and Eleanor A. Evans (Alliance for Justice)

By Hook or By Crook, Stealth Lobbying: Tactics and Counter Strategies, by the Advocacy Institute (Advocacy Institute)

Getting Action, How to Petition State Government, by Carol Oshiro and Harry Snyder (Consumers Union, San Francisco)

The Joy of Lobbying, by Dierdre Kent (Gateway Lobbyskills, Wellington, New Zealand)

The People Rising by Michael Pertschuk and Wendy Schaetzel
Alliance for Justice
11 Dupont Circle N.W., 2nd Floor
Washington, D.C. 20036
Tel: 202-822-6070 / Fax: 202-822-6068
alliance@afj.org / www.afj.org

Independent Sector
1200 Eighteenth Street, N.W., Suite 200
Washington, D.C. 20036
Tel: 202-467-6100 / Fax: 202-467-6101
info@independentsector.org / www.independentsector.org

Ballot Initiatives

The Initiative Cookbook—Recipes and Stories from California's Ballot Wars, by Jim Shultz (The Democracy Center, San Francisco)

Seize the Initiative, by Gregory L. Colvin and Lowell Finley (Alliance for Justice)

Initiative & Referendum Institute
1825 I Street, N.W., Suite 400
Washington, D.C. 20006
Tel: 202-429-5539 / Fax: 202-986-3001
info@iandrinstitute.org / www.iandrinstitute.org

New Technology

E-Advocacy for Nonprofits: The Law of Lobbying and Election Related Activity on the Net by Elizabeth Kingsley, Gail Harmon, John Pomeranz, and Kay Guinane (Alliance for Justice)

In the Absence of the Sacred, by Jerry Mander (Sierra Club Books)

Net Action
601 Van Ness Avenue, #631
San Francisco, Calif. 94102
Tel: 415-775-8674 / Fax: 415-673-3813
audrie@netaction.org / www.netaction.org

OMB Watch
1742 Connecticut Avenue N.W.
Washington, D.C. 20009
Tel: 202-234-8494 / Fax: 202-234-8584
ombwatch@ombwatch.org / www.ombwatch.org

Benton Foundation
950 18th Street N.W.
Washington D.C. 20006
Tel: 202-638-5770 / Fax: 202-638-5771
benton@benton.org / www.benton.org

✳ ✳ ✳ *Notes* ✳ ✳ ✳

Introduction

1. Fareed Zakaria, "The Rise of Illiberal Democracy," *Foreign Affairs* (November/December 1997): 23.
2. Robert D. Putnam, "Bowling Alone: America's Declining Social Capital," *Journal of Democracy* (January 1995): 67–68.

Chapter 1, What Is Government's Job?

1. Niccolò Machiavelli, *The Prince* (Toronto: Bantam Books, 1981), 53–54.
2. "Assessing The Costs," report on the PBS NewsHour, March 13, 1998, http://www.pbs.org/newshour/bb/middle_east/jan-june98/iraq_3-13a.html
3. John Nichols, "Jesse Jackson Jr.: A Different Vision," *The Nation* (September 18/25, 2000): 18.
4. Sonoma County Family Action, *Sonoma County Realities,"*(Santa Rosa, Calif.: Sonoma County Family Action, 1998), 1.

Chapter 2, The Rules of Politics

1. Quoted in Center for Responsive Politics, "A Brief History of Money in Politics," fact sheet (Washington, D.C.: Center for Responsive Politics).
2. Center for Voting and Democracy, "Voter Turnout," fact sheet (Takoma Park, Md.: Center for Voting and Democracy, 1999).
3. Common Cause, "Overall Campaign Spending at the Federal Level," fact sheet (Washington, D.C.: Common Cause, 1999).
4. Common Cause, "House of Representative 1998 Campaign Finance Data," fact sheet (Washington, D.C.: Common Cause, 1998); Common Cause, "U.S. Senate 1998 Campaign Finance Data," fact sheet (Washington, D.C.: Common Cause, 1998); editorial, "Getting the Money Out," *The Nation* (January 29, 2001): 3.
5. California Common Cause, "The Last Waltz," executive summary (Sacramento: California Common Cause, 1997).
6. Connecticut Common Cause, "State House and Senate Challengers Overwhelmed By Incumbents' Wall Of Money," news release (Hartford: Connecticut Common Cause, 1997).
7. Common Cause, "Top "Double Giver" Soft Money Donors Of $50,000 Or More to Both Parties," fact sheet (Washington, D.C.: Common Cause, 1999).
8. Common Cause, "Return on Investment," fact sheet (Washington, D.C.: Common Cause, 1997).
9. Common Cause, "House of Representatives 1998 Campaign Finance Data."
10. Ibid.
11. California Common Cause, "The Last Waltz," and, Connecticut Common Cause, "State House and Senate Challengers."

12. Public Campaign, "The Color of Money: Campaign Contributions and Race," (Washington, D.C.: Public Campaign, 1999).

13. Steve Phillips, from an e-mail interview with the author, San Francisco, June 2000.

14. Center for Responsive Politics, "Sex, Money and Politics: The Gender Gap in Campaign Contributions" (Washington, D.C.: Center for Responsive Politics, 1999).

15. William Greider, "Unfinished Business, Clinton's Lost Presidency," *The Nation* (February 14, 2000): 16.

16. Center for Responsive Politics, "A Brief History of Money in Politics—The States: 'Laboratories of Reform," fact sheet (Washington, D.C.: Center for Responsive Politics, 1999).

17. Quoted in California Commission on Campaign Financing, Democracy by Initiative (Los Angeles, 1992): 37.

18. Quoted in Center for Responsive Politics, "A Brief History of Money in Politics. The States: Laboratories for Reform."

19. Center for Responsive Politics, "A Brief History of Money in Politics—Reform Attempts at the Federal Level," fact sheet (Washington, D.C.: Center for Responsive Politics, 1999).

20. Derek Cressman, "Testimony on Campaign Finance Reform before the Senate Rules Committee (Washington, D.C.: USPIRG, March 29, 2000).

21. Robert Glass, "Senator says Clinton's Finance Reform is a Sham," *Detroit News* (October 5, 1997), http://www.detroitnews.com/1997/nation/9710/05/10050061.htm.

22. Quoted in editorial, "Campaign Finance—Good News," *The Nation* (February 14, 2000): 7.

23. Center for Responsive Politics, "A Brief History of Money in Politics—Reform Attempts at the Federal Level."

24. Bradley A. Smith, "Campaign Finance Regulation: Faulty Assumptions and Undemocratic Consequences," Cato Policy Analysis no. 238 (Washington, D.C.: Cato Institute, 1995).

25. Center for Responsive Politics, "A Brief History of Money in Politics—The States."

26. Quoted in Public Campaign, "Clean Money Campaign Reform," fact sheet, (Washington, D.C.: Public Campaign, 1999).

27. Center for Responsive Politics, "A Brief History of Money in Politics—The States."

28. Human Serve, "A National Plan Of Action," fact sheet (New York, Human Serve, 1995).

29. William Morris, "Gerrymander," *American Heritage Dictionary of the English Language* (Boston: Houghton Mifflin, 1976), 553.

30. Common Cause, "Common Cause Issue: Reapportionment and Redistricting," fact sheet (Washington, D.C.: Common Cause).

31. Common Cause, "Open Meetings," fact sheet (Washington, D.C.: Common Cause, 1998).

32. Ibid.

33. Daniel Bellow, "Vermont, the Pure Food State," *The Nation* (March 18, 1999): 19.

34. Donald Barlett and James Steele, "How to Become a Top Banana," *Time* (February 7, 2000): 25.

Chapter 3, Taxes and Budgets: Following the Money

1. Milton Friedman and Rose Friedman, *Free to Choose* (New York: Harcourt Brace Jovanovich, 1980), 264.

2. Robert S. McIntyre, "Inequality & The Federal Budget Deficit," in *Growth and Tax Equity, Tax Policy Challenges for the 1990s*, ed. Bruce L. Fisher and Robert S. McIntyre (Washington, D.C.: Citizens for Tax Justice, 1990), 7.

3. California Budget Project, "Fact Sheet on the Governor's Tax Cut Proposal" (Sacramento: California Budget Project, 1996).

4. Staff of the California Senate Revenue and Taxation Committee, "Frequently Asked Ques-

tions About Business Tax Incentives" (Sacramento: California Senate Revenue and Taxation Committee, 1993), 1.

5. Lenny Goldberg, executive director of the California Tax Reform Association, from an e-mail interview with the author, Sacramento, California, March 1999.

6. Bill Bradley, "The Case for Tax Progressivity," in *Growth*, ed. Fisher and McIntyre 33.

7. Blaine Greenberg, "Don't Hate Me Because I'm Rich," *Los Angles Times* (October 11, 1992): B.7.

8. Quoted from Steve Forbes presidential campaign Web site, http://www.Forbes2000.com/cp/tax/index.html.

9. U.S. Office of Management and Budget, *Analytical Perspectives, Budget of the United States Government, Fiscal Year 2000* (Washington, D.C.: U.S. Office of Management and Budget, 1999), 105.

10. California Legislative Analyst, "California Tax Expenditure Programs," (Sacramento: California Legislative Analyst, February 1999).

11. California Budget Project, "Budget Watch" (Sacramento: California Budget Project, April 1998).

12. U.S. Office of Management and Budget, *Analytical Perspectives, 2000*, 107; and Congressional Joint Committee on Taxation, "Estimates of Federal Exemptions for Fiscal Years 1993–1997" (Washington, D.C.: Congressional Joint Committee on Taxation, 1992), cited in Center on Budget and Policy Priorities, "Getting Started" a tax issues training manual (Washington, D.C.: Center on Budget and Policy Priorities, 1995).

13. Bradley, "The Case for Tax Progressivity," 33.

14. John Bryan Jr., "The Business Case for Tax Reform," in *Growth*, ed. Fisher and McIntyre, 95.

15. Citizens for Tax Justice, "A Far Cry from Fair" (Washington, D.C.: Citizens for Tax Justice, 1991), cited in Center on Budget, "Getting Started."

16. Iris J. Lav, Edward B. Lazere, Jim St. George, *A Tale of Two Futures*, (Washington, D.C.: Center on Budget and Policy Priorities, 1994), 13.

17. Ibid.,16.

18. California Department of Health Services, Model for Change, the California Experience in Tobacco Control (Sacramento: California Department of Health Services, 1998), 4.

19. James R. St. George, "Critical Condition—The State of School Building Repairs in Massachusetts," Team Education Fund, Boston, 1999, p. 2.

20. Ibid., 3.

21. California Legislative Analyst, "Cal Facts" (Sacramento: California Legislative Analyst, 1998).

Chapter 4, Making Public Rules for Business and the Marketplace

1. Henry Hazlitt, *Economics in One Lesson* (New York: Crown, 1979), 17.

2. Milton Friedman and Rose Friedman, *Free to Choose* (New York: Harcourt Brace Jovanovich, 1980), 11–13.

3. Friedman and Friedman, *Free*, 14.

4. George Lakoff, *Moral Politics* (Chicago: University of Chicago Press, 1996), 210–211.

5. Rose Hughes, from an interview with the author, Petaluma, California, December 1989.

6. Robert Kuttner, *Everything for Sale* (New York: Alfred A. Knopf, 1997), 281.

7. Friedman and Friedman, *Free*, 194.

8. Ibid., 206.

9. Friedman and Friedman, *Free*, 223.

10. Sarah Tippit, "California Jury Orders GM To Pay $4.9 Billion," Reuters News Service [Net Service], Los Angeles, July 9, 1999.

11. Friedman and Friedman, *Free*, 214.
12. Jeremy Brecher and Tim Costello, *Global Village or Global Pillage* (Boston: South End Press, 1994), 23.
13. Kuttner, *Everything*, 86.
14. National Priorities Project, "Working Hard, Earning Less" (Boston: National Priorities Project, 1998), 5.
15. Kuttner, *Everything*, 234.
16. Charles L. Schultze, *The Public Use of Private Interest* (Washington, D.C.: The Brookings Institution,1977), 18.
17. Kuttner, *Everything*, 108.
18. Ibid., 318.
19. Cynthia A. Williams, "Corporate Compliance with the Law in the Era of Efficiency," *North Carolina Law Review* 76 (April 1998): 1265.
20. Kuttner, *Everything*, 313.
21. Kaiser Family Foundation, "Uninsured in America" brochure (Menlo Park, Calif.: Kaiser Family Foundation, 1998).
22. Kuttner, *Everything*, 112, 147.
23. Ibid., 155.
24. Brecher and Costello, *Global,* 13–33.
25. Tim McNamar, letter to the editor, *Time* (March 8, 1999): 5.
26. Jonathan Schlefer, "What Price Economic Growth," *Atlantic Monthly* (December 1992): 117.
27. Brecher and Costello, *Global*, 58.
28. Ibid., 60.

Chapter 5, Civil Rights and Criminal Wrongs: Society's Rules for Individuals

1. Congressional Debate on Immigration Restrictions (1921), published by *American Civil Rights Review*: http://webusers.anet-stl.com/~civil/docs-immigration1921.htm.
2. Mortimer B. Zuckerman, "Beyond Proposition 18,7, *U.S. News and World Report* (December 12, 1994): http://www.usnews.com/usnews/wash/187oped.htm.
3. Margaret Marr, civil rights attorney, from an interview with the author, Santa Cruz, California, July 2000.
4. Quoted in Morris J. MacGregor Jr., "Integration Of The Armed Forces 1940–1965" (Washington, D.C.: Center of Military History United States Army, 1985), http://www.army.mil/cmh-pg/books/integration/IAF-02.htm.
5. Los Angeles Times News Service, "McCain Against Avowed Gays in Military," *Los Angeles Times* (December 20, 1999): 24.
6. Robert Maginnis, quoted in a January 2000 forum sponsored by PBS *NewsHour*: http://www.pbs.org/newshour/forum/january00/gays_military1.html.
7. Quoted in David Schwalbe, "Interracial Marriage in America": http://americanhistory.about.com/homework/americanhistory/library/weekly/aa061499.htm.
8. Robert H. Knight, "How Domestic Partnerships and 'Gay Marriage' Threaten the Family," fact sheet (Washington, D.C.: Family Research Council).
9. Paul Kivel, "Affirmative Action Works!" *In Motion Magazine*: http://www.inmotion-magazine.com/pkivel.html.
10. "The Struggle for Women's Equality and the Defense of Affirmative Action," *Liberator*, journal of the Coalition to Defend Affirmative Action by Any Means Necessary (February 1998): http://www.bamn.com/liberator/liberator-2.htm#women.

11. Dinesh D'Souza, quoted from comments made at a roundtable sponsored by *Atlantic Monthly*, http://www.policy.com/issuewk/1999/0222%5F58/index.html.

12. Quoted in Alicia Montgomery, "A 'Poison' Divides Us," *Salon* (March 27, 2000): http://www.salon.com/politics2000/feature/2000/03/27/connerly/index.html.

13. National Organization for Women, "Talking About Affirmative Action," fact sheet (Washington: National Organization for Women).

14. Lani Guinier, "An Equal Choice," *New York Times* (April 23, 1998): 25.

15. Christopher Edley, quoted in a February 16, 1999 interview with PBS *Frontline*: http://www.pbs.org/wgbh/pages/frontline/shows/race/interviews/edley.html.

16. Family Research Council statement on "Crime and Drugs" (Washington, D.C.: Family Research Council).

17. Justice Policy Institute, Center on Juvenile and Criminal Justice, "Poor Prescription: The Costs of Imprisoning Drug Offenders in the United States" (San Francisco and Washington, D.C.: Justice Policy Institute, Center on Juvenile and Criminal Justice, July 2000).

18. Anthony Lewis, "Breaking the Silence," *New York Times* (July 29, 2000): 13.

19. Barry R. McCaffery, "Testimony of Barry R. McCaffery before the House Government Reform and Oversight Committee," (Washington, D.C.: U.S. Office of National Drug Control Policy, June 16, 1999).

20. Cited in Lewis, "Breaking the Silence."

21. This summary borrows from, "Sentencing Alternatives: From Incarceration to Diversion" (Berkeley, Calif.: Nolo Press, 2000).

22. William J. Sabol and James P. Lynch, "Did Getting Tough on Crime Pay?" (Washington, D.C.: Urban Institute, October 2, 1997).

23. Justice Policy Institute, "Poor Prescription."

24. Pete du Pont, "Taking the Profit Out of Crime" (Dallas: National Center for Policy Analysis, October 19, 1999): 3.

25. Vincent Schiraldi, "How Distorted Coverage of Juvenile Crime Affects Public Policy," *Los Angeles Times* (November 22, 1999): B7.

26. John Jacobs, "California's Growth Industry," *The Sacramento Bee* (August 11, 1994): B8.

27. Justice Policy Institute, Center on Juvenile and Criminal Justice, "Education v. Incarceration: A South Carolina Case Study" (San Francisco and Washington, D.C.: Justice Policy Institute, Center on Juvenile Justice).

28. Vincent Schiraldi, "Want to Get Tough on Crime? Start by Studying Three Strikes," *San Francisco Chronicle* (September 1, 1999): A25.

29. Peter W. Greenwood, C. Peter Rydell, Allan F. Abrahamse, Nathan P. Caulkins, James Chiesa, Karyn E. Model, Stephen P. Klein, "Three Strikes and You're Out: Estimated Benefits and Costs of California's New Mandatory-Sentencing Law," executive summary (Santa Monica, Calif.: RAND, 1994).

Chapter 6, Developing a Strategy: Advocacy's Road Map

1. Maryann O'Sullivan, from an e-mail interview with the author, Oakland, California, March 2000.

2. Theda Skocpol, "Lessons From History" (Santa Monica, Calif.: The Children's Partnership, 1997), 9.

3. Jim Shultz, *The Initiative Cookbook—Recipes and Stories from California's Ballot Wars*, (San Francisco: The Democracy Center, 1996), 76.

4. Sabin Russell, from an interview with the author, San Francisco, May 1996.

5. Emily Goldfarb, from an interview with the author, San Francisco, April 1996.

6. Randy Shaw, *The Activist's Handbook* (Berkeley, Calif.: University of California Press, 1996), 225.
7. Martin Luther King, "Letter from the Birmingham Jail" (1963): http://www.msstate.edu/Archives/History/USA/Afro-Amer/birmingham.king
8. People for the American Way, *A Community Battles the Religious Right* (Washington, D.C.: People for the American Way, 1993), 20.
9. Ibid., 19.
10. Quoted in C. Douglas Lummis, *Radical Democracy* (Ithaca, N.Y.: Cornell University Press, 1996), 35.

Chapter 7, Advocacy by Fact, Not fiction

1. Eugene Bardach, *The Eight-Step Path of Policy Analysis* (Berkeley, Calif.: Berkeley Academic Press, 1996), 6–10.
2. Jamie Court and Francis Smith, *Making a Killing: HMOs and the Threat to Your Health*, Monroe, Me.: Common Courage Press,1999), chapter 1.
3. Rosa de la Vega, *Advocacy Learning Initiative,* (Washington, D.C.: The Advocacy Institute, 1999), 2:87.
4. Albert Norman, "Eight Ways to Stop the Store," *The Nation* (March 28, 1994): 418.
5. Advocacy Institute, "Bridging," 20.
6. de la Vega, *Advocacy*, 2:90.

Chapter 8, Organizing: Bringing People Together to Make Social Change

1. Fred Ross Sr., *Axioms for Organizers* (San Francisco: Neighbor to Neighbor Education Fund), 15.
2. Alexis de Tocqueville, *Democracy in America*, (1835; New York: New American Library, 1956), 95.
3. Kim Bobo, Jackie Kendall, Steve Max, *Organizing for Social Change*, (Washington, D.C.: Seven Locks Press, 1996), 8.
4. Francisco Herrera, from an interview with the author, San Francisco, September 1998.
5. Ross, *Axioms*, 3.
6. Advocacy Institute, "Bridging," 24.
7. Ibid., 25.
8. Margaret Brodkin, *From Sand Boxes to Ballot Boxes* (San Francisco: Coleman Advocates for Children and Youth, 1994), 28.
9. Rinku Sen, "Building Black-Brown Unity: Rhode Island's Home Daycare Campaign," *Colorlines* (summer 1998): 33–35.
10. Ross, *Axioms*, 41.
11. Martha Kowalick, from an interview with the author, San Francisco, March 1998.
12. From a "Yes on 186" Campaign memo to volunteers (Fall 1996).
13. California Institute for Rural Studies, *Organizing for Social Action* (Davis, Calif.: California Institute for Rural Studies), 72.
14. Richard C. Paddock and Maura Dolan, "Environment an Issue for Industry, Celebrities," *Los Angeles Times* (October 25, 1990): 3.
15. Kim Klein, "The Perennial Question of Clean and Dirty Money," *Grassroots Fundraising Journal* (April 2000). For a more detailed look at fund-raising strategies for activist work, see Kim Klein, *Fundraising for Social Change* (Oakland, Calif.: Chardon Press, 2000).
16. Bobo, Kendall, Max, *Organizing*, 8.

17. Quoted in Xenia P. Kobylarz, "The Spirit Girls (Real Girl Power)," *Third Force* (March/April 1999): 18.
18. King, "Letter."
19. Ibid.
20. Saul Alinsky, *Rules for Radicals: A Practical Primer for Realistic Radicals* (New York: Random House, 1972), 127.
21. Ibid., 139.
22. Shultz, *The Initiative*, 77–78.
23. U.S. Out of Central America, *The USOC Cookbook, Recipes for Organizing* (San Francisco: U.S. Out of Central America, 1983), 73–74.

Chapter 9, Building and Maintaining Advocacy Coalitions

1. William M. LeoGrande, *Our Own Backyard: The United States in Central America, 1977–1992* (Chapel Hill: University of North Carolina Press, 1998), 421.
2. Lee Cridland, from an interview with the author, San Francisco, June 1998.
3. Advocacy Institute, "Bridging," 18.
4. Ibid., 38.
5. Maryann O'Sullivan, *Taking Action* (Oakland, Calif.: Women Against Gun Violence, 1995), 18.
6. Shultz, *The Initiative*, 38.
7. Quoted in Rachel Timoner, "Ready or Not, An Assessment of Low-Income Advocacy in California" (Oakland, Calif.: Applied Research Center, 1996): 9.
8. Advocacy Institute, "Bridging," 4.

Chapter 10, Messages and Media: Democracy's Megaphone

1. Quoted in Lawrence Wallack, Katie Woodruff, Lori Dorfman, Iris Diaz, *News for a Change* (Thousand Oaks, Calif.: Sage, 1999), ix.
2. Tony Schwartz, *Media, The Second God* (Garden City, N.Y.: Anchor Press/Doubleday, 1983), 2–3.
3. Quoted in Lawrence Wallack, Lori Dorfman, David Jernigan, Makani Themba, *Media Advocacy and Public Health* (Thousand Oaks, Calif.: Sage, 1993), 61.
4. Jim Shultz, quoted in George Hacker, Liberty Aldrich, *Taking Initiative* (Washington, D.C.: Advocacy Institute, 1992), appendix 10.
5. Kare Anderson, *Cutting Deals with Unlikely Allies, Volume One* (Berkeley, Calif.: Anderson Negotiations/Communications, Inc. 1981), 54.
6. Leo McElroy, from an interview with the author, Sacramento, California, March 1996.
7. O'Sullivan, *Taking Action* , 4.
8. Cited in Michael Pertschuk, "Message Framing for Grassroots Advocates," fact sheet (Washington, D.C.: Advocacy Institute, 1995).
9. Quoted from a "Media Bite" list developed by the Berkeley Media Studies Group, Berkeley, California.
10. Suzanne Espinosa, "Female Immigrants Tell of Abuse," *San Francisco Chronicle* (March 9, 1993): A11.
11. Quoted from "Media Bite" list, Berkeley Media Studies Group.
12. O'Sullivan, *Taking Action*, 3–4.
13. Northern California Immigrant Rights Coalition, "Myths and Facts: Immigration and the United States," fact sheet (San Francisco: Northern California Immigrant Rights Coalition, 1994).
14. Daniel Sneider, from an e-mail interview with the author, San Jose, July 2000.

15. Communication Works, "Nike Blinks," (San Francisco: Communication Works quarterly newsletter, summer 1998): 1.
16. George Skelton, from an interview with the author, Sacramento, California, June 1998.
17. Advocacy Institute, *By Hook or by Crook, Stealth Lobbying: Tactics and Counter Strategies* (Washington, D.C.: Advocacy Institute, 1995), 25.
18. Dierdre Kent, *The Joy of Lobbying*, (Wellington, New Zealand: Gateway Lobbyskills, 1998), 29.
19. Virginia Ellis, from an e-mail interview with the author, Sacramento California, June 2000.
20. Sabin Russell, from an interview with the author, San Francisco, May 1996.
21. Wallack et al., *Media*, 159–161.
22. Amy Dominguez-Arms, from an e-mail interview with the author, Oakland, California, March 2000.
23. Shaw, *The Activist's Handbook*, 216.
24. James Boyd, from an e-mail interview with the author, July 2000.
25. John Diaz, "What Makes a Good Letter," *San Francisco Chronicle* (January 30, 2000): S1.
26. Quoted from a transcript of a "Seminar on Managing Public Issues," sponsored by *The Washington Post* (September 15, 1988), 2.
27. Anne Marie O'Keefe, "A Case for Paid Media," *Media Advocacy* (Washington, D.C.: The Benton Foundation, 1991): 29–30.
28. Quoted from a presentation to a 1998 Democracy Center media advocacy workshop in San Francisco.
29. Quoted in Don Hazen, Julie Winokur, *We the Media: A Citizens Guide to Fighting for Media Democracy* (New York: The New Press), vii.
30. For an excellent summary of the issues of media democracy and a complete listing of groups working in this area see Hazen and Winokur, We *the Media.*

Chapter 11, Lobbying: The Art of Influencing Public Officials

1. Anderson, *Cutting Deals*, 25.
2. Quoted in Advocacy Institute, *By Hook*, 10–13. This book also contains a wonderful description of stealth lobbying and how to combat it.
3. harlotte Lopez-Rojas, "The Road to a Motorcycle Helmet Law in California" (Sacramento, Calif.: The Center for California Studies, 1999): 74.
4. Beth Capell, from an interview with the author, Sacramento, California, August 1998.
5. Anderson, *Cutting Deals*, 8.
6. Timoner, "Ready or Not," 18.
7. These categories come originally from the trainings of David Cohen and Kathleen Sheekey of the Advocacy Institute.
8. Judith Bell, from an e-mail interview with the author, Oakland, California, March 2000.
9. Wendy Lazarus, from an e-mail interview with the author, Los Angeles, October 1999.
10. Angie Wei, from an e-mail interview with the author, Oakland, California, June 2000.
11. Advocacy Institute, "Bridging," 12.
12. Ibid., 11.
13. Lopez-Rojas, "The Road," 77.
14. Carol Oshiro, Harry Snyder, *Getting Action, How to Petition State Government* (San Francisco: Consumers Union, 1979), 10.

Chapter 12, Initiatives: The Power of the Ballot

1. M. Dane Waters, *Century of Citizen Lawmaking, An American Experiment in Self-Governance* (Washington, D.C.: The Initiative & Referendum Institute, 1998).

2. Ibid.
3. Harvey Rosenfield, from an interview with the author, Los Angeles, April 1996.
4. M. Dane Waters, from an e-mail interview with the author, Washington, D.C., February 2000.
5. Karen Kupler, from an interview with the author San Francisco, February 1996.
6. David Binder, from an interview with the author, San Francisco, March 1996.
7. David Roe, from an interview with the author, San Francisco, January 1996.
8. Gerald Meral, from an interview with the author, Sacramento, California, March 1996.
9. Sabin Russell, from an interview with the author, San Francisco, May 1996.

Chapter 13, The Internet: Democracy's Newest Tool

1. Katherine Hobson, "Do E-Mail Petitions Work?" *Salon* (May 10, 1999): http://www.salon-mag.com/tech/feature/1999/05/10/petitions/index.html.
2. From the group's Web site at: http://www.moveon.org.
3. http://cgi.ttd.org/foxweb.exe/ttddltsr.
4. http://www.moveon.org.
5. OMB Watch, "Democracy at Work: Nonprofit Use of Internet Technology for Public Policy Purposes" (Washington: OMB Watch, 1998): 12.
6. Hobson, "Do E-Mail Petitions Work?"
7. Howard Fineman, "Pressing the Flesh Online," *Newsweek* (September 20, 1999): 50–51.
8. http://www.actionnetwork.org/
9. Phil Agre, "Against Chain-Letter Petitions on the Internet" (Los Angeles: University of California at Los Angeles, Department of Information Studies).
10. The Benton Foundation, "What's Working: Advocacy on the 'Net" (Washington: The Benton Foundation, 2000).
11. This discussion about lists and forums borrows generously from the online "Virtual Activist" training guide provided by Net Action, Children Now, and WomensWork at: www.netaction.org.
12. Jerry Mander, *In the Absence of the Sacred* (San Francisco: Sierra Club Books, 1991), 64.

✵ ✵ ✵ *Index* ✵ ✵ ✵

* * * *About the Author* * * *

JIM SHULTZ is a native of Whittier, California. Educated at the University of California at Berkeley and Harvard University, he has served as staff to the California legislature, as an advocate with California Common Cause and Consumers Union, and has taught public policy and public administration to undergraduate and graduate students at San Francisco State University. As executive director of the Advocacy Institute West and later the Democracy Center, he founded the California Budget Project and has trained and counseled hundreds of public activists throughout the United States, Latin America, and Africa. He is the author of *The Initiative Cookbook—Recipes and Stories from California's Ballot Wars* as well as numerous articles on democracy and public affairs published in *The Nation*, *In These Times*, the *San Jose Mercury News*, *Sacramento Bee*, *Minneapolis Star-Tribune*, *San Francisco Chronicle*, and elsewhere. He lives with his wife, Lynn, and their two children, Elizabeth and Miguel, in Cochabamba, Bolivia.

Note: Comments about this book are warmly welcomed, as are requests for a free subscription to the Democracy Center's monthly e-mail newsletter. Both can be sent to info@democracyctr.org.